Google Tools Meets
Middle School

To our families: Thank you for supporting us through this work.

Google Tools Meets Middle School

Michael J. Graham
Jason Borgen

CORWIN
A SAGE Publishing Company

FOR INFORMATION:

Corwin
A SAGE Company
2455 Teller Road
Thousand Oaks, California 91320
(800) 233-9936
www.corwin.com

SAGE Publications Ltd.
1 Oliver's Yard
55 City Road
London EC1Y 1SP
United Kingdom

SAGE Publications India Pvt. Ltd.
B 1/I 1 Mohan Cooperative Industrial Area
Mathura Road, New Delhi 110 044
India

SAGE Publications Asia-Pacific Pte. Ltd.
3 Church Street
#10-04 Samsung Hub
Singapore 049483

Acquisitions Editor: Ariel Bartlett
Senior Associate Editor: Desirée A. Bartlett
Editorial Assistant: Kaitlyn Irwin
Production Editor: Bennie Clark Allen
Copy Editor: Lana Todorovic-Arndt
Typesetter: C&M Digitals (P) Ltd.
Proofreader: Barbara Coster
Indexer: Wendy Allex
Cover Designer: Candice Harman
Marketing Manager: Anna Mesick

Printed in the United States of America

ISBN: 978-1-5063-6016-4

This book is printed on acid-free paper.

SUSTAINABLE FORESTRY INITIATIVE
Certified Chain of Custody
Promoting Sustainable Forestry
www.sfiprogram.org
SFI-01268
SFI label applies to text stock

17 18 19 20 21 10 9 8 7 6 5 4 3 2 1

Contents

Preface

Every student deserves a high-quality, technology-rich learning environment. Students who enter kindergarten today will retire sometime in the 2070s. No one knows what education, the world economy, and jobs will look like then, but one thing is certain—the future will be increasingly technology dependent. Educators have a mandate to ensure that students will be ready to enter college and the workplace with the necessary skills to perform in the technology-based economy. That is why college- and career-readiness state standards across the United States focus on preparing students for the unknown challenges of the 21st century. Given this reality, the most pressing questions for educators today are the following:

- How will educators incorporate technology into their lesson plans to meet the expectations of the various college- and career-ready standards?
- To be successful, how proficient do teachers and students need to be in using technology?
- What are the technology and software products available that will help educators meet the rigorous standards, while also offering students experiences that will ensure their success in high school and beyond?

One of the best ways to tackle meeting standards and preparing students for the future is to take advantage of Google's free service built exclusively for schools, called G Suite for Education. Google provides a robust and vigorous suite of educational tools for schools that include everything necessary to meet and exceed the technology integration components of the various college- and career-ready standards. Over 40 million students and teachers around the world are using G Suite for Education every day. If your school uses Gmail as its email, then your school is a G Suite for Education school. If your school is not a G Suite institution, it is easy to get started. Direct your technology department to www.google.com/edu/products/productivity-tools/ to get signed up. Even if your district does not sign up for G Suite for Education, individual educators may still use most of these tools to organize, collaborate, and share content with students and faculty.

WHAT'S NEW IN THE SECOND EDITION?

Middle School Focused. The second edition has a middle school focus with clear examples of how to use G Suite with young adolescents in mind. Jason and Michael are both middle-level educators who can share their experience about why these tools will be useful to you and your students.

All New Screenshots. It has been 3 years since the first edition. Several buttons have moved in the G Suite. The updated screenshots will help you see where and why to click.

Addition of Google Classroom to G Suite. Since the publication of the first edition, Google has added Google Classroom to the G Suite. It has made the suite even stronger. Classroom gives students and teachers a learning management system (LMS) to assign work, turn in assignments, communicate with parents, and organize students' and teachers' digital work.

Broadened Focus to All Standards. The book has shifted from an exclusive Common Core State Standards to a variety of standard sets including Next Generation Science Standards to the updated International Society for Technology in Education Standards (ISTE). The Common Core Standards are of course also still a focus, but the book is no longer limited to just Common Core.

New Coauthor. Jason Borgen brings so much to the table. As a California educator and former school teacher, he has a wide range of experience. Currently working as a Curriculum and Technology Director in a small district in the Silicon Valley, he supports Google tools across all grade levels. Jason also is a Google Certified Innovator and Google Education Trainer. He has worked with schools and districts across the country in training teachers and building strategic plans focused on innovation.

Focus on Transformative Use of Technology. Teachers can integrate technology day-in and day-out, but is it truly transforming teaching and learning? The SAMR Model of technology integration focuses on how teachers integrate technology from substituting a physical instructional strategy with technology, which does not change the functionality of the lesson, to redefining how technology is used to transform the lesson. Each chapter now has examples of how each Google tool written about in the book can modify or completely redefine the lesson.

New Chapters. In the new edition, new chapters include an overview of digital learning and the SAMR Model. There is an introduction to Google Classroom, which didn't exist during the first edition. Also, several new features that Google offers through G Suite are also included, such as Quizzes in Google Forms and Add-ons with all core Google Drive applications.

PURPOSE

Based on our experience in the trenches of education, we have heard over and over again how difficult teachers and administrators find it to incorporate technology into their lessons, maximize learning, and meet the college and career standards of their particular state. We offer this guide to the G Suite for Education as a solution to that ongoing effort. The book offers step-by-step tutorials that can help any teacher master G Suite. It also appeals to the needs of tech-savvy teachers by challenging them to think of new ways of learning with tech. For each app, the book provides lesson plan ideas for how to implement technology with a focus on the standards. Ultimately, this book is written as a resource and a guide for educators to use G Suite for Education to meet and exceed standards and help students be prepared for tools that they will inevitably work with in college and their careers. It is as if Google's education team reviewed the various state standards, polled teachers, and then created free software to meet and exceed their wildest dreams. The G Suite is almost perfect.

TARGET AUDIENCE

All middle school stakeholders will find this book to be a valuable source of how to implement technology into the teaching and learning environment. Technology integration is the book's main focus aligned with rigorous standards, but the step-by-step tutorials are helpful for educators from any nation, state, or educational institution. College and career readiness is a worldwide goal. It is not restricted to the United States. Teachers, curriculum specialists, administrators, and college instructors alike will find the information in this book worthwhile and meaningful. Professors of education at universities are encouraged to read and recommend this work to their students. Teachers who come directly out of college with the skills and understanding of this book will be ready to lead in the fight to get students college and career ready.

A note to veteran teachers: Many experienced educators we have talked to are contemplating retirement because of the changes brought about by new standards such as the Common Core and its mandatory technology integration. If you are one of these educators, please consider using this book. Although it may seem difficult to implement technology as an older teacher, we strongly encourage you to try because your wisdom and experience as a veteran teacher is sorely needed and plays a vital role in the school community. This book can dispel your fears, but also challenge you to break out of your comfort level to try something new. We're willing to bet you'll find renewed energy and inspiration that will transform your teaching practice.

HOW THIS BOOK IS UNIQUE

There is nothing like this book available for educators. Most books about Google only tell educators about the wide swath of tools that Google provides. If you plan on incorporating G Suite into your classroom, this book is essential because it can help educators match specific state standards to the most appropriate Google app, while also offering step-by-step tutorials for implementation that will maximize learning. It is meant as a tool to smooth your path to successful integration of technology into your classroom. The beauty of G Suite is that you don't have to scour the Internet for a hodge-podge of tools to use. At Google, the apps are all easily accessible in one place and all follow the same basic principles of use. Much of the work is already done for you!

Another key aspect of the book is that it is written by two educators who still work with students and teachers every day. They practice what they preach. Michael and Jason live over 2,000 miles apart, but they have collaborated in real time to author this book. This book was written primarily using Google Docs and discussed over video conference using Google Hangouts. Jason Borgen is the Director of Learning & Innovation for Portola Valley School District in California. Michael J. Graham is the principal at Westside High School in Arkansas. Before becoming an administrator, he taught fifth through eighth grade at a local middle school. One of our specialties is to provide professional development to teachers who are scared of implementing technology because they feel that it is too complicated or out of their skillset. We are eager to show you that with a little guidance, the path doesn't have to be scary at all—we hope you'll find it fun and exciting!

ORGANIZATION OF THE BOOK

Each chapter is designed to highlight specific standards. Each standard discussed is followed by how G Suite for Education can be used to meet or exceed it with real classroom examples. Along the way, some authentic student work is displayed showcasing the power of G Suite for Education. Each core chapter of the book has a similar structure including

- Key Features: Highlights that will be covered in the book
- Standards Identified: Specific academic and/or technology standards that are evident and can be related to the tool
- Technology-Infused Teaching Tip: A quick example of how technology can leverage the use of each tool
- Lesson in Focus: A short objective and procedure on implementing a relevant lesson relating to the tool being written about in the chapter
- SAMR Implications—Transforming Instruction: Examples of how the tool written about can be applied to transformative teaching and learning
- Summary: A short summary of how the specific tool(s) can be used in the middle school classroom

STEP-BY-STEP TUTORIALS

Every chapter contains clear instructions illustrated by screenshots that show exactly when and where to click. These tutorials make it easy for anyone to access the features of G Suite no matter what level of experience they have with technology. For an example, see the short tutorial below.

How to Use Google's URL Shortener

Links to web addresses can often be long and complex. Google offers a tool to shorten links to make them more accessible. For example, this is a link to a Google Doc that I want readers to access: https://docs.google.com/document/d/1gYavpNndG8vJtnE-Dr_hWpjSjosh-rGEms1-cgt-I_E/edit. It would be very difficult to type all of this into a web browser. But Google's URL Shortener can convert the link to http://goo.gl/Kaz6M. This shorter link can easily be typed into a web browser to access the file. The shortened links created by Google never expire. All links are case sensitive, meaning that capital and lowercase letters must be typed in exactly as shown. Follow the steps below to use Google's URL Shortener.

1. Go to http://goo.gl in a web browser.

2. Copy any web address to shorten.

3. Paste the web address in the box shown in Figure P.1.

Figure P.1

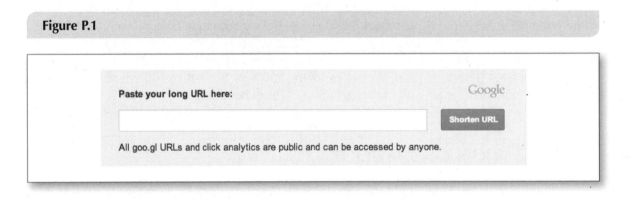

4. Click the ███████ button to reveal the shortened link found in Figure P.2.

5. Email, tweet, post on Facebook, or write the shortened link down to access it later or share with friends.

Figure P.2

TECHNOLOGY-INFUSED TEACHING TIPS

Throughout the book, notice the boxed feature Technology-Infused Teaching Tip. This feature offers readers commentary on how to explicitly use G Suite to meet the rigors of college- and career-ready standards. These boxes often contain lesson plan ideas and short descriptions on how to maximize learning using technology.

RESOURCES

Resources is a boxed feature at the end of each chapter. Resources provide the reader with links to full lesson plans that use various G Suite tools for the middle-level student. It will direct the reader to the appropriate part of the Resource section that contains lesson plans found on the website. The web content is a collection of the following:

- Links to lesson plans at various grade levels and subjects found on the web
- Links to videos
- Links to video tutorials
- Additional resources

Find the entire collection of web resources that we have gathered or created at www.corwin.com/googlemeetsms.

Lesson plans are included on the website because most of the lesson plans developed use more than one G Suite app. To help the reader align the various G Suite apps and standards of the lesson plans, the website also contains a Lesson Plan Correlation Chart at the beginning of the Resource section. Using the chart, readers can connect various apps they are learning about with real-world lesson plans found in the Resource section.

FOUR REASONS TO BUY THIS BOOK

1. *Simplicity:* This book is an easy-to-use guide to help you implement G Suite for Education into your classroom with step-by-step instructions.

2. *Innovation:* This book will enhance your teaching practice with cutting-edge, classroom-tested ideas that implement technology in your classroom.

3. *Standards Connected:* This book is organized around common college- and career-ready standards that are applicable and adaptable to meet state mandates.

4. *Google Certified Authors:* Graham and Borgen are certified by Google to provide professional development to teachers and others who use G Suite for Education.

Acknowledgments

Corwin wishes to acknowledge the following peer reviewers for their editorial insight and guidance:

Lisa Graham, Program Supervisor, Special Education
Berkeley Unified School District
Berkeley, CA

Heidi Guadagni, Learning Specialist
French Prairie Middle School
Woodburn, OR

Deborah Howard
Teacher of the Deaf, Teacher ESL, Teacher EFL
Consultant with several school districts
Pownal, ME

Michelle Kocar, Curriculum Specialist
North Olmsted City Schools
North Olmsted, OH

Betty Rivinus, Special Education Teacher
Canby School District
Canby, OR

Susan Stewart, Assistant Professor
Ashland University
Ashland, OH

About the Authors

Michael J. Graham is the principal of Westside High School in Jonesboro, Arkansas. Michael specializes in providing professional development to teachers on his staff and across the nation to maximize the learning experience for students through the implementation of technology into the classroom. His strength lies in working directly with teachers, motivating them to become 21st-century learners so they can pass on those skills directly to students. Michael received a BA in chemistry and MSE in educational leadership from Arkansas State University. He has finished his EdS from Arkansas Tech University, credentialing him to become a superintendent. His teaching experience includes 5 years of eighth-grade mathematics and 2 years as instructional technologist at Harrisburg Middle School. In 2014, Michael moved back home to become an administrator of his alma mater. Michael is involved with the Arkansas Department of Education's Technology Information Center for Administrative Leadership Cadre and board member on the Arkansas ASCD. Michael has a new baby, Katherine Olivia, with his wife Jessica. In between changing diapers, Michael continues to write and think about creating the best learning environment possible.

Michael is a Google Certified Education Trainer, providing professional development to teachers and others who use G Suite for Education.

Jason Borgen is a native to using technology in education. Jason taught middle school science and AVID from 2001 to 2007 in the Silicon Valley area. Focused in the use of project-based learning through collaborative projects, he helped many students succeed through 24/7 learning environments. Jason earned his master's degree in educational leadership from San Jose State University. He spent 8 years with the Technology Information Center for Administrative Leadership (TICAL), a statewide project in California, funded by the Department of Education. TICAL's mission is to assist administrators across the state with technology integration and support. TICAL also provides services to the state of Arkansas. During his tenure working out of the Santa Cruz County Office of

Education, Jason also provided professional development workshops and credential coursework to local teachers and administrators. Jason currently is Director of Learning & Innovation for Portola Valley School District overseeing Curriculum, Assessment, Professional Development, Information and Education Technology. Jason presents at regional, statewide, and national and international conferences, and he also leads workshops for CUE, International Society for Technology in Education (ISTE), and CASCD. Jason has worked with several schools and districts in technology planning and providing professional development in integrating technology to engage students, increase achievements, and develop higher-order, college- and career-ready skills in the 21st century. Jason has helped design curriculum for the nationally recognized Leading Edge Certification program to support innovative educators. He is a Google Certified Innovator (Mountain View, 2008) and a Google Education Trainer. Jason serves on CUE, Inc.'s Board of Directors. To disconnect, Jason enjoys traveling, hiking, playing drums, and spending time with his family and two dogs.

Both Jason and Michael are cofounders of the DigitalEdAlliance, LLC, a professional development consulting company focused on innovative professional learning for the education community. Their flagship event, the Midsouth Summit Featuring Google for Education, occurs every July in Trumann, Arkansas.

1 Becoming a Master of Learning

Key Features

- Identify Future Ready Learning initiative
- Understand the technology-specific academic standards
- Compare and contrast 20th-century and 21st-century education
- Describe ISTE Standards for Students
- Synthesize the SAMR Model of Technology Integration
- Describe the features of G Suite for Education
- Formulate an understanding of when and how to use Google Tools

"If we teach today's students as we taught yesterday's, we rob them of tomorrow."

—John Dewey

Preparing students for college and careers in the 21st century is our goal as educators. What are these skills? How do we foster them? How do we keep students interested? Most of all, how do we ensure relevancy and authenticity as we approach the 20% mark of the 21st century? Middle school is a time in a young adolescent's life where he or she must gain skills that incorporate self-direction, self-discovery, and self-discipline. However, this does not just include the physical world anymore. Educators, community members, and parents must all engage our young adolescents in respectful and appropriate interactions in the digital world. Becoming a digital citizen involves not only respecting the global connected world, but also participating in this still-young new world. After all, Google has only been a company since 1998, and now more than 40 million students use the tools to engage in content mastery, increased productivity, and open dialogue with their teachers and peers around the globe.

FUTURE READY LEARNING

In 2015, the U.S. Department of Education launched an initiative to support personalized digital learning called Future Ready Schools (Resource 1.1). This initiative established a framework focused on Curriculum and Instruction, Community Engagement, Budget and Resources, Use of Space and Time, Infrastructure, Professional Learning, and Data and Privacy. These seven gears are at the crux of our modern (and future) educational environment. With a new set of content standards and a motivation to prepare for high school, college, and/or a career, we as educators must redefine and transform our practices. Middle school educators must be aware of national best practices to reform our schools in order to stay competitive, focus on change, and grow our adolescent youth. Aligning to this framework can assist teachers in becoming true masters of learning and being privy to national directions, possible grants, and other aspects of educational reform.

INSTRUCTIONAL STANDARDS

The Common Core State Standards (CCSS) and various other state standards have been a catalyst for change in schools focused on college and career readiness. They force educators to rethink their instruction and provide opportunities for deeper learning by lending itself to collaboration, inquiry, and project design. In fact, these various standards as well as the Next Generation Science Standards (NGSS) are the first set of standards to specifically embed references to digital learning. What follows is a set of college- and career-ready CCSS anchor standards that explicitly references digital learning.

Reading

- **R.CCR.7**: Integrate and evaluate content presented in diverse media and formats, including visually and quantitatively, as well as in words.

Writing

- **W.CCR.6**: Use technology, including the Internet, to produce and publish writing and to interact and collaborate with others.
- **W.CCR.8**: Gather relevant information from multiple print and digital sources, assess the credibility and accuracy of each source, and integrate the information while avoiding plagiarism.

Speaking & Listening

- **SL.CCR.2**: Integrate and evaluate information presented in diverse media and formats, including visually, quantitatively, and orally.
- **SL.CCR.5**: Make strategic use of digital media and visual displays of data to express information and enhance understanding of presentations.

Furthermore, the college- and career-ready standards imply cross-curricular connections. Take for example students learning about viruses in seventh-grade science. Students must effectively research the science behind viruses at the microscopic level, but they also must explore how viruses have affected society. Students can then develop a video via a third-party Google app, such as WeVideo, to demonstrate their understanding of how viruses attack cells, and how we can learn from our previous experiences through history about how to protect ourselves and each other from potential harm. Students have to learn the science, write a script, present the information, and publish a video through collaborating with others. This powerful project involves deeper learning at all levels, but most importantly, it shifts the role of the teacher from the distributor of content to the facilitator of learning.

PEDAGOGY

Prior to the age of Internet research, the teacher was the content authority in the room, and the library was the place to access a fixed set of content and information. Things have changed now with primary sources, encyclopedia, textbooks, and news being available at our fingertips. Literacy has shifted from just being able to read, write, and communicate, to being able to comfortably do these things with technology. Figure 1.1 provides a visual of this shift of access to information.

Figure 1.1 20th- Versus 21st-Century Knowledge Taxonomy in Schools

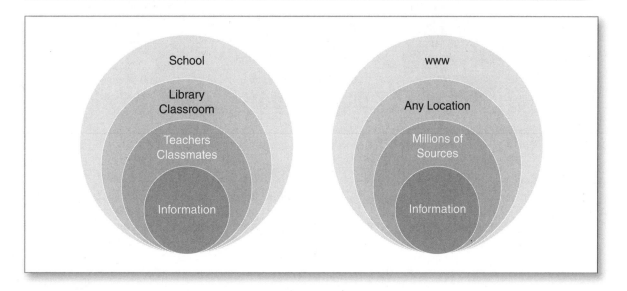

So how do teachers shift their art and practice to support this new way of accessing knowledge? There are several frameworks to align to. First, the International Society for Technology in Education (ISTE) has developed a set of standards shown in Figure 1.2 that focuses on elements of a new approach to teaching. These standards can develop a foundation for practices in the classroom. Each focus area of student standards implies relevant and timely skills needed for success in the 21st century. By using these standards as a guide, teachers have the ability to ensure students engage in activities that promote student agency, innovation, and appropriate use of interactive and communicative technologies. Furthermore, middle school students can use the indicators ISTE provides in the standards (Resource 1.2) to begin (or continue) their pathways toward college and career readiness.

Think about the virus project above and how you as a teacher would develop a lesson plan. Would you provide direct instruction? Would you involve global collaboration, such as having real doctors or historians view the videos and offer feedback or have students in a different state or country share some connections to viruses that are dominant near them? No matter how you would write this up, most likely it would be a lesson design that would have been impossible to accomplish 10+ years ago. This is where you as an instructional designer have the power to completely transform your classroom. However, it takes time.

Dr. Ruben Puentedura, an educational researcher, developed a framework of how we use technology and media to transform instruction and redefine learning. The SAMR Model (Substitution, Augmentation, Modification, and Redefinition) is is now used to design high-quality, standards-based lessons that use technology as a catalyst for redefining the learning-integrated lessons. The acronym provides a spectrum of how we can use technology to transform learning practices. See Figure 1.3 for how SAMR is used to define technology integration and the stages that lead to transformation.

Figure 1.2 ISTE Standards 2016

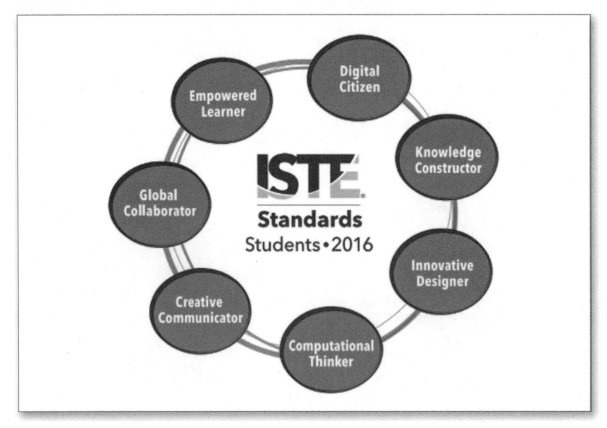

Figure 1.3 The SAMR Model

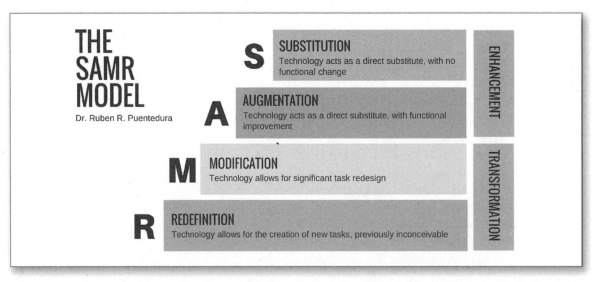

For example, creating digital flash cards with tools such as Quizlet allows you to substitute the old-fashioned index cards for easier access to study tools. This example lends itself to only enhancement of the activity (substitution or augmentation). However, using the same flash card tool (Quizlet), students can search, build, and share their own flash cards, while also including images with their peers in class and in other countries allowing for global collaboration and collaborative study techniques. The latter task allows redefined approaches to instruction.

As we look to apply any technology, we must think about how it allows for tasks that were once inconceivable, as we know our students will be in careers in the next 10–20 years that are also inconceivable today. As we explore G Suite in middle school, we will provide applications specific for the transformative aspect of the SAMR Model since education today should innovate for tomorrow!

Technology-Infused Teaching Tip

Try searching for SAMR resources on Twitter (Resource 1.3 https://goo.gl/1i9qEO)! You will find a great deal of images, examples, and methods to apply in your classroom. Twitter is also a great tool to connect with teachers and classrooms. Whether you are looking to build your personal learning network (PLN) or create more global opportunities for your students, Twitter will open the door for extended learning for both you and your students.

FEATURES OF G SUITE FOR EDUCATION

Why G Suite?

Have you ever read a book and wanted to know if is based on a true story or not? Or, perhaps you were watching a documentary about John F. Kennedy and wanted to know what his parents did for a living. Well, if you ask 9 out of 10 people, they would use the commonly used phrase—*google it*! Recently, while walking through a sixth-grade history class, students were discussing World War II. One student wanted to know why Hawaii was the first place attacked in America. The teacher, instead of just explaining the geographic location of Hawaii, asked students to load Google Maps, navigate to Hawaii, and use the measurement tools to measure the distance from Hawaii to Japan. They then compared that distance from mainland USA. Without any explanation, students just nodded, and one said, "This makes total sense!"

Google.com in 1997 was officially registered as a website. From then on, it became increasingly utilized at first as a search engine and then more readily as other relevant applications including mail, maps, news, and office productivity. The simplicity, ease of use, and benefits of the tools became internationally recognized as the go-to company for information. Google has provided many benefits to education as well. They provide G Suite for Education, a *free* suite of district-managed applications that are safeguarded by district IT staff and have always been focused on student safety, privacy, and security. All users who are logged into G Suite for Education have ad-free searching and unlimited storage of any type of data in Google Drive, including images, videos, and documents. Perhaps Google wants to create the next generation of Google users, but regardless, if the tool works, if it helps with student engagement, productivity, and creativity, it will enable student achievement! Teaching the importance of evaluating tools and consumerism can be also embedded in the breadth of the entire curriculum.

Hardware

G Suite for Education apps are unique because they operate on any device that is connected to the Internet. Users may access their content in Google Drive and create Docs, Sheets, and Slides from any laptop, tablet, or smartphone. For example, students could work on an interdisciplinary writing project comparing and contrasting ideas from a historical document in history class on their classroom PC. Later when students move to English class, they will be able to finalize the writing portion for grammar and syntax on the classroom's Mac. Finally, at lunch, students can share the work with a partner on their smartphones and work collaboratively to edit the final work.

Chromebooks

Chromebooks are laptop computers that solely run Google apps and Google's operating system called Chrome OS. Many manufacturers make the Chromebook, but all run Google's free apps and other apps from the Chrome Web Store. Chromebooks are a different kind of laptop computer. The device has a small hard drive and is made to run in the cloud connected to the Internet. It is perfect for students because it is inexpensive, easy to use, and does not require updates. For example, our technology coordinator never has to update a single Chromebook since the initiative started. Each time the computer is turned on, it downloads in the background the newest version of Chrome OS. The devices have a small hard drive for storing files locally, but this is not required or used very often because of the unlimited cloud storage of G Suite for Education's Google Drive.

Chromebook Management Console

All Chromebooks come with the option of pre-installed software called the Chromebook Management Console. This software allows the technology professionals at the school to manage each Chromebook to prepare for testing, force install certain Google apps, and block apps, websites, and other harmful Internet content. For example, when state-mandated testing season approaches, technology coordinators that have the Management Console installed can tell the Chromebooks to enter testing mode remotely. This means that the technology department does not have to physically prepare machines for security, updates, and other system configurations. Another example is end of the year preparation. At the end of the school year all Chromebooks will be turned into the technology department for repairs and maintenance. The process of updating, deleting student files, and restoring settings for the next year is a simple push of the button. The Chromebook Management Console may be purchased from vendors and preloaded on devices when ordered. Save headaches, man-hours, and money by installing this much-needed application.

Choosing a Chromebook Device

As two practicing administrators, Michael and Jason are both overseeing 1:1 Chromebook initiatives for about 1,700 students K–12 and 500 students K–8, respectively. We know choosing the best Chromebook for your students could be daunting because of the many different models and manufacturers. Each Chromebook model has different features. We have broken down the process and have provided reviews to help you in your search. The information below has pointers on the things to look for in a Chromebook for student use.

- Tough power adapter: Schools with take-home initiatives seem to have a lot of issues with weak power adapters. For example, some Chromebooks have a thick power insert, as shown in the first image below. The power plug is thin and can be bent, rendering it useless. The power adapter plug in the second image is 5.5 mm thick and could not be easily bent. Accidents happen in the middle school classroom and at home. It is better to be prepared with a strong power adapter to keep repair costs down.

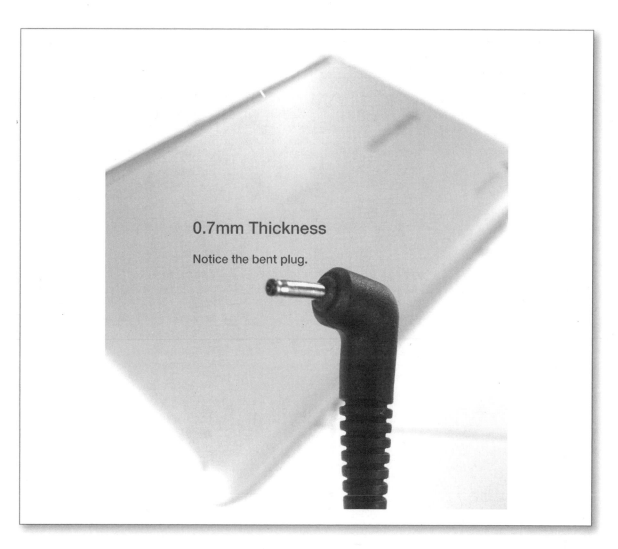

0.7mm Thickness

Notice the bent plug.

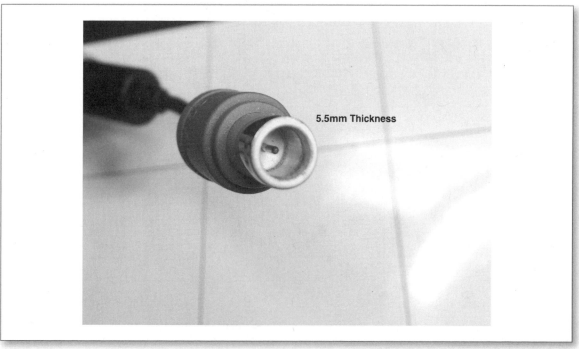

5.5mm Thickness

- Screen hinges: The screen hinges are vulnerable to breakage. Choose a Chromebook that has durable hinges that will last potentially 100 openings and closings per day.

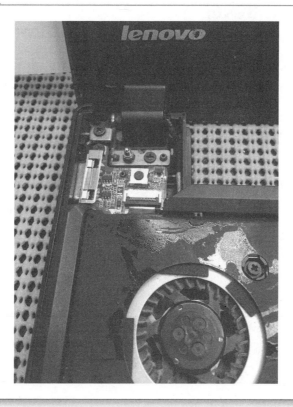

- Battery life: Constant Internet surfing causes the battery life to drain on many devices. Choose a Chromebook with at least an 8-hour battery life.
- Durability: We both taught middle school for several years before becoming administrators. We have seen our fair share of fragile technology be destroyed by various methods of annihilation. Finding a Chromebook that is tough, durable, and has spill-resistant keyboards is essential for students of any grade.

Best excuse from our Technology Department for a broken Chromebook: "My cat jumped on my Chromebook and broke it."

—Sixth-Grade Student

Best Chromebook survival story: "I put my Chromebook on top of my mom's car when she was picking me up from school. . . . It fell off about 2 miles down the road. It is a little scratched up, but it still worked when we found it."

—Eighth-Grade Student

Technology-Infused Teaching Tip

Students and parents can come up with some real MacGyver-like ways to fix a broken Chromebook. Look for duct tape, superglue, or mismatching screws as you generally inspect student devices.

GOOGLE USER EXPERIENCE

So why Google? Thousands of schools, districts, nonprofits, government agencies, and businesses have adopted G Suite for Education as their core suite of tools. We know Microsoft Office has been the go-to industry-standard set of productivity tools for more than 20 years, but with the movement toward cloud computing and Google's jump-on easy-to-use collaborative web-based software, we are seeing a definite paradigm shift in industry standards. Who will win, we don't really know, but Google is a great place to start for several reasons.

- It is free, and Google said it plans to keep it free forever for education users as a donation to education (See Figure 1.4). (Resource 1.4)
- Unlimited storage
- Device neutrality
- Features like Hangouts and Google Voice
- The Google ecosystem has the same user experience for each of their apps. At the same time, Apple's iPad has millions of apps that all have different sets of user rules. The G Suite has the exact same user experience no matter what device you access it from. Google Docs works identically on a Mac, PC, or Chromebook.

Figure 1.4   G Suite for Education Free Statement

How much is G Suite for Education?

G Suite for Education is free. We plan to keep the core offering of G Suite for Education free. This offering includes user accounts for future incoming students. As you may know, Google was founded by a research project at Stanford University, and this is just one way we can give back to the educational community.

To see the available features included in G Suite for Education, visit the G Suite for Education homepage.

For more information, review our Terms of Service.

WHY GOOGLE?

One reason why G Suite for Education is the best solution for implementing technology for today's classroom is because the service is device neutral. Device neutrality means that no matter what device the student is using, he or she will have access to G Suite for Education. On the other hand, Apple's word-processing software Pages can only be accessed on an Apple device. Using the programs available through G Suite for Education only requires access to the Internet and a web browser. With G Suite, students can access and produce their documents, files, and other work from any device (PC, Mac, Android tablet, or iPad). That is a large combination of devices to prepare students to work with. G Suite for Education helps students become ready for an ever-changing device market and to be nimble and ready for any device that their employer or college throws their way.

Teaching and learning in the 21st century and beyond sets high expectations for both students and educators. One of the most challenging expectations for educators is finding the right way to integrate technology into the learning environment. Educators everywhere know that one thing is for sure: Technology integration into our lives and work environments will be ever-increasing. The kindergartner that starts school this year will retire sometime between 2070 and 2080. The iPhone was first released in 2007. Think how much the world has changed in the past years since its debut. Fast forward to 2040, the year kindergartners of 2016 will be in the first years of their career. What skills will they need to thrive in the work environment of the day?

G Suite for Education provides nearly all of the tools to get educators on the path of using technology while implementing various college- and career-readiness standards. Google's apps are free, easy to use, and are trusted by more than 40 million students and teachers worldwide and expected to reach 110 million users by 2020. The services Google offers follow the company's motto of "do no harm." Google is providing free software to schools that works on any device from anywhere. This contribution of any device gives students a diverse technology experience. They are providing the most sophisticated, easy-to-use software experience for free, because Google feels that it is the right thing to do for teachers and students.

Figure 1.5 Growth of G Suite for Education (Formerly Google Apps for Education) Boost eLearning

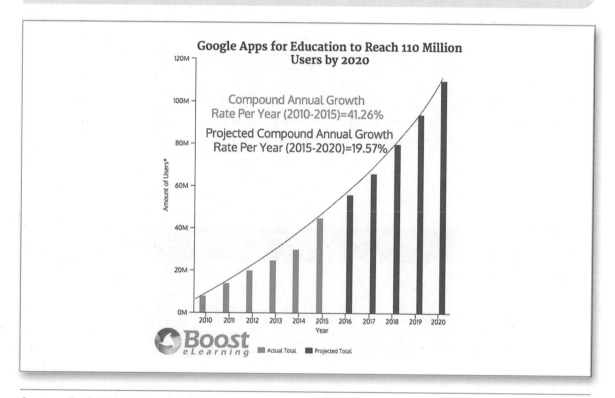

Source: Alhadeff, V. (2015, July 1). Google Apps for Education Anticipated to Reach 110 Million Users by 2020. Retrieved from http://www.prnewswire.com/news-releases/google-apps-for-education-anticipated-to-reach-110-million-users-by-2020-300107878.html

Note: *Includes teachers, students, and administrators.

This book is filled with exciting new ideas and processes for the middle school educator to get started with G Suite for Education, demonstrating how it can be used to meet and exceed the various college, career, and technology readiness standards. Hopefully, it can excite the veteran teacher to implement new strategies, while calming fears, and it will help the novice teacher get familiar with the much-needed technology integration components students need for success in high school and later in life. This book will offer step-by-step tutorials with screenshots to explain in detail how to get your students learning and working with these amazing 21st-century tools, as well as full lesson plans on the companion website.

Google has a vision for their users. Their aspirations were as follows:

The Google User Experience team aims to create designs that are useful, fast, simple, engaging, innovative, universal, profitable, beautiful, trustworthy, and personable. Achieving a harmonious balance of these 10 principles is a constant challenge. A product that gets the balance right is "Googley"—and will satisfy entire district deployments. G Suite is seamless to implement across any size school or district big or small. Furthermore, Google is committed to student safety, privacy, and data, ensuring no data will be shared nor used for advertising purposes, much different than traditional Google accounts. (Resource 1.5)

SUMMARY

As you begin to think about transforming your middle school classroom experiences, how will you set the tone for our future generations? What makes your classroom "Googley"? Whether you see the need for applying these tools to various sets of standards such as Common Core or ISTE, or you want to really transform your classroom using the SAMR Model as a guide, one thing is for certain—our world is changing, and what we are preparing students for in their careers will be something we may never have a full grasp on. Google will be a service that will be essential for many decades to come.

Many of you are already immersing transformative practices into teaching and learning, but are you creating a sustainable system to allow for deeper learning and content acquisition that is relevant, rigorous, and applicable to students near and far? In order to do so, you must think of yourself as the master of learning, not necessarily the master of content. Throughout this book, you will immerse yourself in a set of tools to add to your toolbox to be the true facilitator of lifelong learning for the remaining four-fifths of the 21st century.

RESOURCES

For more information about G Suite for Education, including

- lesson plans related to chapter content,
- domain setup for tech administrators' videos,
- overviews and Google training materials,
- the authors' favorite websites, and
- testimonials and interviews of schools currently using G Suite,

access Resources from this chapter on the companion website.

online resources http://resources.corwin.com/googlemeetsms

2 G Suite for Education: Overview

Key Features

- G Suite is free . . . forever.
- Core apps Docs, Sheets, Slides, and Classroom overview
- The Cloud: Definition and why it is important
- Sharing: What it means and how it has changed classrooms
- Domain administrator: How schools can control access to parts of Google

Walking through a sixth-grade English Language Art class one day in Portola Valley, CA, Jason saw students searching Google for a variety of controversial issues in society. One student searched for dog rescues in California. Another student searched for trash found on beaches. They were all taking notes in Google Docs. Jason asked the teacher what the objective of the project was, and she said students were to present the importance of a specific cause being supported by several individuals and organizations. Some of the following tasks were to email a representative from a nonprofit representing the cause, develop an informational narrative that includes some research (in a blog or article), and create a multimedia presentation or video summarizing the cause. Of course, *every* tool used was a G Suite for Education app. One significant observation was that students were engaged in relevant and collaborative products! Computer skills such as writing documents, creating presentations, writing email, and collecting data on spreadsheets must be commonplace in the classroom because they are commonplace in high school, college, and in a career. Many K–12 and higher education institutions across the country are using G Suite for Education in their schools to help provide this vital experience.

G Suite for Education is a suite of applications offered at no cost and advertisement-free to educational institutions. These applications provide educators with the tools to successfully integrate technology into their teaching, and they prepare students to be college and career ready with relevant 21st-century skills. Standards like Common Core, ISTE Standards, and other college- and career-readiness standards require teachers and students to be fluent in digital technologies. The architects of the standards address the need for students to be able to work and learn in a technologically based society. That is why many standards demand that students be able to work in an atmosphere of collaboration, with special emphasis on creating and sharing learning. G Suite for Education will make these goals a reality in the classroom by providing teachers and students with the ability to create, collaborate, and share their work.

THE APPS

Google offers Search, Gmail, Google Calendar, Google Drive (which includes Docs, Sheets, Slides, Drawings, and Forms), Google Classroom, and Google Sites in a package that students and faculty can access from anywhere. This virtually unlimited access of Google apps allows students and teachers to extend learning and work beyond the school walls. This gives users vital real-world experience with digital tools to manage their work and life.

Search

Google is the king of search. Although it is not one of the core applications, it is the most synonymous with Google. When you have a question, what do you do? *Google it.* Caution to teachers: If you are asking the majority of questions to your students that can be answered by "google it," then you are asking the wrong questions. Teachers who can craft questions that elicit a thoughtful response will be more successful at solidifying understanding. For example, middle school students could be assigned to learn about internment camps that forced Japanese Americans to be essentially jailed during WWII. Instead of asking students to list three places where the internment camps were located, the teacher could ask, "Explain the local weather conditions of the various internment camps. How were the conditions of the prisoners different or the same from camp to camp?" This example allows the students to use Google to point them to articles where they can read and conceptualize understanding. The same objective was met, and the students know not only where the camps were located, but also so much more.

Gmail

Gmail is a web-based email service that provides students and school employees with a school-managed email account. This is done under a school's unique *domain* that users can access from any Internet-enabled device. For example, a student or faculty member at a G Suite for Education school will have a Gmail address with this format: username@yourschool.org. This is different from personal Gmail accounts that have the format username@gmail.com. Features located within Gmail for schools keep Gmail safe, secure, and controlled by the school's *domain administrator.* Gmail can be accessed from home, school, a smartphone, or any Internet-enabled device. Gmail is packed with features like search, Hangouts, and even a free telephone that will ring your Google account. These features extend the user experience. For example, when enabled by the domain administrator in the Hangouts app, Google will allow users to send SMS text messages to cell phones, and it allows teachers to call any phone number directly from their Gmail account. This is great for teachers, giving them a phone in their classrooms that provides a way for easy parent contact. With the ability to text or call directly from their Gmail account, teachers can stay in touch with parents regardless of the parents' communication hurdles. To learn how to access Google Voice and get your own telephone number associated with your Google account, follow the steps in Chapter 10.

Google Calendar

Google Calendar is a web-based calendar that lets users make appointments, schedule meetings, set due dates, and share that information with others in a live online calendar. Teachers can create class calendars and share them with specific students or with groups of contacts organized by class period, making it easy to share material with large numbers of students. Teachers and students can also create multiple calendars that manage their busy lives. For example, the student council secretary could create a calendar of the meetings and events for the organization. He could then share that calendar with the members of student council. That calendar will appear along with each member's basketball game schedule, freshman English assignment calendar, and personal calendar. All of the calendars are color-coded accordingly, making them easy to distinguish from one another. Calendar makes it possible to see events of multiple friends, classmates, or teachers' schedules in one online calendar. Figure 2.1 shows how different calendars are represented by different colors. Each event that belongs to a particular calendar has the same color.

Figure 2.1 Calendar

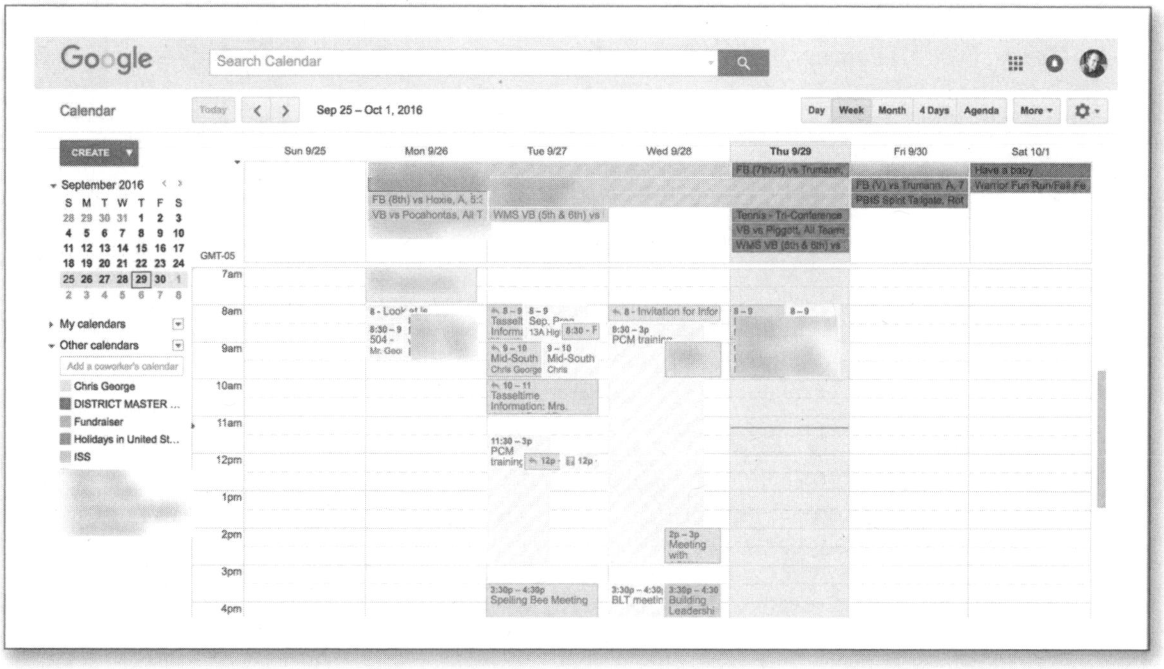

Google Drive

Google Drive is the storage component of G Suite for Education. Drive has unlimited storage for any file type. Students and teachers can store any file like videos, PDFs, Microsoft Word Documents, and of course, Google Docs, Sheets, and Slides. This is the user's cloud-based storage drive that can be accessed anywhere there is an Internet connection.

Technology-Infused Teaching Tip

Mobile Applications and Google

Download applications made by Google for the iPhone, iPad, or Android mobile OS in their respective app stores. Follow this link to Resource 2.1 at https://goo.gl/zdM2oD for access to all of the Google apps for iOS. Google apps are preloaded on the Android OS.

Google Drive includes a web-based software package that includes document, presentation, spreadsheet, form, and drawing applications that can fully replace expensive office software. In Google Docs, students have the ability to share a document with teachers or peers, allowing for a collaborative writing experience. Students can write on the same document at the same time, but be on different devices. In addition, students can share the document with the teacher allowing immediate feedback on writing assignments.

Google Docs is where the work gets done using G Suite for Education. Built into Google Docs is the ability to share. Sharing provides a collective environment where student work that is created in any of the Google Drive programs can be collaboratively viewed, edited, or published to the web. Google Docs saves the user's work every few seconds to Google Drive. Google Docs and Google's cloud storage service eliminate the need for physical student data storage devices such as USB flash drives, which reduces clutter and decreases the chances that the dog will eat their homework.

Figure 2.2 displays how to access Google Drive. Clicking on the boxes ⚏ at the top right of the screen while signed into any of the Google apps will take the user here. Clicking on the **New** button will enable the user to choose what type of Doc to create. The Google Drive homepage includes links to Docs, Slides, Sheets, Forms, Drawings, Sites, Maps, and more programs under the �⬚NEW⬚ button.

Figure 2.2 Google Drive

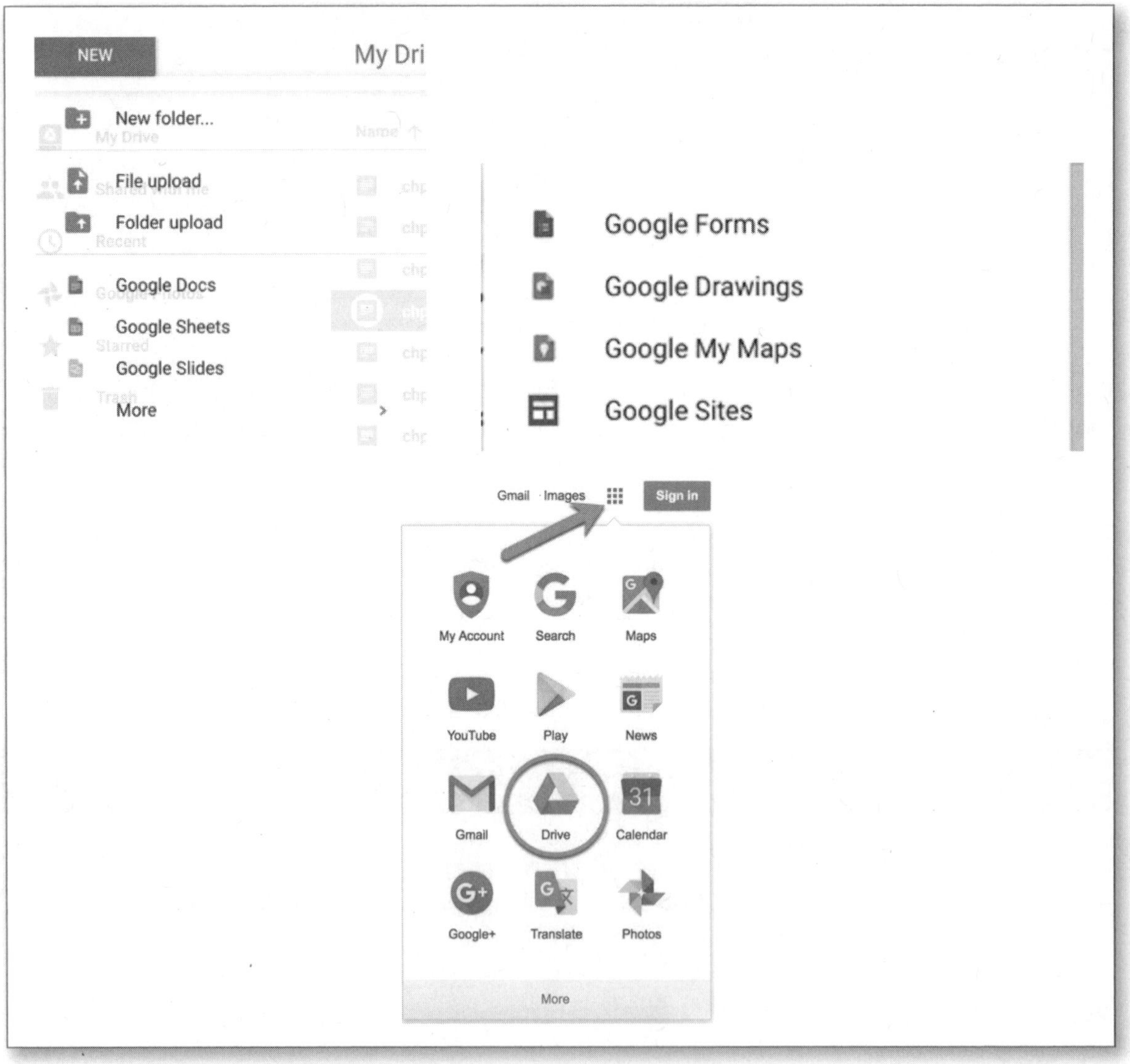

Google Classroom

Have you ever taken an online class? All online classes provide an online community space for curriculum delivery, assignment submissions, and ongoing discussions. Google Classroom, similar to an online class community space, is a digital version of your classroom, allowing you to create announcements, deliver assignments, engage students in online discussions, and share curricular resources. It provides an integrated calendar and a one-stop shop for any or all assignments. You can ask students to review videos, websites, and/or submit their projects with Google Classroom. Submissions are automatically organized for the teacher so you can easily provide feedback to students anytime/anywhere. You also have the ability to invite parents to view your Google Classroom activity and receive notifications if and when assignments are overdue. Figure 2.3 shows the different items that you can post in a Google Classroom.

Figure 2.3 New Google Classroom Post

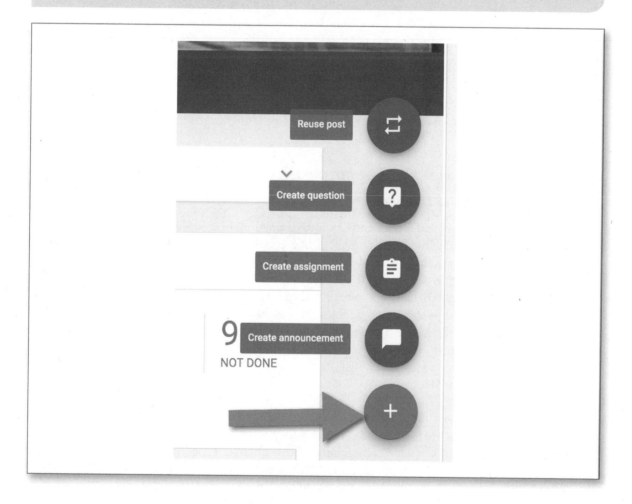

Google Sites

Google Sites is a free website creator that allows teachers and students to make websites that are fully compatible with Google Calendar and Google Docs. These are kept under the school domain, and students may share websites with the outside world if approved by the domain administrator. Google Sites does not require the use of complicated web design language such as HTML.

Figure 2.4 displays the Classic Google Sites main menu. The new version of Google Sites is actually available directly in Google Drive. Sites that are created under the school's G Suite domain are listed here. If Sites are enabled for students and teachers in a large district, then it is possible that a large number of sites would be listed here. Using the *search bar* to narrow down sites is the most efficient way to find the site the user is looking for. In 2016, Google introduced a new version of Sites that saves all your sites into Google Drive.

Figure 2.4 Google Sites Main Menu

Gmail and Google Sites in This Book

Google's mail application called Gmail and Google Sites will not be addressed in detail in this book. Gmail and Google Sites are important and should be considered as part of a school's solution for delivering high-quality technology-related instruction. The purpose of this book is to directly relate G Suite for Education, while connecting to college- and career-readiness standards to offer teachers lesson plan ideas and insight to make that possible. Gmail is a very high-quality program that is ubiquitous and easy to use. Additionally, Google Sites' user controls are complex and would require more space than is suitable for this work. The focus of this book is to get the most out of G Suite to help teachers increase student achievement.

THE CLOUD

G Suite for Education apps are cloud based, meaning they can be accessed anywhere from any device that has an Internet connection. Cloud computing makes it possible for users to store, create, and share content without saving it to a physical hard drive. For example, a student writing an essay in Google Docs on a laptop in English class can save the file to her Google Drive and later access that file from her home computer. With Google Drive, it doesn't matter if the computer gets a virus and is completely destroyed. The student's essay can be accessed anywhere there is an Internet connection through the user's G Suite for Education account. This ability allows students and teachers to create, collaborate, and share their work across any device using any platform. It does not matter if students are working on a Mac, PC, or smartphone. Students may even upload other formats of student work such as Microsoft Word, Excel, PowerPoint, Apple Pages, .PDF, or .CSV data files and share them with anyone.

If the student or teacher uploads a format other than Google Docs to his or her Google Drive, the user may not edit the document in the Google Docs program. In that case, Google Drive would be used just for storage. Alternatively, the user could convert the file to Google Docs format, creating a new Google Doc that may be edited in the corresponding Google program. During the upload process, Google Docs will ask the user if he or she wants to convert the document to its matching Doc format (see Figure 2.5). This allows the user to edit the document with the corresponding Google Docs program.

1. To access upload settings, click the settings gear ⚙ in the upper right-hand corner of Google Drive.

2. Then click the **Convert uploaded** box shown in Figure 2.5.

Figure 2.5 Upload Settings

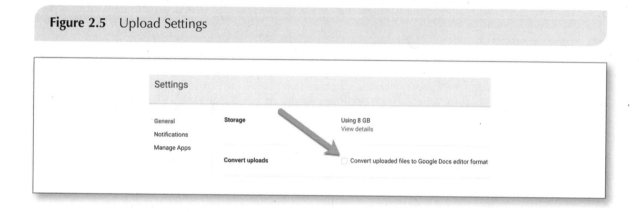

Share

Sharing is one of the unique features of Google Docs that gives it the upper hand by offering collaboration to users. Traditional office software packages that reside on the hard drives of computers do not offer the ability of collaboration and sharing. Sharing in Google Docs allows users to be able to work collaboratively in any of the programs. The user can give others the rights to edit, view, or comment on any document that they own in real time by setting visibility options and share settings. The default share setting is private (unless your domain administrator changed the settings), but users can share with anyone through a URL or use share settings to send the person an email notification alerting them that a document is being shared. Options in sharing allow the user to make the Google Doc searchable on the web, public for users in your domain only, or public for anyone with the web link.

Students' motivation for doing high-quality work will increase because they are doing the work not only for the teacher to read, but they are also producing work that can be shared with parents, peers, and other adults, giving them a sense of pride and responsibility to produce excellent work.

Vannessa, a sixth-grade student at Harrisburg Middle School, was quoted saying, "Using Google Docs is way easier than writing our essays on paper; it also gives me a way to show off my writing. . . . I can really share it with anyone . . . plus, we're not killing all of the trees we used to." Vannessa now has another purpose for her writing. Her writing has the possibility of being read by parents, peers, and professionals around the world, giving her pride, motivation, and validation. Sharing work with others outside the student–teacher relationship is a possibility, not a requirement. Students, teachers, and parents may have conversations on what is appropriate for sharing with parents, peers, or the world.

With G Suite for Education, users can share Google Docs within their domain or, if their domain administrator has approved out-of-domain sharing, students and teachers may share with anyone. This includes neighboring school districts, professionals in the field, or colleges and universities. One of the hallmarks of the Common Core State Standards is learning through collaboration. Through sharing and collaborating, students gain a sense of community and responsibility for the group's work. G Suite for Education gives students the tools to create, collaborate, and share their understanding of the world and to find their place in technologically rich college and career settings. Figure 2.6 is a screenshot of the share settings in G Suite. Follow the steps to share and restrict times people may access documents.

1. Click the **Share** button to open the sharing center.
2. Click the **Advanced** button as shown in Figure 2.6.

Figure 2.6 Advanced Sharing Access

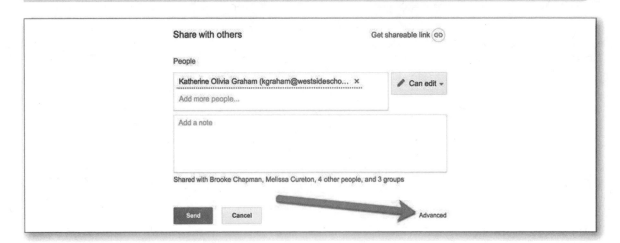

Figure 2.7 Advanced Sharing—Limit Sharing by Time

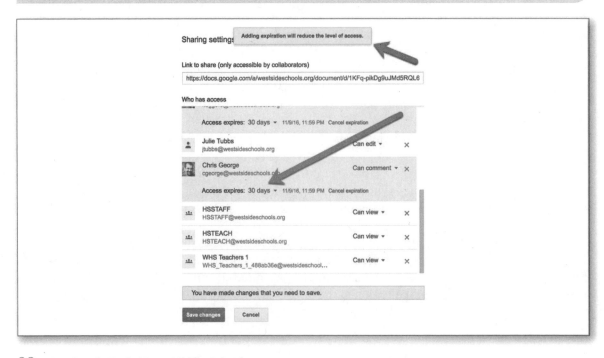

By clicking on the arrow in Figure 2.7, the user can set the time limit a particular user may have access to the document.

THE DOMAIN ADMINISTRATOR: BEHIND THE SCENES

G Suite for Education is hosted by Google, which means all of the content created by students and teachers is safely stored on Google's servers. However, the data that students and teachers create with their G Suite account are the property of the school and the user. G Suite for Education customers benefit from two features that will help district technology personnel allocate human and financial resources more appropriately. There is no software to install and no hardware to purchase: Google provides the entire apps package, services, and support for free. The ability of the school domain administrator to manage the G Suite for Education service adds the special security measures that are appropriate for the school setting.

The domain administrator can control virtually all features of G Suite for Education. For example, the domain administrator can select certain features to become available to groups of users. He or she may allow teachers and support staff to access Hangouts and Google Voice, but they may be turned off for students. Your school community would benefit from a committee that is designated to review what features of G Suite for Education are available for use by students and teachers so that they may reflect the values of the community. The domain administrator may add features or take them away at any time for individual users or groups of users. For example, if a middle school student sends an email to a fellow student that contains bullying language, then the domain administrator may disable Gmail for the offending student, but leave on Google Calendar and Docs so that the student may complete assignments. After the student has been held accountable and counseled on the proper way to communicate online and has earned the trust back, the domain administrator can restore the privilege of Gmail to the student. All emails sent to the student during that time will be saved and may be accessed when the student's Gmail is reactivated. Groups of users from an elementary setting may benefit from more restricted access to sharing and Gmail outside the domain, while middle and high school students may need to contact peers, parents, or professionals outside the domain.

Technology-Infused Teaching Tip

In Michael's first year as a middle school teacher in 2006, he had no projector and no computer, and he had a hard copy spreadsheet for a gradebook. Michael had just come out of college working and learning with Google and its evolving products, and when he got to the classroom, he felt stifled and unaccustomed to the technology resources he had to work with. Beginning teachers from any year will possibly face this scenario or something similar. If you are reading this book and your school is not a G Suite for Education school or your principal or domain administrator does not "like" Google or think it is unimportant, then find ways to interact and show off some of the time-saving tools administrators can use to communicate better. In 2006, Michael's principal and domain administrator just did not know what was possible with technology. He had to prove it to them that it was beneficial. If you feel like your school is in the Dark Ages, take on the responsibility to educate your building and district leaders.

Although dangers exist, proper classroom management and student online safety education will create a student who is ready for college and a career. Blocking outside forms of communication may leave the student unprepared to handle the digital world. Relaxing the content filters and share settings can educate students about dangers such as bullying and access to inappropriate content. When a student abuses the trust, the student can be counseled on the appropriate way to use digital tools. If left uneducated, students may not know how to behave properly online once out of the more secure G Suite for Education setting.

RESOURCES

For more information about G Suite for Education, including

- lesson plans related to chapter content,
- domain setup for tech administrators' videos,
- overviews and Google training materials,
- the authors' favorite websites, and
- testimonials and interviews of schools currently using G Suite,

access Resources from this chapter on the companion website.

online resources http://resources.corwin.com/googlemeetsms

3 Google Classroom

Key Features

- Develop an online repository of resources
- Engage an online community with your students
- Engage students in online discussions
- Share relevant curricular resources in diverse formats
- Create and deliver assignments paperlessly
- Evaluate and provide feedback on student work

Jason was helping an English language arts and history teacher (we call this two-period class Core) recently with some lessons around Google Maps. As students walked into class after lunch, they all picked up a Chromebook and immediately navigated to Google Classroom. Looking over a shoulder of one student, he noticed in Google Classroom the core teacher had several activities to be completed. The first activity was a question, "How do you think racism affects our country? Give at least two examples." Jason was mesmerized by the engagement and immediate active learning happening. The teacher did not say a word, but students knew exactly where to go and what to do! The next task asked students to watch a video about the rise of racism during the Civil War, and the final task asked students to read one article about various forms of racism and write a letter to their Congressional representative explaining ways society should combat racism. The letter would be written in Google Docs and submitted at exactly the same location where they started—in Google Classroom.

When you visit most college and many high school campuses, you may notice students accessing their materials digitally through a Learning Management System (LMS). Think about it: curriculum, assignments, online discussions, announcements, class calendar, gradebook, and much more all in one place. Some elementary and middle schools are even moving toward this 24/7 access to classrooms to meet the needs of state standards and/or Common Core Standards. Students now have the ability to access research, prepare and evaluate multimedia, and engage in conversations from anywhere via an LMS approach. The foundation to any 21st-century middle school classroom should include some type of online classroom system that provides a one-stop shop for all classroom materials. This system should also seamlessly integrate other tools used across the learning environment.

As we explore the most significant aspects of using G Suite for Education, a foundational element is setting up your Google Classroom—an LMS*lite*, if you will—which will provide the location where you will deliver content, assignments, and announcements as well as engage students in ongoing dialogue. How is this different from a class website? Well, this could definitely replace the class website, but more significantly, Google Classroom is made to be interactive where students can submit and engage in conversations. A class website acts as a read-only informational site to view general class information where Google Classroom is a one-stop shop for true active learning. You can still deliver and link to your entire curriculum on the website, but instruction and assignments are completed in Google Classroom. Think of the class website as the textbook and Google Classroom as the workbook. Please note: Your district must be a G Suite for Education (formerly known as Google Apps for Education) customer, and Google Classroom must be turned on by your administrator. Ask your IT administrators for details.

Figure 3.1 shows an example of your Google Classroom homepage, which will list each class you teach. Every time you create a new Class, there is a corresponding Google Drive folder associated with it for all assignments and projects.

Figure 3.1   Google Classroom Homepage

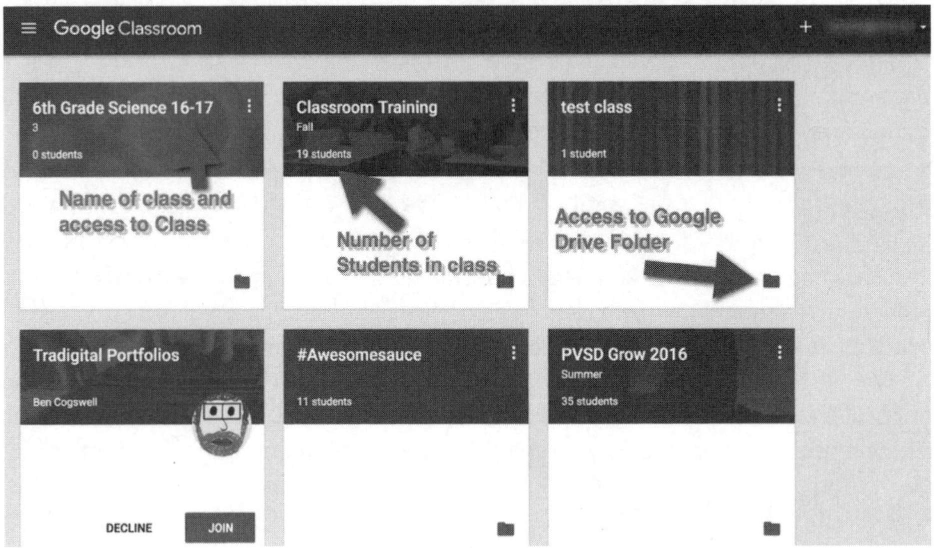

SETTING UP YOUR CLASS

Creating Your Class

When you first launch Google Classroom, it will ask you if you are a student or teacher. You will need to select **Teacher** as this will add you to a group on the administrative backend. You either will then be able to begin adding classes, or you may have to communicate with your IT staff to accept you to the teachers' group to allow you to create classes. This is dependent upon how restrictive your district's settings are.

Once you are set up as a teacher, follow these steps to add your class or classes:

1. Click the + **sign** in the upper right of the screen.

Figure 3.2   Creating a Class

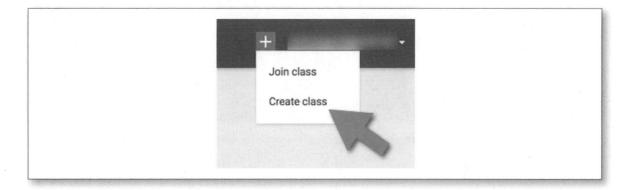

2. Select **Create class**. (Figure 3.2)

3. Type in the name of your class (a good practice is to also add the year), section, or period number:

Figure 3.3   Class Details

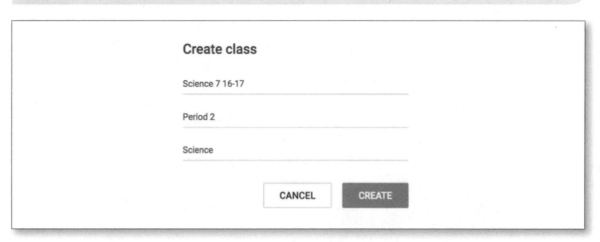

4. Type in the name of the subject (be consistent with naming conventions). (Figure 3.3)

5. Click **Create.**

6. Repeat this for each period you teach.

Branding Your Class

As you begin to develop an online community for your students, it is important to brand your classroom with your class personality and image. You can do this several ways—use existing themes or create a logo. A great idea is to take a landscape picture of your students and/or classroom and upload the image. The image must be at least 800 pixels × 200 pixels. There are several online services available to resize images, including ReSizeImage.net.

Figure 3.4   Classroom Banner Photo

To change the theme or use your own photo, simply click on **Select theme** or **Upload photo** from the right side of your Classroom banner, as shown in Figure 3.4.

The next thing to notice in your Google Classroom are the three tabs at the top center: **Stream, Students,** and **About.** Each tab navigates to a different area of the classroom. Figure 3.5 summarizes each tab, which we will go into detail on.

Figure 3.5   Tabs in Google Classroom

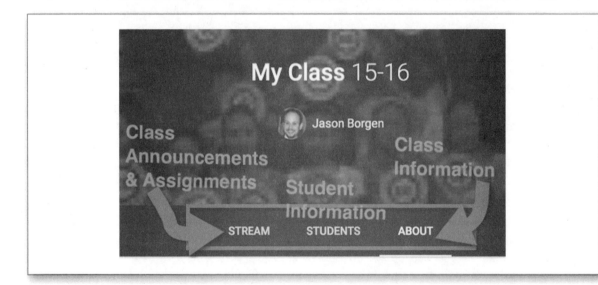

About Tab

Before you invite students and post information to your Classroom, it is important to post the materials that will be pertinent throughout the year (e.g., syllabus, class website, reading lists). Think of this section as your classroom bulletin board where you post items that stay constant for the entire year. See Figure 3.6.

1. Add your classroom name, description of your class, and room number.

2. Access your corresponding Google Drive folder and Google Calendar that is automatically created for every Classroom you create. (*Note:* Any file your students submit online through

Google Classroom will be accessible in this folder, and any due date will automatically be added to the Classroom Google Calendar for both you and your students.)

3. Click on **Add class materials** to add resources.

4. There are four resources you can add, represented by icons:

   a. Attach files from your computer, such as a class photo of the school handbook.

   b. Attach files from Google Drive, such as videos or documents you have stored in the cloud, like a syllabus.

   c. Attach a YouTube video or videos that perhaps represent your class and/or your interests.

   d. Attach links that provide students more resources for your class such as websites related to your content areas (e.g., National Geographic, Newsela, Library of Congress).

   e. Click on **Post** to post the materials.

5. If you have co-teachers, mentor teachers, administrators, etc. and would like to share the responsibility of posting and monitoring class activities with others, you can invite others to be listed and act as teachers in the classroom. Simply click on **Invite Teacher.**

Figure 3.6 About Tab

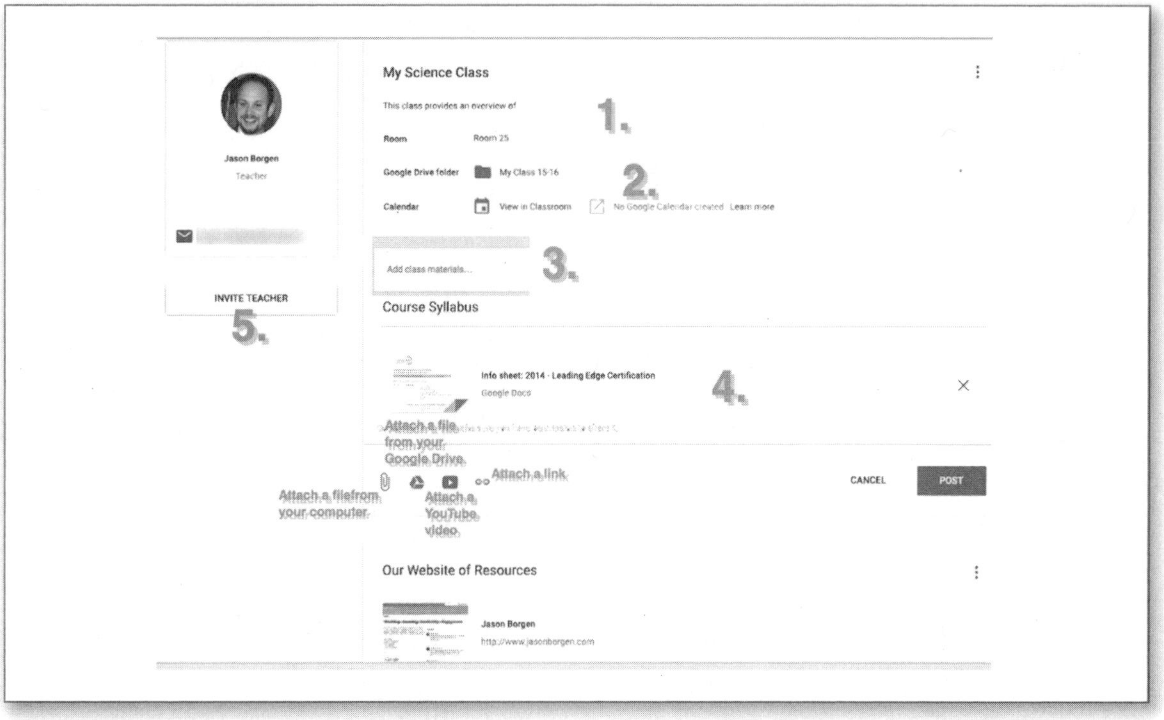

Student Tab

The **Student** tab allows you to view your students, invite students and parents/guardians, and communicate with them. You also have the ability to turn on or off student posting and commenting for the entire class.

When you first set up your classroom, you want to either invite students, or share the unique class code with students so they can join themselves. It is much less tedious to simply write down the invite code on the board and tell students to go to Google Classroom at classroom.google.com and click on the + **icon** in the top-right corner of the screen to join the class. They will then be able to type in the code associated with your class and click **Join.** This will immediately add them to your class. If you get new students at any point throughout the year, you can then use the **Invite Students** button to send them an email invitation individually. Or, once invited, students can navigate to Google Classroom, and the invitation will be waiting for them on their Google Classroom homepage.

Finally, you have the ability of emailing (if Gmail is turned on in your domain) your students. You can either check the box at the top to email all, or check individual students. By checking one or more students, you can click on the **Actions** button to email, remove them from your class, or "mute" them, which will not allow them to post or comment. Muting can be helpful for students who post inappropriate content.

CLASS ACTIVITIES

Stream Tab

Once your classroom is set up and you have invited students, you will spend the majority of your time on the **Stream** tab to post announcements, assignments, discussion questions, poll questions, and to access student work. To post anything in Google Classroom, click on the + **icon** in the bottom right of the **Stream** tab, and you will see the options you have, as shown in Figure 3.7.

Figure 3.7 Posting Options

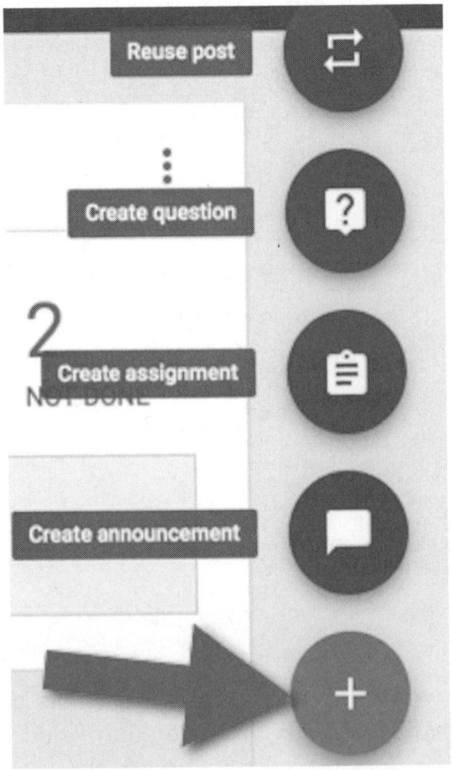

Announcements

Announcements are exactly what they sound like: quick items to announce that may or may not require a response. Maybe you want to share with students an interesting article or video about asteroids in a science class or remind students to bring their field trip forms back to class tomorrow. You can even pose a question where students can comment on the post. Students will receive a notification in their email or on the Classroom mobile app once anything is added to the stream. Announcements do not have a grade associated with them. You have the option of adding attachments (PDFs, images, etc.), Google Drive files, YouTube videos, and/or links to webpages to your announcement. CCSS focuses on being able to interpret information in diverse media formats, and you have many options of media you can add to the announcement. You can make announcements of simple tasks for students to complete in class that you will not grade. For example, you may want students to review a PDF of a poem, then watch a video of the poem, and finally read a biography of the author. You can attach as many resources as you would like to an announcement. Once you are ready to post, click on **Post,** and students will immediately see this in their stream. You can click on the drop-down arrow next to **Post** for more options including scheduling the post, saving as a draft, and/or editing later.

Table 3.1 Common Core State Standards: Reading Information Text

CCSS 7.7RI: *Compare and contrast a text to an audio, video, or multimedia version of the text, analyzing each medium's portrayal of the subject.*

Look at Figure 3.8. This example assignment allows students to easily access text of a narrative, a video, and an interactive website to review Edgar Allan Poe's rich literary mind. Students can better understand how the medium portrays the author and discuss the benefits of each medium correlating directly to CCSS 7.7 RI (shown above in Table 3.1).

Figure 3.8 Example Post: Reading Informational Text Post With Poe

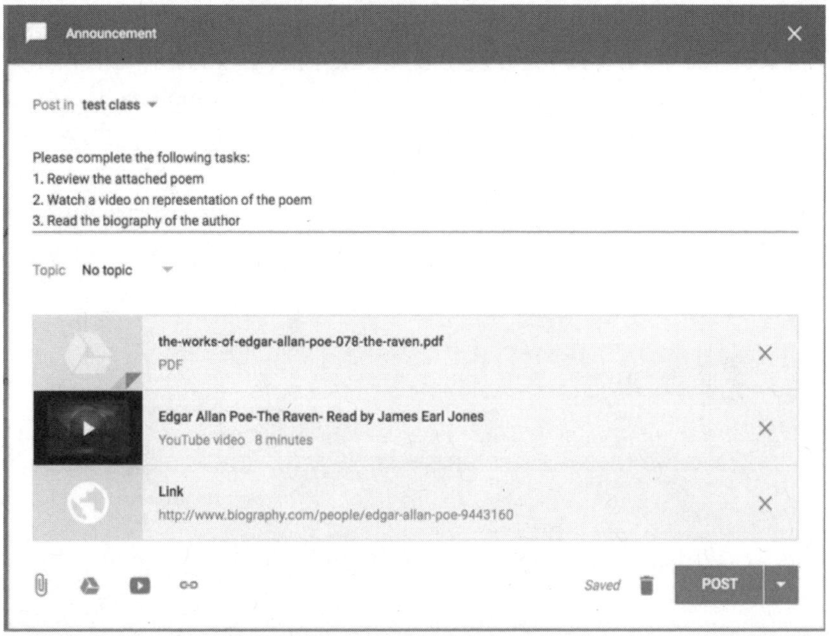

Assignments

Assignments are more significant tasks and/or graded work. Students have the ability to share their work via link, attachment, or they can create Google Drive files such as documents, spreadsheets, presentations, etc. You have the ability of also adding attachments, YouTube videos, web links, and Google Drive files. You can even add a Google Drive file as a type of worksheet or template and make a copy for each student, as shown in Figure 3.9. By doing this, students will have the templated document such as an essay format, lab report format, etc. Google Classroom will automatically append the title of the file with each student's name. You can also allow all students to edit the same file via Google Drive if you want all your students to share the work

Figure 3.9 Adding Google Drive File

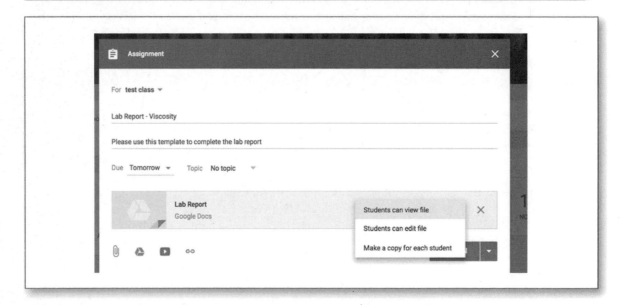

Perhaps the greatest advantage of Assignments is viewing students' completion in real time. Every assignment on the Stream list shows real-time completion status. If students are working on Google Files, there will be a **Turn In** button on top of the file. Or, students can manually click **Done** on the assignment in Google Classroom to let you know they have completed it. You can monitor this when appropriate and intervene for students who are struggling, as seen in Figure 3.10.

Figure 3.10 Monitoring Student Progress

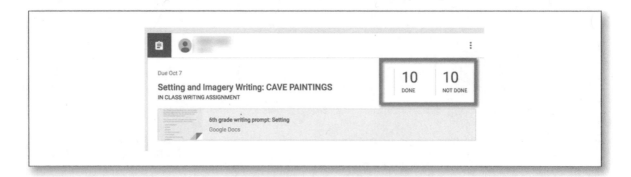

Once assignments are complete, you have the option of providing a grade and direct, private feedback to students by simply clicking on the assignment title to see their work.

Questions

Table 3.2 Common Core State Standards: Speaking and Listening

CCSS 7.2SL: Analyze the main ideas and supporting details presented in diverse media and formats (e.g., visually, quantitatively, orally) and explain how the ideas clarify a topic, text, or issue under study.

Questions are similar to assignments, but ask students to respond directly in Google Classroom. You have the option of creating open-ended discussion-type questions where students can respond to each other (but not before they respond to the prompt initially). This type of interaction allows students to have meaningful, academic conversations as your middle school students begin to develop their voices and opinions. This could be an excellent way for students to develop arguments as they prepare for more significant presentation. Students have the ability to discuss main ideas from reading and other relevant topics via Google Classroom Questions anytime/anywhere (see Figure 3.11)! Questions in Google Classroom also allows you to create multiple-choice questions for quick formative assessments and checks for understanding.

Figure 3.11 Online Discussion

Technology-Infused Teaching Tip

For advanced users, install the Google Classroom Chrome extension in Resource 3.1 on the companion website. This will allow you to push any website you are on to your Google Classroom as a resource, assignment, and/or question. Maybe you are searching YouTube for a video relating to idioms; you can then simply click on the **Extension** in Chrome, and the website will automatically populate in your Google Classroom with no need to copy and paste.

GRADES

Both assignments and questions can have grades associated with them, giving you the ability to provide students with quantitative feedback demonstrated in Figure 3.12. Students can always resubmit assignments, and every submission is recorded. By clicking on each assignment or question, you can modify the points total, review each student's work, and return their work with a private comment/narrative feedback. Students will receive an email (if your students are using Gmail with their school account).

Figure 3.12 Quantitative Feedback

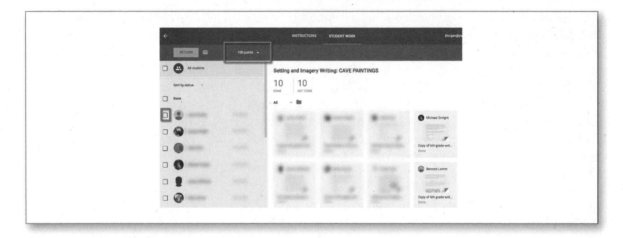

COMMUNICATE WITH PARENTS

Creating transparency in your classroom is essential. You have the ability to send notifications to parents so they see assignments and announcements and can track their child's completion. (*Note: You must be a verified teacher in G Suite for Education. Ask your IT administrators to verify you if you do not see this option.*) Inviting parents or guardians allows them to see upcoming assignments, daily posts, and any late assignments not turned in. They can get daily or weekly emails. Parents or guardians will receive an email invite (see Figure 3.13) and will need to set up a Google account to receive the notifications. You will need to type in parent or guardian emails one at a time. You will need to turn on notifications for parents and guardians in the bottom left of the **Students** tab.

Figure 3.13 Parent Access

Argumentative Writing

The teacher will

1. Create a question asking about a controversial topic (e.g., climate change, cell phones in schools, homework)

2. Create a rubric for students to see how they will be evaluated on their responses (i.e., meets standard by sharing three details referencing valid/credible resources *and* responds with relevant and thoughtful ideas to at least two other students)

3. Discuss effective argumentative writing strategies with students

4. Assign Google Classroom discussion

5. Debrief online discussion the following day

SAMR IMPLICATIONS—TRANSFORMING INSTRUCTION

Modification	Allowing students to engage in online discussions encourages students to be able to create thoughtful responses to a specific prompt where they can then reply and engage in ongoing conversations in and out of class by providing links to research, videos, articles, and more.
Redefinition	You have the ability of sharing classes with classrooms around the world to discuss similar content. You just need to ask your IT administrators to whitelist the domains of these schools/districts. This will allow students to discuss and work together on assignments in this class at a global level! Students need to be able to interact and collaborate with students from varying geographic locations and cultures.

EVEN MORE

Drafts and Scheduling

Sometimes you want to create a bunch of posts at once for your stream. Maybe you are working on a unit, and you want to create one announcement, question, and assignment, but you want them to be displayed at different times. You can either save them all as drafts and go back to the draft when you are ready to push them out. Or, you can schedule the release of a post at a certain date and time. Simply click the drop-down menu adjacent to the words **Post, Assign,** or **Ask** and select **Schedule** or **Save draft** (Figure 3.14). If you select **Schedule**, a window will appear where you can specify the date and time the post will become live on the stream. Michael uses this feature as an administrator when teachers turn in lesson plans. Each week by Sunday night his teachers are automatically assigned to turn in their lesson plans in Google Classroom. It is set up for each week of school and it automatically posts each week. Lesson plans are then reviewed and feedback can be given with comments on Google Docs.

All your drafts will be saved at the top of your Classroom and accessible anytime for posting when appropriate.

Figure 3.14   Saving and Scheduling Posts

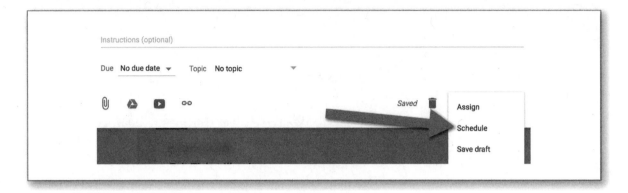

Quick Access to All Assignments and Classes

Sometimes you or your students want quick access to all assignments, due dates, or other classes. The three lines on the top right (**Quick Access** menu) of the screen give you access to toggle to all assignments, class calendars, and classes as shown in Figure 3.15. This allows you to either go from one classroom to the next quickly or focus on accessing the work that needs reviewing.

Figure 3.15   Quick Access Menu

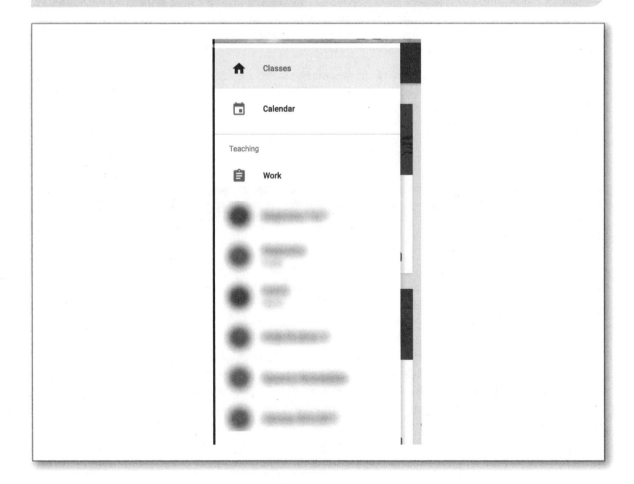

SUMMARY

Google Classroom is your one-stop shop for students to keep all their assignments and tasks in one location. It is the foundation for any successful use of Google tools in your classroom. From creating a 24/7 classroom community to engaging students in peer and student–teacher dialogue, Google Classroom allows you to streamline ways you deliver content and evaluate assignments and/ or projects. As middle school students continue to develop organizational strategies, they can become more self-directed and develop a community voice. As you become more proficient in using Google tools, you will continue to find ways to organize your physical classroom through the virtual Google Classroom. In the subsequent chapters, you will get a better idea of how to assign *all* Google tools in Google Classroom to create a transformative learning environment. Interested in many resources and a Google Classroom genius? Check out Alice Keeler and her resource at Resource 3.2 on the companion website.

RESOURCES

For more information about G Suite for Education, including

- lesson plans related to chapter content,
- domain setup for tech administrators' videos,
- overviews and Google training materials,
- the authors' favorite websites, and
- testimonials and interviews of schools currently using G Suite,

access Resources from this chapter on the companion website.

online resources ↘ http://resources.corwin.com/googlemeetsms

4 Google Documents

> ## Key Features
>
> - Create original documents
> - Share documents with peers, parents, and teachers
> - Store all documents in one cloud storage account
> - Work collaboratively among peers, parents, and teachers
> - Publish work to web and social networking sites
> - Integrate with Google Classroom
> - Explore tool

Google Documents (Google Docs) is the word-processing software offered by Google as part of G Suite for Education. Google Docs is free and can replace conventional word-processing programs such as Microsoft Word or Apple Pages. An advantage of Google Docs over Word, Pages, or other word-processing programs is the convenience of storing student and teacher work in the cloud. Google's cloud storage space is called Google Drive. Storing in Google Drive helps users avoid being tethered to multiple hard drives that students and teachers may encounter during the school day. Cloud computing means that users may store their work on Google's servers and have access to that content anywhere an Internet connection exists. Google offers unlimited storage for G Suite for Education users. Students can take advantage of this storage capacity to start to create electronic portfolios that can showcase their academic progress throughout their school career. With the ability to store work in the cloud, students become mobile learners. For example, students are able to start a writing project in the school's computer lab on an iMac, then later add content during English class on an iPad or Android tablet, and finally revise the paper at home on the family's PC.

With Google Docs, students can work on a document from home, school, or any place where they have an Internet connection. Up to 50 people can work on the same document at the same time from anywhere in the world or in the same room. Google Docs differs from traditional word-processing programs because it goes where the user goes. Students and teachers never have to worry about what programs are installed on which computers. Anywhere there is a web browser, your personal Google Docs are always available. In addition, sharing and collaboration become a reality with a click of the mouse. This ability to be anywhere and work collaboratively on a document without saving multiple versions of the same document on multiple devices is great for students and teachers. This is important because it can provide a method for organization to keep up with the ever-increasing digital content that is created.

G Suite for Education is gaining popularity in a time of deep changes in our educational system. College- and career-readiness standards have arrived in most states, creating a paradigm shift in education. The Future Ready Schools movement puts this in a framework for school districts. The framework defines the resources needed to build the Future Ready School. This along with strong leadership and a focus on this effort will make these things a reality. Attention school leaders: Visit Resource 4.1 on the companion website to view the framework. The shift that movements like Future Ready lay out will cut the number of standards and push for the increased integration of technology to prepare students to become college and career ready. This chapter will connect G Suite for Education directly to college- and career-readiness standards standards like ISTE Nets and the Common Core State Standards that will help the teacher meet the needs of students to prepare them for college and beyond. It will also connect to the SAMR Model of technology integration highlighted in detail in Chapter 1. Look for the boxed feature at the end of the chapter.

Table 4.1 highlights three Common Core Anchor Standards for Writing and the ISTE Standards for Students that are particularly important when using Google Docs. Anchor Standards provide a broad understanding of writing that spans all grade levels in the Common Core State Standards. In Anchor Standard 5, revision, editing, and rewriting are key features. Google Docs has a feature that will allow students and teachers to see a revision history of their work giving the students the ability to return to a previous version. Google Docs saves the work with every keystroke automatically. This creates a trail of revisions that can be accessed by the teacher and the student. For example, if a student is struggling about a particular paragraph in their writing, a student could delete or edit the paragraph without worrying it will be deleted forever. The student then can make a copy of the work and return to the previous version. This is helpful during the editing process. The teacher now can give feedback to the student, guiding him in the right direction.

Using Google Docs to meet and exceed Anchor Standard 6 is important for student growth. This Anchor Standard aligns fully with the use of Google Docs in the classroom. Students are able to produce writing using the Internet and publish writing to collaborate with peers, parents, and teachers. For example, students working on a piece of writing may create a Google Doc and then share the document with the teacher. When sharing is complete, the teacher will be able to comment on the writing and see its progress. Immediate feedback may be given, steering the student in the right direction by leaving comments. For more on giving meaningful feedback, see Resource 4.2 by John Hattie. After adjusting the share settings learned in Chapter 2, students can publish their content to anywhere on the web or select specific people with a click of a button.

In Anchor Standard 10, Google Docs could be used to collect research from the web. For example, when starting a new research project, the student may create a document titled "Research." The student will perform the research and use the copy-and-paste features to gather links, text, or pictures explaining the topic from the Internet. This material is easily saved in Google Docs for review or shared with other members of the research group. It is important to realize that research takes time. Google Docs is a nice way to write over extended time periods because it allows the user to save the work and access it from anywhere. Students are no longer tied to the computer in which they started their work.

Let the Common Core State Standards in Table 4.1 guide you through the chapter. G Suite for Education, in particular Google Docs, will be used to focus on these standards and more Common Core State Standards in teaching. These provide a road map so you can refer to key standards and see how G Suite for Education can make a connection to the Common Core in your teaching.

Table 4.1 Selected Anchor Standards for Writing

Selected Common Core State Standards: Anchor Standards for Writing 5, 6, and 10

5. Develop and strengthen writing as needed by planning, revising, editing, rewriting, or trying a new approach.
6. Use technology, including the Internet, to produce and publish writing and to interact and collaborate with others.
10. Write routinely over extended time frames (time for research, reflection, and revision) and shorter time frames (a single sitting or a day or two) for a range of tasks, purposes, and audiences.

Selected ISTE Standards: Ages 8–11

2. Digital Citizen Students recognize the rights, responsibilities and opportunities of living, learning and working in an interconnected digital world, and they act in ways that are safe, legal and ethical.
   - 2.a. Students demonstrate an understanding of the role an online identity plays in the digital world and learn the permanence of their decisions when interacting online.
   - 2.b. Students practice and encourage others in safe, legal and ethical behavior when using technology and interacting online, with guidance from an educator.
   - 2.c. Students learn about, demonstrate and encourage respect for intellectual property with both print and digital media when using and sharing the work of others.
   - 2.d. Students demonstrate an understanding of what personal data is, how to keep it private and how it might be shared online.

6. Creative Communicator Students communicate clearly and express themselves creatively for a variety of purposes using the platforms, tools, styles, formats and digital media appropriate to their goals.
   - 6.a. Students recognize and utilize the features and functions of a variety of creation or communication tools.
   - 6.b. Students create original works and learn strategies for remixing or repurposing to create new artifacts.
   - 6.c. Students create digital artifacts to communicate ideas visually and graphically.
   - 6.d. Students learn about audience and consider their expected audience when creating digital artifacts and presentations.

Google Classroom Connection

Google Classroom integrates fully with any of the programs in the G Suite. When teachers make an assignment, Google Classroom makes a copy of the document and places it into a folder in the student's and teacher's drive. Google Classroom is the perfect command center for the teacher and student to keep up with assignments and due dates. This learning management system is cloud based and accessible anywhere there is an Internet connection, even on a smartphone. For example, Reilee Jones, a former middle school teacher, uses her Android smartphone to grade writing assignments on the go. Google Classroom's mobile application for Android and iOS gives teachers the ability to comment on assignments, leaving feedback that can help students get back on track with their work. For a more detailed explanation of Google Classroom, read Chapter 3.

GOOGLE DOCS BASICS AND STATE-MANDATED TESTING

The Every Student Succeeds Act (ESSA) mandates that states assess their students toward proficiency in college and career readiness. States must test each Grades 3 through 10. The majority of states that have adopted Common Core State Standards or their own college- and career-readiness standards will employ an online computer-based, next-generation assessment. Smarter Balanced, PARCC (Partnership for Assessment of Readiness for College and Careers), ACT Aspire, and other testing vendors have contracts with nearly each state to develop assessments. These next-generation assessments are tied to the same various college and career standards mandated by ESSA. These assessments will be used to measure student achievement in English language arts, science, reading, and mathematics. Access to some of these sample assessment pieces offered by the various testing companies (Resource 4.3) may be found at www.discoveractaspire.org/assessments/test-items/. These items provide a piece of informational text and ask the students to read the passage, research a particular part of the passage on the Internet, answer questions regarding the passage, and create a product of student work describing the passage and research. After the product is complete, the students are asked to upload the document to the testing center's website for scoring.

To perform successfully on these types of questions, students in the middle grades must be familiar with the general use of word-processing programs over a wide platform, and they must practice those skills frequently, because nearly all students will be taking the state-mandated writing exam on an electronic device. That means they must know the conventions of writing a formal paper on an electronic device. They must be able to navigate simple toolbars like the ones in Google Docs to shape the piece they are writing—for example, center, justified, margins, bullets, numbering, and so on, as shown in Figure 4.1.

Figure 4.1 Google Documents Toolbar

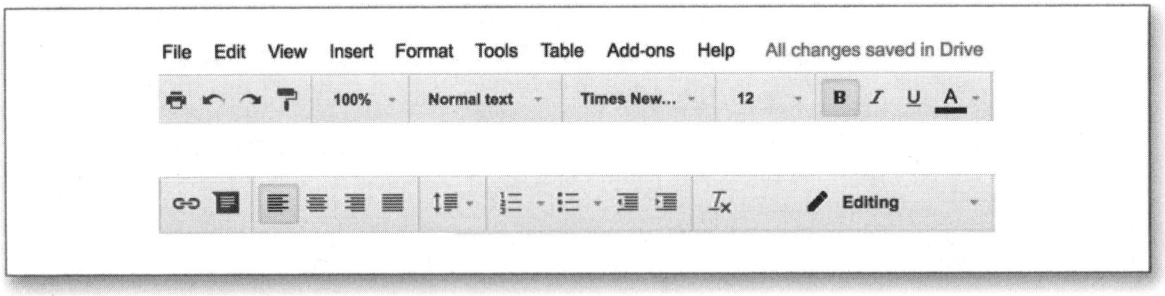

Note: Each anchor standard is a guide for the entire K–12 levels. Each anchor is broken down into grade bands that will specify what the students will do in a particular grade.

Spell Check

Google Documents offers an automatic spell checker that works the same in all of the G Suite for Education programs. It does not have a specific button like Microsoft Word that checks the spelling of the document at once. Instead, Google places the familiar red line underneath words that are spelled incorrectly as they are typed on the page.

This type of spelling check has its advantages when addressing the college and career standards. The CCSS Anchor Standards for Production and Distribution of Writing indicate that students must produce writing using digital tools starting in kindergarten and continuing throughout the grade levels. Correcting mistakes during the writing process makes for more efficient writing and lets the students practice producing writing on the device. The procedures for writing are evolving with the

Figure 4.2 Correcting Misspelled Words

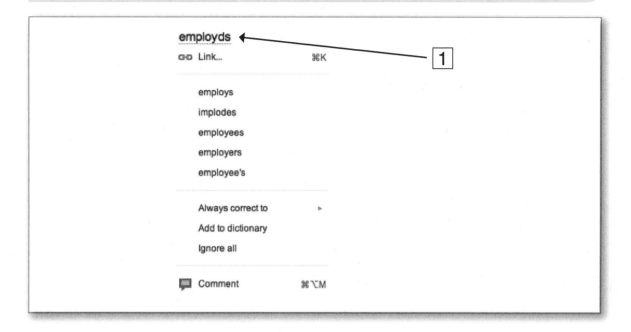

integration of technology into the classroom. In the past, students wrote the content using a pencil and then transferred the writing to a word-processing program. With technical advances and the way the world now communicates, students must produce writing on the electronic device, then use the device to edit and revise the work. Google Docs makes this task a reality in the classroom, practicing for the next generation assessments and writing beyond middle and high school.

1. Right-click on the red underlined misspelled word as shown in Figure 4.2 (Mac users Command+Click).

2. Click on the appropriate word to replace the misspelled word.
   - **Always correct to** automatically corrects chronically misspelled words. This feature is nice because whatever device is used to type a document, Google Docs remembers the user's list of trouble words if she is signed in to her Google account.
   - **Add to dictionary** lets the user add words to his own personal spell-check dictionary to avoid placing the red underline. Popular items to place in the dictionary include proper nouns such as people's names or places. Students will automatically recognize their own names being underlined if their name has an uncommon spelling. Instruct them to add their name to their personal spell-check dictionary.

Keyboarding and Technology in the Middle Grades

Beginning in kindergarten, many college- and career-readiness standards will mandate the use of technology in an effort to help our students have a wealth of 21st-century skills. The use of technology rapidly increases throughout the years in CCSS Anchor Standard 6, Production and Distribution of Writing, and in Standard 6 of the ISTE Nets. This standard wants students to be Creative Communicators where "students communicate clearly and express themselves creatively for a variety of purposes using the platforms, tools, styles, formats and digital media appropriate to their goals" (ISTE Standards 2016) located in Resource 4.4 on the companion website. The kindergarten portion of this standard indicates that students will explore various technologically enhanced tools to create writing. The wording only differs slightly for students in the first and second grades; the standard says *use* digital tools, suggesting that students actually get their hands on devices to input their content. Table 4.2 provides information about technology and writing, especially the use of the keyboard in the middle school Grades 4–8.

Since Google Docs can be accessed through any Internet-enabled device, it does not require a traditional keyboard like other word-processing software. Students in the early grades could benefit greatly by writing on devices such as the iPod Touch, iPad, Android tablet, or another similar device without a physical keyboard. By the fourth grade, students will be expected to have a sufficient grasp of keyboarding skills so they are able to type one page in a single writing event as well as collaborate with peers and adults using technology. One page per grade year is added through the sixth grade. By the time they reach middle school, students should be given experience using the traditional keyboard for input.

Table 4.2 provides grade-level standards for Common Core Anchor Standards 3, 6, and 8. This table offers guidance about how Google Docs can drive student learning within these Anchor Standards. It is important for the reader to realize that Google Docs is an Internet-based word-processing program much like what students will be exposed to during online next-generation assessments. The more experience students get using technology to publish, produce, interact, and collaborate while using the Internet, the better students will do on the high-stakes tests.

Anchor Standard 6 of the Common Core State Standards refers to using the Internet to produce, publish, and collaborate on writing throughout every grade level. Google Docs makes this standard a reality. Anchor Standard 6 can be linked to most of the other writing standards. For example, Standard W.12.1 wants students to write arguments and support claims in reference to complex text. To produce this type of writing, the student must use skills taken from Anchor Standard 6, Production and Distribution of Writing. To compete globally in a 21st-century economy, students must have relevant skills to produce and distribute quality writing using high-tech tools such as Google Docs. Most of the Common Core State Standards for Writing involve production and distribution of writing; therefore, most standards of writing could be exceeded with the use of Google Docs.

Table 4.2 Writing Standards and Breakdown

Grade	Common Core State Standard	Breakdown
Grade 4		
W.4.6	With some guidance and support from adults, use technology, including the Internet, to produce and publish writing as well as to interact and collaborate with others; demonstrate sufficient command of keyboarding skills to type a minimum of one page in a single sitting.	Students in the fourth grade must have a grasp of collaboration and keyboarding skills to create and edit a one-page document. Students will need constant practice using the keyboard to attain the stamina to type one whole page in a single setting. One example to prepare students for this task is to create a recipe book. Students can use Google Docs to type family recipes from home with an added narrative about their experience with the food. Incorporate Standard W.4.3 to create a narrative of their experience, giving supporting details in their writing. Students share the documents with the teacher for grading and feedback. After revisions are made, share with parents, peers, and other adults. Collect all pages into a single document. Share the cookbook through share settings, making it easy to post to relevant Facebook Fan Pages or Twitter accounts for community involvement.
W.4.3	Write narratives to develop real or imagined experiences or events using effective technique, descriptive details, and clear event sequences.	

Grade	Common Core State Standard	Breakdown
Grade 5		
W.5.6	With some guidance and support from adults, use technology, including the Internet, to produce and publish writing as well as to interact and collaborate with others; demonstrate sufficient command of keyboarding skills to type a minimum of two pages in a single sitting.	Two pages are required for fifth grade, further reiterating that keyboarding should be practiced as an important skill used for college and career preparation. Fifth-grade students may use Google Docs in writing to produce content-specific writing that also meets other writing standards. Teachers meeting Standard W.5.8 could use Google Docs to create a list of content-specific search terms and websites that describe their topic for the lesson. The teacher will share the document with the class, giving them directions to only choose from these websites listed in the teacher document to research their topic using these specific search terms. The students can click the links that the teacher has embedded (instead of typing in a long URL into the address bar) to navigate to the site. Students research and summarize on a separate document, providing a list of sources. Copy and paste specific links within the website the student chose. Teach students how to hyperlink in Google Docs to create an easy-to-read piece without cumbersome URLs.
W.5.8	Recall relevant information from experiences or gather relevant information from print and digital sources; summarize or paraphrase information in notes and finished work, and provide a list of sources.	

Collaborative Note-Taking Example

Table 4.3 highlights an eighth-grade mathematics standard from the ISTE Nets and the Common Core State Standards. This standard is represented in Figure 4.3 and Figure 4.4, where students are taking collaborative notes while writing on the same document at the same time. The students are instructed to type only in their assigned box; if they did not follow these instructions, students would be trying to type on the same line from different computers creating confusion. As the class discussion proceeds, the students are typing what they believe is important about the subject. Later the teacher will help the students revise their notes concentrating on the key parts of the lesson. When they are finished, this document is automatically saved into every student's Google Drive for later review from any location with Internet access.

Table 4.3 Expressions and Equations Common Core Mathematics Eighth Grade

(8.EE.5) Graph proportional relationships, interpreting the unit rate as the slope of the graph. Compare two different proportional relationships represented in different ways. For example, compare a distance-time graph to a distance-time equation to determine which of two moving objects has greater speed.

In Figure 4.4, students are in the act of typing on the same document. Notice as they type their username appears highlighted in a color to help differentiate who is typing where. If Connor is typing in Gavin's box, the whole class will know, decreasing the chance for disruption from a discipline problem.

Figure 4.3   Collective Note-Taking Part I

1. Noah	2.	3.	4. Joey Hi	5.Allie. I learned to get the velocity
6.Connor	7.Dalton	8.	9.john : a ill	10.Ashton Hello
11.	12. gavin Ms.	13.	14.	15.GABBIE
16.	17.	18.	19.Hayden :3	20.Rebecka
21.	22.Savannah :)	23.	24.	25.
26.	27.	28.	29.	30.

Technology-Infused Teaching Tip

Middle school students are children. They have a unique desire to test limits and break boundaries. Let them know the rules for new technologies early in the process. At the school where Michael is principal, breaking a rule with technology is no different than a student breaking a rule with pencil and paper. Bad behavior is bad behavior. It may be the educator's first impulse to take away the technology if a student acts inappropriately with it. Would a teacher take away a student's pencil for the rest of the school year because he or she wrote a dirty note? No, there are discipline policies written to redirect, counsel, and admonish the bad behavior. My school takes the same approach to bad behavior perpetrated using technology. Wrong is wrong, no matter how the behavior is displayed. Be consistent, and technology integration will be smooth for your students.

Figure 4.4 displays the final product. The teacher has facilitated discussion, and with the help of other students and the teacher, each student has refined his or her notes. The teacher, Mrs. Strawn, reported a pleasant surprise during the activity. Katie and Madlyn spontaneously performed a Google Image Search to find examples of distance-versus-time graphs and inserted them into their explanation. This happened live on everyone's screen, and the discussion quickly became more in-depth because the *student* was explaining why it was important not only to have notes about distance versus time, but also to see a picture.

Figure 4.4   Collective Note-Taking Part II

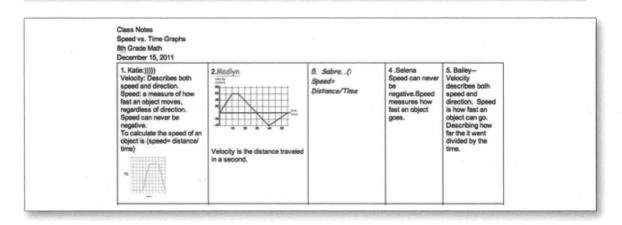

Opening Google Docs

To access Google Docs, follow these steps:

1. Sign in to your Google account as described in Chapter 3 in Figures 3.2 and 3.3.
2. Click on  located at the top right hand of the screen as shown in Figure 4.5 of any G Suite application.
3. Click the button to reveal a drop-down menu shown in Figure 4.6.
4. Click **Google Docs** as shown in Figure 4.7 to create a new document.

Figure 4.5 G Suite Icon

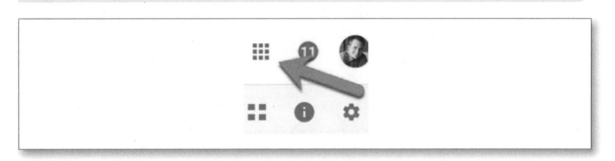

Figure 4.6 Opening Google Documents

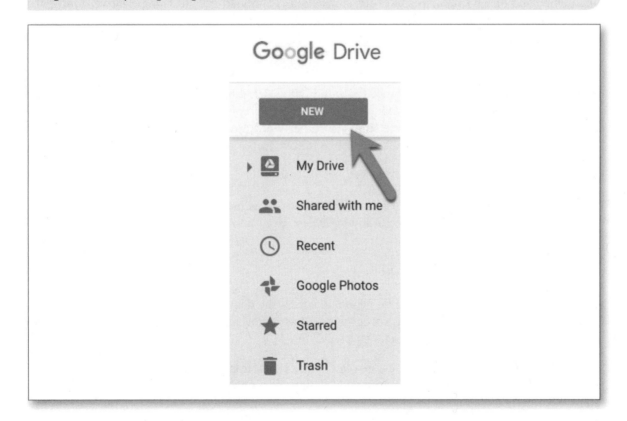

Figure 4.7 Accessing the Documents Program

Upload

Uploading files and folders to be stored in the user's Google Drive makes mobile learning a reality. Google allows the uploading of any file type to its servers for access anywhere there is an Internet connection. For example, if a student uses Microsoft Word to produce writing on a home computer, then the student can upload that work to her Google cloud from home. During the upload process, Google asks if the document should be converted to Google Docs version or uploaded in Microsoft Word format. If the user chooses Microsoft Word format, then the document can be downloaded to any device and opened if Microsoft Word is installed. To upload files to Google Drive, follow the steps outlined in Chapter 9: "Google Drive."

FILE MENU

After the user completes the steps associated with Figures 4.5, 4.6, and 4.7, the Google Docs program will open. The following describes the contents of the **File** command located in the Google Docs toolbar section. These commands are similar to other word-processing programs, but they contain cutting-edge features that take them a step above for classroom use.

Share

Sharing allows the user to give access to a Google Doc to as many or as few people as they prefer. Users may share the document in the following ways:

- Email as an attachment
- Anyone with the **Shareable Link**
- Public—on the web
- Private—allowing only specific people to access the document
- Set Expiration ⏱ by hovering over the user's name reveals the clock icon, and this option can set time limits on the share settings

Sharing is one of the hallmark features in Google Docs. It is used in every part of Google Docs to work collaboratively and publish content. To share documents from Google Docs, follow these steps. Sharing is discussed at length in Chapter 2.

1. Select **Share** from the **File** menu in the toolbar in Google Docs or click on the blue button in the upper right-hand corner of any Google Doc program to reveal the share settings as shown in Figure 4.8.

2. Click **Get shareable link** in Arrow #1 in Figure 4.8 to share the document via link sharing.

   a. Paste it into one of these places to link share:

      i. Email

      ii. Social media (Facebook, Twitter, other social media)

      iii. Another web browser's address bar

3. Type in the names, email, or groups of people that you would like to directly share the Google Doc with in the bar near Arrow #2.

   a. Click the **Can edit** drop-down menu to select the type of access you would like others to have.

4. Click to Done.

5. Click **Advanced** to show all of the people the document is shared with and to make changes to share settings as well as time limits on sharing. This is shown in Figure 4.8.

Figure 4.8   Share With Others

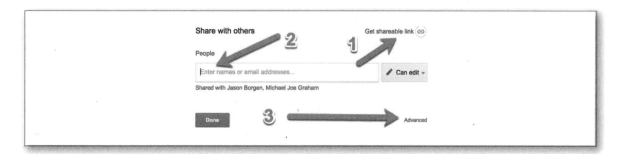

Figure 4.9   Share Settings

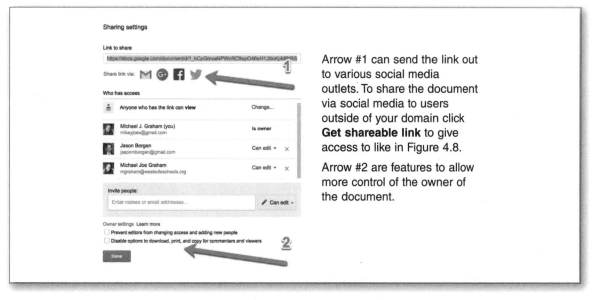

Arrow #1 can send the link out to various social media outlets. To share the document via social media to users outside of your domain click **Get shareable link** to give access to like in Figure 4.8.

Arrow #2 are features to allow more control of the owner of the document.

Figure 4.10 Who Has Access

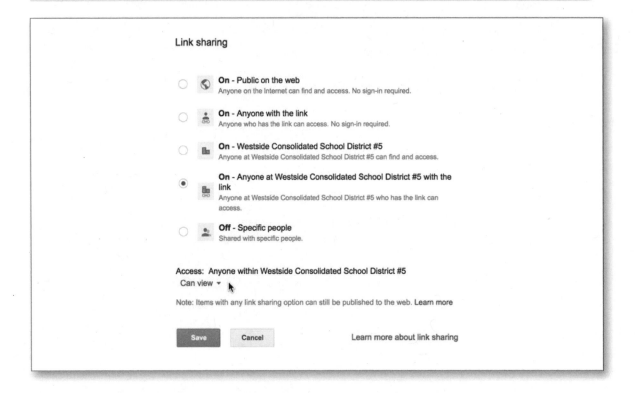

Figure 4.11 New Google Doc

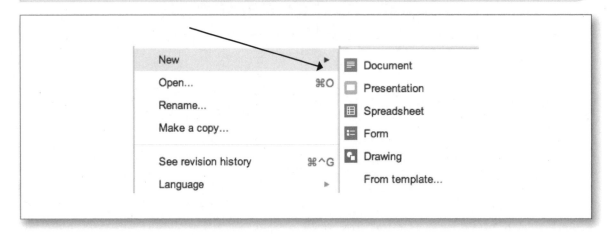

New

Click **New** in the **File** menu to open a new Google Doc as shown in Figure 4.11. This option opens the new Google Doc in another tab or browser window.

Open

Click **Open** in the **File** menu to return to the documents view, also called Google Drive. This is the equivalent of a My Documents folder on a PC. This is where folders are created and files are managed, allowing for management of your cloud storage.

Make a Copy

This option lets the user make a copy of the work. This will be helpful when sharing documents with students. For example, the teacher could share a writing prompt document with a class and assign the students to answer questions on the page; the students make a copy of the work, answer the questions, and re-share the document by email or share settings to be graded. If the students did not make a copy, all of the students would be typing on the same document at the same time unless the document is made view-only by the teacher. There is an option in Google Classroom explored in Chapter 3 (see Figure 3.9) that will allow the teacher to force the document to make a copy automatically.

Revision History

Revision history will allow the user to go back to any point in time to see how the work is progressing. This tool allows you to see all edits made to the document. In the Common Core Writing Standards, Anchor Standard 5, Production and Distribution of Writing, wants students to "develop and strengthen writing as needed by planning, revising, editing, rewriting, or trying a new approach." This standard is clearly met with the use of this feature in Google Docs. For example, students learning to write informative pieces that examine complex concepts may need to revisit a previous idea. Seeing a revision history will allow the student to look back in time at the writing examining how the progression was made. This allows students to return to a previous version down to a specific keystroke. If two or more people are working on the document collaboratively, then each person could see their revisions and who made the changes. Figures 4.12a, b, and c show multiple revisions. This is great when sharing a document with several people to edit. To see the revision history of a document, follow these steps:

1. Select **See Revision History** from the **File** menu in the Document's Toolbar.

2. Click on a revision timestamp in Figures 4.12a and b to roll back the changes to that particular time.

3. Click to see wider time intervals.

Figures 4.12a and 4.12b   Revisions Menu

Figure 4.12c More Revisions in Menu

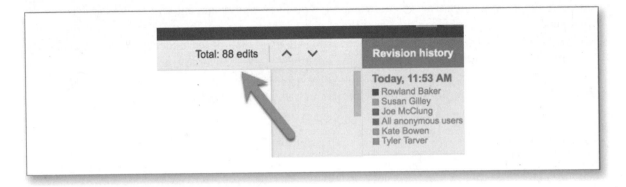

Figure 4.13 In-Text Revisions

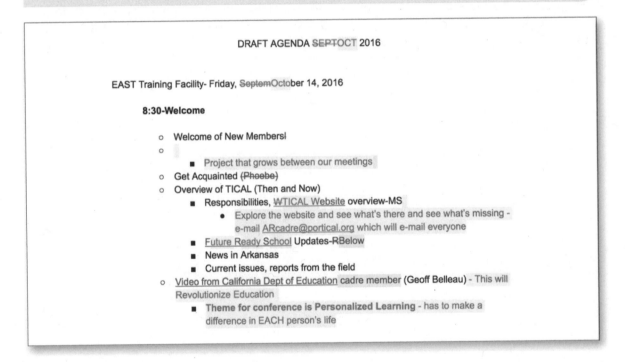

Language

The use of the Language feature allows the user to change the language of the dictionary Google Docs uses to spell-check words. For example, if a student is writing a translation of several words in a foreign language, the student may choose to use spell check in that language. It is also useful when students need special characters when writing. For example, the word *niña* in Spanish has the tilde over the second *n,* denoting a different sound associated with that letter when spoken in Spanish. If the student chose the Spanish dictionary to spell-check the document, he or she could right-click (Command+Click for Mac users) the word to reveal suggested spellings and choose appropriately from words that appear in the Spanish dictionary.

Download As

Choose this option to save the work to your computer's hard drive in various formats. Google doesn't discriminate. It even lets the work be saved in Microsoft Word format for sharing with others who do not use Google Docs. Plus, Google offers a variety of formats, including PDF, TXT, and HTML.

Publish to the Web

Publish to the web is a sharing option that is similar to the **Anyone with the link** option shown in Figure 4.10. It gives instant access to publish work directly to the web from the document to anyone, not just collaborators. Publish to the web if you want others to view the document and see changes through the unique web address but without inviting them to become a collaborator. Stop publishing any time by selecting the option in Figure 4.14 (toggle between **Start Publishing** and **Stop Publishing**). In addition to publishing the document's link, there is also an option that gives the document the HTML **Embed code** shown in Figure 4.14. This code may be placed into websites and modified to fit the user's needs.

Technology-Infused Teaching Tip

Use the publishing features to share student work through social media websites. For example, Westside School District has an official Facebook page. We use this page to communicate with our school community on the web. Often, we publish examples of award-winning student work or links to student projects that were made with Google Docs. Since each Doc is given a web address, it is easy to post the link of the work to the page for our community to view.

Email Collaborators

Click **Email Collaborators** to send an email message to all who are working on the document. In-document chat is also available for instant feedback of student work. Teachers may assign a writing exercise and be online while the students are creating. This allows the teacher to give immediate feedback during the writing process. Common Core Anchor Standard 6 in Grades 11 and 12 wants students to receive ongoing feedback from writing that is collaborative. The screenshot in Figure 4.15 shows the message feature, which allows teachers to send feedback directly to students.

Figure 4.14   Publish to the Web

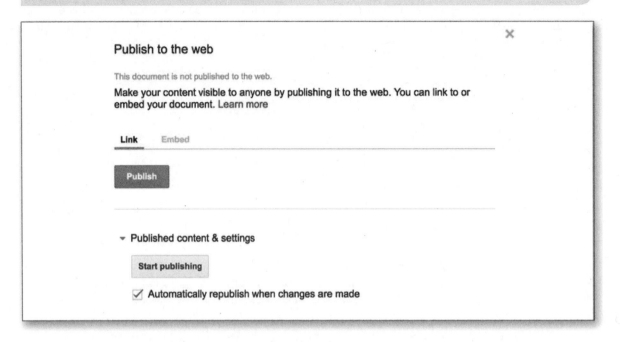

Figure 4.15   Email Collaborators

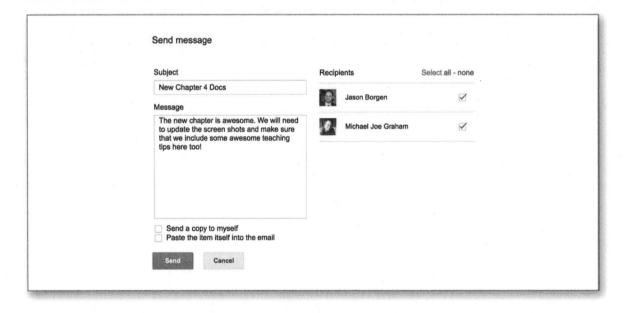

Email as Attachment

All of the core G Suite applications let the user email documents as attachments in a variety of formats as shown in the drop-down menu featured in the circle in Figure 4.16. Use the email as attachment feature to bypass the old and time-consuming way of attaching documents to emails. In the past, people were forced to save the document, open an email, click attach file, find the document on the computer's hard drive, then email it. With Google Docs, click **Email as attachment** under the **File** menu to send the doc directly from Google Docs.

Figure 4.16 Email as Attachment

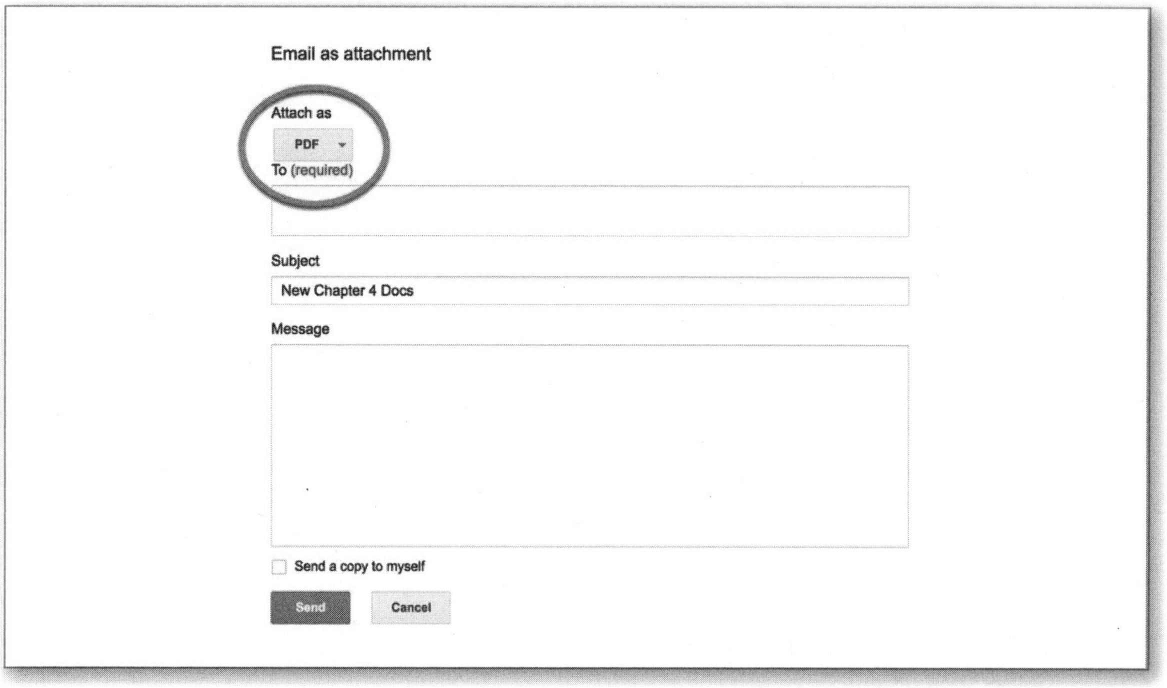

Figure 4.17 Email as Attachment File Types

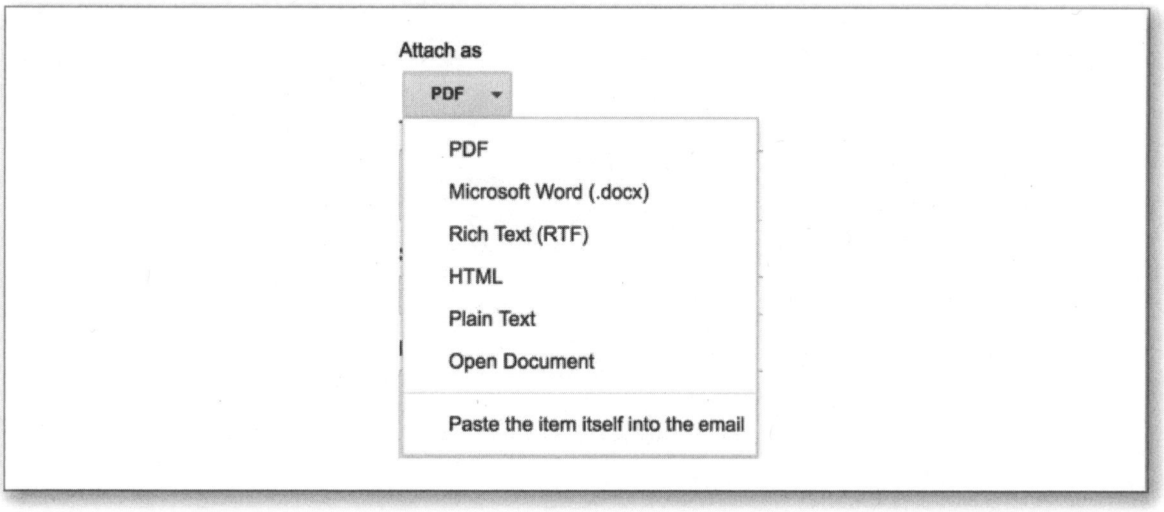

Page Setup

Use the tools in Figure 4.18 to switch to landscape or portrait views as well as manage the margins and paper size. As students start to share their work, this will allow them to use tools that are more creative. Anchor Standard 5 in Speaking and Listening stresses that students use digital tools to express their understanding by enhancing presentations. Adjusting paper sizes, orientation, and page color can make printed or web-shared documents more visually appealing.

Figure 4.18 Page Setup

Page setup

Orientation	Margins (inches)
⦿ Portrait ○ Landscape	Top 1
Paper Size	Bottom 1
Letter (8.5" x 11") ⇕	Left 1
Page Color	Right 1
▣ ▾	

OK   Cancel   Set as default

Print

To print a Google Doc, follow these steps:

1. Click **Print** from the **File** menu or press **Command+P** for Mac or **CTRL+P** for PC to bring up the Print menu.
2. Click as shown in Figure 4.19.
3. Click to switch printers.

Figure 4.19 Print

Print

Total: 1 sheet of paper

Cancel   Print   [2]

Destination   🖶 Brother Graham

Change...   [3]

Pages   ⦿ All

○ e.g. 1-5, 8, 11-13

Copies   1   + –

Margins   Default   ▾

Options   ☐ Two-sided

Print using system dialog... (⌥⌘P)
Open PDF in Preview

EDIT MENU

The **Edit** menu is very similar to other word-processing programs. See the Google Docs **Edit** menu in Figure 4.20. Be aware that some Internet browsers do not allow right-clicking to copy and paste in the G Suite. If this is the case, PC users press CTRL+C for copy, CTRL+V for paste, and CTRL+X for cut. Macintosh users press Command+C for copy, Command+V for paste, and Command+X for cut.

Other options in this menu include **Paste without formatting**. This option will allow the user to copy text from anywhere on the Internet (from another Google Doc or a webpage) and paste the text without any of the original text's formatting. This is great for students and teachers who want a particular style or formatting on their Google Doc.

Figure 4.20   Edit Menu

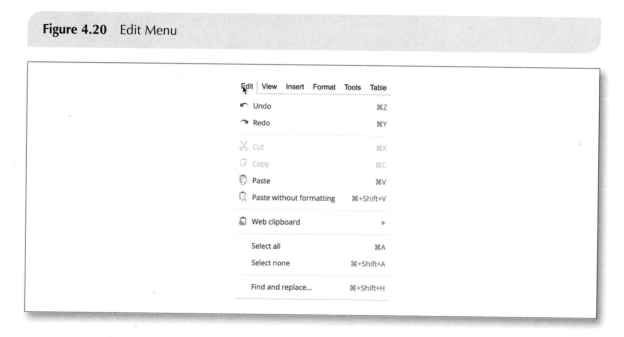

VIEW MENU

The **View** menu displays commands to control the way the users visualize the document they are editing. These options are common in various word-processing programs and are easy to understand. Figure 4.21 shows the **View** menu.

Figure 4.21   View Menu

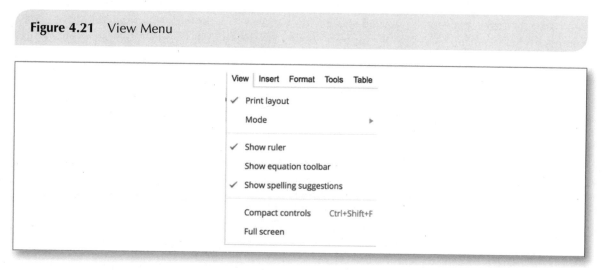

Mode: Editing, Suggesting, Viewing

Mode is a command that lets the user set how they interact with the document. The owner of the document sets the permission to others such as edit, view, and/or comment. When the user gives permission to edit, the other person editing the document could choose **Suggesting** to track the changes of the document. See Figure 4.22 for an example.

Figure 4.22 Mode

The figure shows that when clicked, the suggestion will be made part of the document. It is similar to the Track Changes feature in Microsoft Word. Just like Word, the other user must accept the changes for them to become part of the document without the edit flags and strikethroughs.

Show Ruler

The show ruler option allows the user to control the margins of the document. Encourage students to bend the rules when displaying informal documents to others in a presentation or when linking to social media. Using innovative ways to display information might spark an artistic flair, making the difference in the document's impact. Instruct students to know when documents should be presented in formal and informal formats to become aware of the audience and to be appropriate to task.

Show Equation Toolbar

With the equation toolbar, teachers and students have the ability to use symbols and other math characters not normally found on the keyboard. Teachers can use this to create assessments, or students can make their own math problems and share with the class. Create shareable math help that can be continually updated and shared with a class or classes anywhere in the world. When the **Show equation toolbar** is enabled, the user will see the options in Figure 4.23.

Figure 4.23 Equation Toolbar

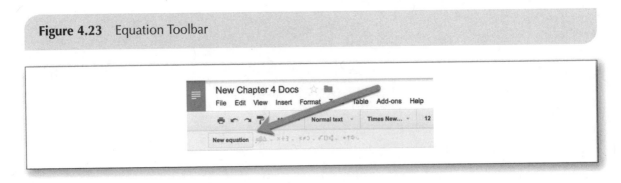

Show Spelling Suggestions

Placing a checkmark beside this option will toggle on the red line under words, denoting spelling errors. Students need to be aware of this to take advantage of the spell check feature of the G Suite.

Compact Controls

Compact controls are used to hide the G Suite's toolbars and the title of the document. This is useful when a user is presenting a document with a projector. More of the document can be seen on the screen without having to scroll.

Full Screen

Full screen allows the user to hide all toolbars and the control panel to maximize space on the screen for the text. Press the **Escape** key to return to normal view. This may be useful when presenting ideas or taking notes collectively to emphasize the importance of the text. Google Docs lets users take collective notes or brainstorm ideas to a shared document. Follow these steps for an example of a quick lesson idea using full screen.

Lesson in Focus

The teacher will

1. Create a document

2. Insert a table with the number of cells matching the number of students in the class

3. Place a number in each cell

4. Assign a number to students, and instruct them to type notes only in their assigned cells

Fifty students may type at once on this document, creating collective notes or ideas for a brainstorming session. Use a projector to show the class the document in real time. The student responses will automatically appear with each keystroke on each student's screen and the projector. Use the full-screen mode to make the presentation visually appealing.

LIVING DOCUMENTS

The G Suite provides a way for students to create documents that are adaptable with the rapid influx of relevant information concerning a topic. In the 21st century and beyond, most material that students read will be on a screen, giving the authors the ability to constantly update information as it presents itself (see CCSS English Language Arts Standards 11–12.W.6–10). Reading interactive text that contains links to other information will change the way students relate with the written word. Students need to learn how to read informational text that comes from webpages and other online materials to extract meaning and purpose. In addition, students in their careers will be writing in these mediums, creating living documents like blogs, wikis, online news articles, and Twitter posts. Most printed material will rapidly become outdated with the use of cloud-based tools, web-based writing, and mobile devices that can interact with this content. One could imagine that as soon as the document is printed on paper, new and useful information may become available. Students need to develop skills of writing digitally, and Google Docs provides ways to acquire these skills. Living documents allow the students to be interactive authors with the ability to change their work with new knowledge learned or the ability to insert links to other ways of thinking about the text they are composing. Students getting ready for college and career need to be exposed to writing ideas that are changing rapidly. Table 4.2 presents standards of writing that embody living documents. Google Docs provides the platform for which students can achieve these standards. For example, when writing, link keywords or phrases to a web address to offer more information that may deepen students' understanding. This differentiation will help students interact with content in multiple ways. The web address can link to other Google Docs created by the student or link to webpages with more information. Adding hyperlinks to text leads the reader to new or supporting ideas. Follow these steps in the Technology-Infused Teaching Tip to add hyperlinks.

Technology-Infused Teaching Tip

Use links in documents to share other information to students within the document. When creating a link in a document, it will turn blue and become a live clickable link. When you click on the blue word, the web browser will open a new tab, opening the webpage to be viewed. Instead of having https://youtu.be/N7ng1AcEFv0 in the document, create a link that packages the entire URL into a descriptive title, such as Westside High School EAST Program Reviews Space Ice Cream (the blue line under text indicates a live URL link). In all college- and career-readiness standards, students are expected to be familiar with the Internet and how to navigate the wealth of information it connects the user to.

1. Highlight any word in a Google Doc that you want to link to.

2. Press **Command+K** (Mac) or **CTRL+K** (PC) to show the menu in Figure 4.24.

3. Enter text into the text box to hide the URL.

4. Enter the URL for the link as shown in Arrow #1

   a. Arrow #1—Paste a link into the box to correspond with the title in the text box.

   b. Arrow #2—Google will search the Internet for you for websites that might match your highlighted term. In this case it suggested the site www.westsideschools.org, which matches my text to link. Click the blue **Apply** button to accept the suggestion.

   c. Arrow #3—This feature searches the user's Google Drive and looks for documents to link to that may match the highlighted text. This is great for students to connect notes from other work to their current document.

Figure 4.24   Link

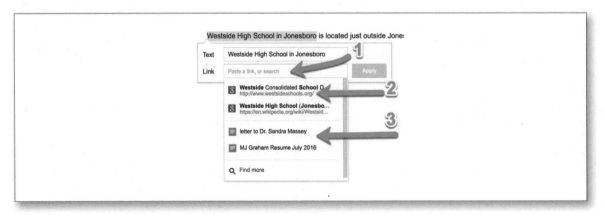

Here are some ideas for linking:

- Link other documents, spreadsheets, presentations, forms, or drawings that the user created. Linking data collected from experiments in math or science into a document is a great way to publish results.
- Link supporting information from websites taken from reputable sources.
- Use Google Forms to collect survey results and add commentary about the study.

Table 4.4 describes Anchor Standard 6 for Writing taken from the Common Core State Standards for Grades 9–12, which directs students to write with "response to ongoing feedback." Google Docs can make this anchor standard come alive with the use of links and living documents.

Table 4.4   Writing Standards for Technology

Sixth- to Eighth-Grade Writing Standards—Anchor Standard 6
Grade 6: Use technology, including the Internet, to produce and publish writing as well as to interact and collaborate with others; demonstrate sufficient command of keyboarding skills to type a minimum of three pages in a single sitting.
Grade 7: Use technology, including the Internet, to produce and publish writing and link to and cite sources as well as to interact and collaborate with others, including *linking* to and *citing sources.*
Grade 8: Use technology, including the Internet, to produce and publish writing and present the relationships between information and ideas efficiently as well as to interact and collaborate with others.

Many college- and career-readiness standards want students to be able to create, collaborate, and share their work as well as be able to update accordingly to accommodate new information. Teaching students to read dynamic information like online newspapers, blogs, Facebook, and Twitter feeds to extract important information, while discarding the unimportant, will be a significant skill for the digital citizen. Learning to write in these elements and produce high-quality work will be equally important.

Notice that the seventh-grade standards for writing include "linking to and citing sources." Programs in the G Suite make this task easy for the student. See the Technology-Infused Teaching Tips and Figure 4.24 to get familiar with the process in the G Suite.

Technology-Infused Teaching Tip

Facebook, Twitter, and blogs are other important sources of information as well as traditional media. For example, a student researching the Syrian Civil War may follow prominent figures of the rebellion on Twitter, gaining very important information in real time directly from the source. Having the courage to explore the benefits and problems new media brings to school settings will have lasting impact on students. Be open-minded to new media.

INSERT MENU

The **Insert** menu in the Google Docs toolbar is packed with features. Google makes it easy to insert graphics, pictures, links, and other important document style options. Many of these same features are offered in the other G Suite programs.

Image

Insert images from your hard drive, a URL, Google Image Search, or Google Photos albums into any Google Doc. The URL import feature is significant because many images that the user would want to use may be housed on the web. For example, a student may want to drive home his point with a picture from a website taken on a battlefield in Afghanistan. The student may browse websites and copy and paste the URL of the photo, and it will appear in the document. Be particularly mindful of copyright. If the user chooses Google Image Search, he or she can search Google Images directly in the Google Docs program without having to go to another window. The user's Google Photos are also available to insert. For example, a middle school writing assignment may ask the students to create a narrative story describing details of a family vacation. The student may use photos taken during the trip and insert these images into the document. This is seamlessly accessed from any computer with an Internet connection. As long as the user is signed into her Google account, Google Photos will link personal photos to any document. When the picture is captured with a GPS enabled smartphone, a geotag of where the photo was taken is embedded into the file. Users of Google Photos may even search for photos where the picture was taken making it easy to find photos from a trip. To insert an image, follow these steps:

1. Select **Image** from the **Insert** menu in Google Docs to reveal the menu shown in Figure 4.25.

2. Click the desired method to insert the image.

3. Click to insert.

Figure 4.25 Insert Image

Methods to Insert Image. Use the methods here to insert an image into Google Docs.

- **Upload:** Click this option to upload an image from your computer's hard drive.
- **Take a snapshot:** Click this option to take a picture from your computer's built-in webcam.
- **By URL:** Click this option to copy and paste an image URL to automatically insert it without saving the image to the hard drive.
- **Your albums:** Click this option to upload an image from your Google Photos Web Albums.
- **Google Drive:** Click this option to insert an image from the user's Google Drive.
- **Search:** Click this option to search photos from Google Image Search, *Life* magazine, and stock photos. All of these images are labeled for reuse by the owner of the picture. That means that they can be used without permission. Investigate further if you plan to sell work with images from this service in it. Look at Figure 4.26 for more information and how-to steps for inserting Google Images Search.
- **Drag Image:** Drag the image into the box to insert into the document. This is denoted by the circle in Figure 4.25.

Figure 4.26 Search Images to Insert

Google Image Search is embedded in Google Docs to insert photos with ease. Type into the search bar any search term (Figure 4.26). After searching, Google displays images according to the query. Students may choose what color is in their photo by selecting the colored boxes underneath the search bar. Look at Figure 4.27, for example; a student searched for frogs, then the student may choose what color of frog to display. Also, notice that you can choose what type of picture the results will display. Choose from **Any type, Face, Photo, Clip Art,** or **Line drawing**. This can insert some excitement into any boring document with a picture. Students will be able to craft and express their understanding visually. For example, students may be studying the Bay of Pigs in history class. While writing their review of the incident and its repercussions, students may search for a photo of Castro and Kennedy and insert it directly into the document. Students aware of these tools can start to become digitally fluent, honing much needed skills for college and career.

"They need to be able to use technology strategically when creating, refining, and collaborating on writing. They have to become adept at gathering information."

—Taken from "Commentary of Standards,"
Common Core State Standards English Language Arts (p. 63)

Figure 4.27   Google Image Search Color

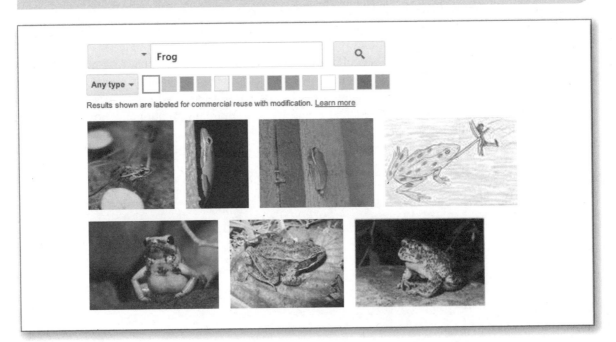

Technology-Infused Teaching Tip

Be aware of licensing. Some images and videos may need permission to be used. Follow all copyright laws. If you need help searching for more items that may be used without restriction, go to Resource 4.5 on the companion website for more information on Google Advanced Image Search. All photos searched in the manner above have permission to be reused.

Drawing

Insert Google Drawings into Docs. For example, students may create flowcharts or graphic organizers explaining what they understand graphically and insert them into any Google Doc. Common Core State Standards for Speaking and Listening Anchor Standard 5 says, "Make strategic use of digital media and visual displays of data to express information and enhance understanding of presentations." Insertion of Drawings to documents published to the web or shared through print or email will meet this standard. See Chapter 8, "Google Drawings," for more details on how to create a drawing. To insert a drawing, click **Drawing** from the **Insert** menu.

Chart

Students may insert charts into Google Docs directly from the **Insert** menu. Figure 4.28 shows the available chart types that may be inserted. For example, a student may want to insert a pie chart into the Google Doc. When the student chooses the **Pie** chart option a generic, editable pie chart appears in the document. Click on the ☑ icon to open the associated Google Sheets (spreadsheet application

Figure 4.28   Insert Chart

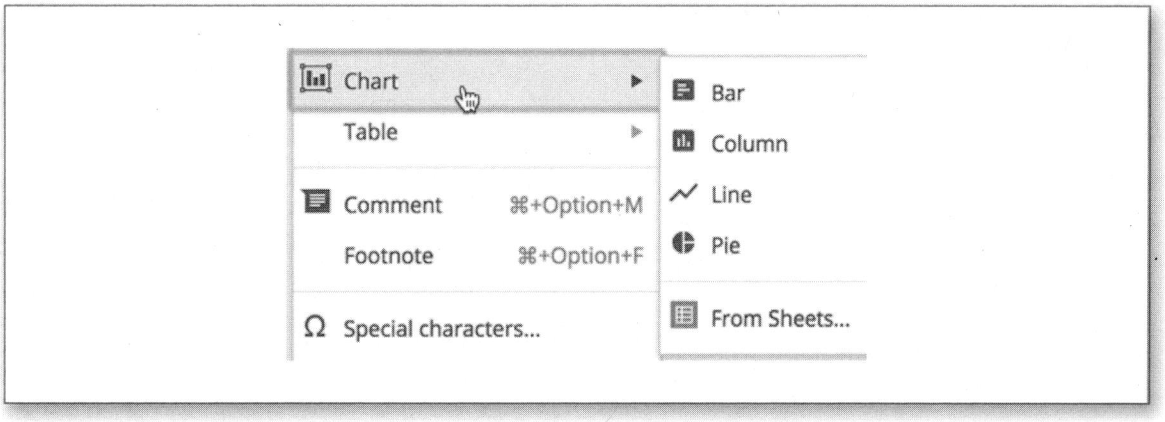

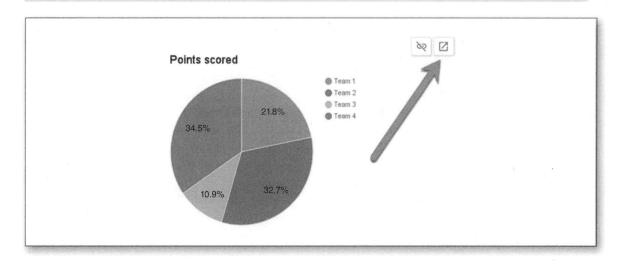

Figure 4.29   Edit Data in Google Sheets

in the G Suite) to edit the chart. When the spreadsheet is edited with the data the student wants to display, it will automatically change in the document. All changes in the spreadsheet data will automatically be changed in the Google Doc. There is no need to save the document again.

In Tables 4.5 and 4.6, the Common Core State Standards call for students to enhance meaning through the use and creation of graphic organizers, graphs, tables, and charts. Using Google tools will help the classroom teacher meet this standard.

Consider the standards in Tables 4.5 and 4.6. Inserting Drawings into Documents and other programs such as Presentations is a great way to meet these standards. The main idea is to get students to analyze and synthesize information in a way that they can graphically represent the idea. Students must have experience using these tools to be successful on the next-generation assessments and in college and a career.

Table 4.5 Middle School Standards for Writing and Speaking and Listening

Fifth-Grade Speaking and Listening	Middle School Writing 6–8
Include multimedia components (e.g., graphics, sound) and visual displays in presentations when appropriate to enhance the development of main ideas or themes.	Introduce a topic clearly, previewing what is to follow; organize ideas, concepts, and information into broader categories; include formatting (e.g., headings), graphics (e.g., charts, tables), and multimedia when useful to aiding comprehension.

Table 4.6 Writing Standards for Literacy in History/Social Studies, Science, and Technical Subjects 6–12

Introduce a topic and organize complex ideas, concepts, and information so that each new element builds on that which precedes it to create a unified whole; include formatting (e.g., headings), graphics (e.g., figures, tables), and multimedia when useful to aiding comprehension.

Comments

Inserting comments is a great way to interact with the content of student writing. As student papers are shared with the teacher, the teacher can give immediate feedback in a comment. Comments are great for revising work and offering suggestions for rough draft corrections. For example, when a student is writing a paper for English class, the student will produce the writing on the computer or via the Google Docs app on a smartphone. During the formation of the paper, the student will share the paper with the teacher, giving the teacher access to the document in real time as the student is typing. The teacher could work with groups of students, providing immediate feedback in the form of comments and in-document chat. Parents, peers, and other adults could share the document to help revise the work, guiding the student's writing. An example of what this looks like is located in Figure 4.33. To insert comments, follow these steps:

1. Highlight the portion of text that you wish to leave a comment on.
2. Right-click the text and choose **Comment.**
   a. Or click **Comment** from the **Insert** menu.
4. Type the comment in the space provided as shown in Figure 4.33.

Technology-Infused Teaching Tip

Comments are powerful ways to give students the ability to get feedback on their work. Sometimes a teacher may assign a large assignment to several students at once and particular students are responsible for certain parts of the work. There is a feature in comments that allows the teacher to assign to a student a selection of work to be done in the document. Another example is when using Google Docs for a leadership team meeting there are several jobs that must be completed and assigned to team members. Our leadership team takes notes and minutes for each meeting shared with everyone in a Google Doc. The team members that are given access to comment or edit the document can assign certain tasks to members of the team. Follow the steps below to assign tasks.

1. Highlight a task in the document to be completed.

2. Right click on the highlighted portion or look for the comment bubble on the right side margin ▣ .

3. In the **Comment** box shown in Figure 4.31, type a plus sign followed by the email address of the person you want to assign the task to. For example, +katherine.graham@westsideschools .org. The first time you do this, the graphic in Figure 4.30 will appear.

Figure 4.30   Assign an Action Item Help Box

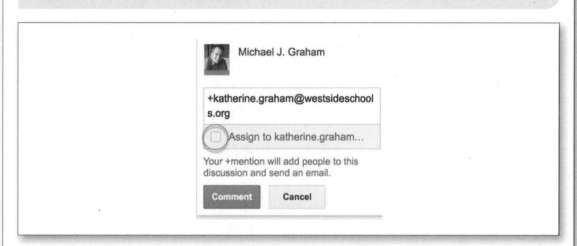

4. Click the **Assign** box as shown in Figure 4.31 to assign the task.

Figure 4.31   Assign to Collaborator

(Continued)

(Continued)

Figure 4.32 Follow-ups

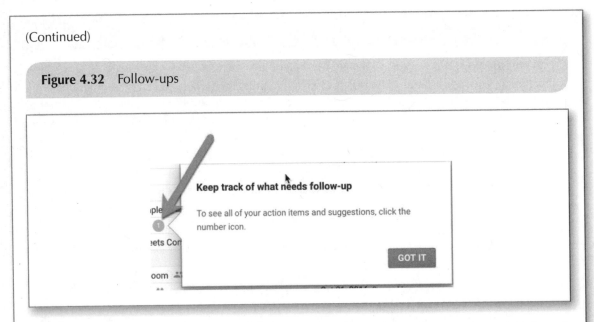

Keep track of what needs follow-up

To see all of your action items and suggestions, click the number icon.

GOT IT

The arrow in Figure 4.32 shows what the other collaborator will see when they are assigned a task by adding the plus sign in front of an email in the **Comment** box (for example, +k.o.graham@mit.edu). If the circle with a number is shown, as shown in the arrow, then you have been assigned a follow-up.

Figure 4.33 is an actual piece of student writing from a sixth-grade student. The teacher, Mrs. Betsy Davis, is a veteran educator with more than 28 years of experience teaching writing. She says that using Google Docs has helped her students with organization and revising more than any other method she has seen in her vast experience. This assignment is a part of an interdisciplinary unit between Mr. Steven Cazort's sixth-grade social studies class and Mrs. Davis's sixth-grade English class. The letter to the president was written in Mr. Cazort's class on Google Docs. Later, the document was accessed in Mrs. Davis's English class to edit and revise. Since this was the first time Mrs. Davis and the students were using Google Docs for the production of writing and editing, she focused on pointing out three revisions at a time. Yellow highlights bring attention to the part needing review. Notice timestamps to denote when the revisions were made and the discussion. This is a fun and exciting way to talk about writing and the writing process.

Also, feedback can be given in the form of the teacher writing directly on the paper with the student. A teacher may choose a different text color than the student and make comments and corrections live in the text.

The other options in the **Insert** menu are easy to understand. So, for the sake of brevity, these will be left for the reader to discover.

Table 4.7   Common Core State Standards Anchor Standard 5 Grade 6

With guidance and support from peers and adults, develop and strengthen writing as needed by planning, revising, editing, rewriting, or trying a new approach. (Editing for conventions should demonstrate command of Language standards.)

Figure 4.33   Student Writing With Comments

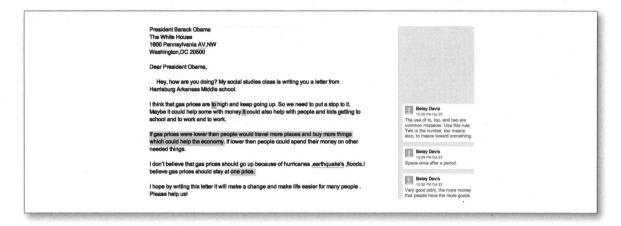

TOOLS MENU

Figure 4.34 shows the **Tools** menu. This menu option has many features that will be helpful to students and teachers. All are discussed in detail in the following section except word count, which is self-explanatory.

Figure 4.34   Tools Menu

Explore

The explore tool in the G Suite is great for student research during a writing event. This feature allows the user to search Google directly from the document and add information from the Internet directly into any of the G Suite programs. Explore creates a tailored search based on the things that you write in documents and other files in your Google Drive. The explore tool attempts to predict suggestions that you may need in the writing. Users can search with the text box and find three sections of search results listed under Topics, Images and Related Research. The explore tool is also accessible in the bottom right-hand corner of any program in the G Suite, . The explore tool will appear on the right-hand side of the document as shown in Figure 4.35. To learn how to use the explore tool, follow these steps:

Figure 4.35 Explore

1. Select **Explore** from the **Tools** menu as shown in Figure 4.34, or right-click on a word in the document to *Explore* the word you clicked on.
2. Type into the search box a search query.
3. Results will appear in the **Explore** window.

Lesson in Focus

The teacher will

1. Share a document with the class through Google Classroom that contains boxes for students to organize their research in and notes for each main idea of their writing
2. When shared through Google Classroom, select the feature that makes a copy of the document. This allows the students to take ownership of the doc and title it accordingly
3. Instruct the students to use the **Explore** tool to research their topics and make notes in the boxes
4. Monitor their progress by viewing their shared documents and offer comments and feedback

Define

The define tool will allow the user to define any word in the document. Highlight the word in the document to be defined and the **Explore** tool will give the user the definition. Additionally, the define tool will display synonyms and antonyms for the word as well as offer the word in a sentence. Basically the define tool acts as a thesaurus, pronunciation guide, and defining resource.

Document Outline

The document outline feature displays headings and subheadings on the left-hand side of the document. The headings and subheadings are linked to their respective sections in the text. Clicking on a heading or subheading takes the user's cursor directly to the location of the appropriate level of the heading. Figure 4.36 shows what this looks like in the Google Doc.

Figure 4.36 Document Outline Tool

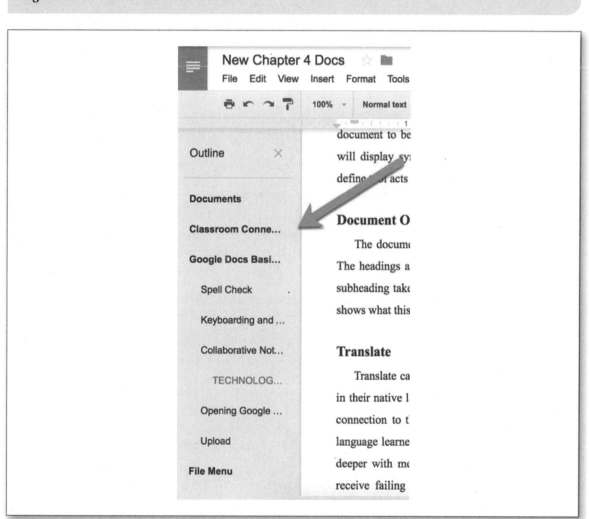

Voice Typing

Voice typing is exactly as it sounds. When enabled, users can dictate speech to text directly in the document. This feature is great for special needs students. For example, a dyslexic student may suffer from severe and chronic misspellings. When using voice typing, a student does not have to worry about trying to spell a difficult word. If the student is trying to type a difficult word, they may try to spell it as close as they can. Sometimes the student will not be able to get close enough to the correct spelling for the spell check feature to correct it. When the student enables voice typing, the student can simply say the word and Google Docs will type it for them. Use the define tool to make sure the student is applying the correct meaning to the word. Follow the steps below to use voice typing:

1. From the **Tools** menu select **Voice Typing** (or use the keyboard shortcut **Command+Shift+S** for Mac or **CTLR+Shift+S** for PC).

2. This will open the voice typing floating icon as seen in Figure 4.37. Floating icons may be moved about the screen by clicking and dragging to a convenient location on the document.

Figure 4.37   Voice Typing

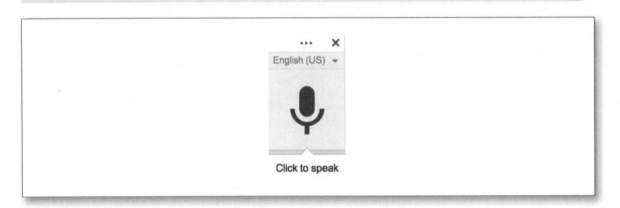

3. Click the **microphone** to enable the microphone on your computer to record words. When the microphone is clicked and ready to record, the microphone icon turns red and has a red circle denoting it is listening as shown in Figure 4.38.

Figure 4.38   Voice Typing Red

4. Start speaking to dictate speech to text. If the user wants to voice type an entire sentence, say "period" or "new line" as shown in Figure 4.39 to automatically add a period or start a new line of text.

Figure 4.39 Voice Typing Features

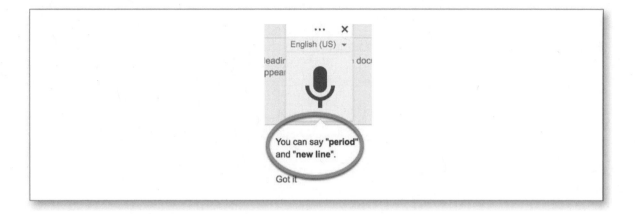

5. Click the **X** in the upper right-hand corner of the icon to close voice typing.

Translate

Translate can be used in foreign language classes or with English language learners. Being able to write in their native language and then to translate key sentences or phrases back to English will give the students connection to the meaning and improve their writing skills. The translate tool should benefit the English language learner and help the teacher understand the English language learner. This allows the student to go deeper with meaning by exploring writing in his or her native tongue. Often English language learners receive failing grades because of the language barrier. They may be fantastic writers but struggle with English. Using **Translate** in Google Docs provides a way for teachers to understand what the student is trying to say other than how well they understand English. This tool will help the students learn English by letting the student translate any document that is shared by the teacher or other students to their native language. Follow these steps to translate Google Docs:

1. Open the document to translate.

2. If a non-Google Doc, convert it to the Google Docs format.

3. Select **Translate** from the **Tools** menu as shown in Figure 4.34.

4. Name the new translated document as shown in Figure 4.40.

5. Choose a language from the drop-down menu.

6. Click.

The document is now translated to the language chosen. Be aware that the original document is still in the user's Google Drive and was not altered. A new translated document was created and will appear next to the original in the *documents* list in Google Drive.

Figure 4.40   Translate Document

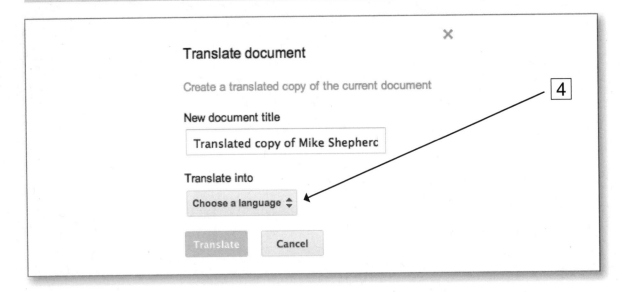

TABLE MENU

Tables are a great way to quickly collect data for mathematics. For example, students studying theoretical versus experimental probability may create a 2 × 10 table to record the results of a coin being flipped. Below the results, students can write about their findings explaining their observations. Share the results of the study with all class periods. Discuss what happens to the percentages of heads and tails as the sample size increases. Follow these steps to insert a table:

1. Select **Table** from the toolbar.
2. Hover and click the mouse over the dimensions of the table to insert as shown in Figure 4.41.
   a. Figure 4.41 only shows a 5 × 8 table, but hover the mouse outside the limits to create a larger table. The largest table in Google Docs is 20 × 20.

Figure 4.41   Insert Table

Table	Help	Last edit was made 5 days ag
Insert table	►	
Insert row above		
Insert row below		
Insert column left		
Insert column right		
Delete table		5 x 8

ADD-ONS

Add-ons are enhancements that can be added to any of the G Suite programs. These enhancements or extra features allow the user to do anything from inserting graphic organizers to creating rubrics to grading student work. To explore add-ons click the **Add-ons** menu bar and select **Get add-ons** to view the list and descriptions of the available add-ons. Add-ons are in all of the G Suite programs and are specific to the type of document. For example, add-ons for Google Docs will be specifically for word processing documents, while add-ons for Google Sheets will be entirely different and specific to extra features that would be appropriate for spreadsheets. The arrow in Figure 4.42 shows where to search for add-ons. Scroll through the list of add-ons or use a keyword for a particular feature that you think may have an add-on. When I do professional development for teachers across the nation I am often told "the reason I do not use Google Docs over Microsoft Word is that Google Docs just does not have all of the features like Word." After I show the participants how to use add-ons, many people in my trainings immediately see how Google Docs is a much better user experience. For example, a teacher told me she does not use Google Docs because there is not a way to print labels. Obviously she was unaware of the add-on displayed in Figure 4.43 called "Avery Label Add-on."

Figure 4.42 Add-ons Search

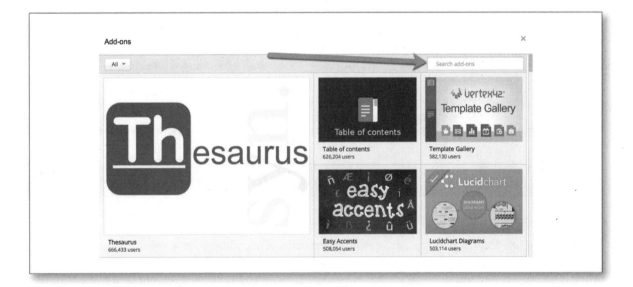

Figure 4.43 Avery Label Add-on

SAMR IMPLICATIONS—TRANSFORMING INSTRUCTION

Substitution	At the lowest level of SAMR Google Docs allows the user to substitute written words on paper for a digital version. This mirrors what is happening on paper and allows the teacher or student to make changes or edits easily.
Redefinition	In the redefinition level of SAMR, Google Docs allows the teacher or student to collaboratively edit documents in real time. To be truly redefined add Google Hangouts to the scenario. Students may share a Google Doc with the teacher while they are in the hospital or some other type of leave where they have an Internet connection. The student could open a Google Hangout to video conference with the teacher while they collaboratively edit the document. The teacher could give live feedback on the video conference while they work on the shared document. This is great for homebound students.
	One particularly awesome redefinition is the example from Heather Eggers. She is a teacher at Westside High School and recently she went on maternity leave. We set up for her English students to a Google Hangout with Mrs. Eggers each week for at least 30 minutes. This time was spent reviewing individual writing projects so they could ask questions of their teacher, while she was away. To make this work for middle school, practice with your students on a snow day by following this template.
	1. Set up a predefined time that you will be available on your first snow day. a. Talk with your students and parents ahead of time and build some excitement. 2. At the determined time, send an email link out to your class of the Google Hangout. 3. Share a Google Form or Google Doc and share some interesting info about a topic or a fun game. 4. Follow up the next time a snow day occurs or when one of your students is homebound.

EVEN MORE

Orange Slice Rubric

Orange Slice has teacher and student versions of rubrics. This add-on has great functionality to give student feedback and peer feedback. The teacher version allows the teacher to create a rubric and push it out via Google Classroom. The student version can be attached to the student work allowing the student to self-assess.

Google Books Ngram Viewer

Google outdoes itself once in awhile. This is an example of its nerdiness gone wild. Google has scanned millions of books totaling over 450 million words and has used an algorithm to turn printed books into digital text. For example, Google has scanned thousands of books from the year 1500 to present day, as well as other papers and publications. Google is still scanning more books every day. Something that has been produced by this is called *ngram*. Ngrams can gauge the popularity of words that have been written over time. Google took the metadata from the books along with the words revealing the author, date of publication, and frequency of words used. In the example in Figure 4.44, the graph compares the popularity of Frankenstein, Albert Einstein, and Sherlock Holmes over the last 200 years. This could be an excellent tool to help students grasp word usage and popularity over time. In a sense, it gives the user a cultural look into the past. Students can see when certain words appear and then disappear from the common language of these books. Visit the ngram viewer, Resource 4.6, at https:// books.google.com/ngrams.

Figure 4.44 Ngram

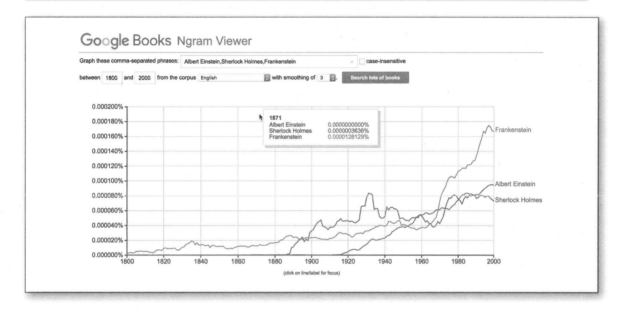

(click on line/label for focus)

SUMMARY

Google Docs gives the teacher and students a dynamic word-processing program attached to the Google account. School districts that use G Suite for Education for their student and faculty have all of these capabilities built in. Google Docs seamlessly integrates with Google Classroom to provide an organized student and teacher workflow in an easy-to-use, cloud-based learning management system. With the ubiquitous next generation often technology dependent, college- and career-readiness standards, school leaders, technology specialists, teachers, and students need to be ready for the coming changes in curriculum and technology. Google offers these services and support for free. Documents are just the beginning. The upcoming chapters are full of interesting, engaging ideas and procedures to motivate students to create, collaborate, and share.

RESOURCES

For more information about G Suite for Education, including

- lesson plans related to chapter content,
- domain setup for tech administrators' videos,
- overviews and Google training materials,

- the authors' favorite websites, and
- testimonials and interviews of schools currently using G Suite,

access Resources from this chapter on the companion website.

Lesson Plans

Lesson Plan Title	All lesson plans and resources can be found on the companion website at: http://resources.corwin.com/googlemeetsms	
Jefferson, Adams, and History	http://goo.gl/rHn33	Resource 4.7
Choose Your Own Adventure Story by Susan Wells	http://goo.gl/Bbu9c	Resource 4.8
Political Campaign	http://goo.gl/rHBmn	Resource 4.9
Writing for Context, Audience, and Purpose by Andrea Zellner	http://goo.gl/gQgnt	Resource 4.10

 http://resources.corwin.com/googlemeetsms

5 Google Slides

Google Slides is a powerful presentation maker that is part of G Suite for Education. Slides has all of the features users have come to expect with traditional presentation software such as Microsoft PowerPoint and Apple's Keynote. Slide transitions, animations, inserting images, and videos are all part of Google Slides. The difference is in sharing, collaboration, and price.

Many of the same tools that are used in Google Docs will be used in Slides. Sharing, cloud-based storage, and download as other formats are available in the same manner as they were in Docs. For example, each presentation made in Google Slides is given a unique web address that when typed into a web browser can be viewed or edited depending on the share settings. This is great for sharing student presentations. For an example of a collaborative presentation made by students, visit Resource 5.1 or snap the quick-response (QR) code in Figure 5.1 to view the presentation on your smartphone or tablet.

Figure 5.1 is a QR code. Using a smartphone or tablet QR code-reader application, follow the link to view the presentation on a mobile device. Accessing information with increased mobility will be a necessary skill. Read more about QR codes in Chapter 10.

SLIDES AND COMMUNICATION

Presentations are key in communication. College- and career-ready students will present information to classmates and coworkers routinely, allowing for Innovative Design and Creative Communication (both ISTE Student Standards). Preparing students to make high-quality presentations in the middle grades will hone their skills as they progress in school. In the Common Core State Standards (CCSS), presenting information in clear, concise ways will prepare students for the rigors of communicating

Figure 5.1   QR Code Student Presentation

to specific audiences. The many college- and career-readiness standards for Speaking and Listening demand that students have an extensive set of skills in presenting information. The standards included in the CCSS English Language Arts Standards are as follows:

> Students must learn to work together, express and listen carefully to ideas, integrate information from oral, visual, quantitative, and media sources, evaluate what they hear, use media and visual displays strategically to help achieve communicative purposes, and adapt speech to context and task.

Google Slides meets this requirement by allowing collaborative work and the ability to easily share that information with peers, parents, and teachers. The standards say that it is the responsibility of all teachers to make sure students are able to speak and listen with clarity in their particular content areas.

Anchor Standard 5 for Speaking and Listening found in Table 5.1 embodies Google Slides. For example, students may make visually stunning displays that capture the attention of the audience. Animations and video may be added to presentations as well as representations of data such as graphs, tables, or charts. All of this can be done in collaboration and can be shared with the world through share settings. Google Slides offer a unique opportunity for students to create, collaborate, and share their work. Presenting about concepts studied is one of the best learning strategies. It provides a forum for students to research the content, summarize the information, display data in the form of charts, tables, or graphs, and create visual representations of content with video and images. Making presentations can teach the student how to organize information, letting it flow seamlessly to the viewer. The educators everywhere believe that it is an important skill to become ready for life after high school. The Anchor Standard in Table 5.1 addresses digital media and displays of data when making presentations.

Table 5.1   Anchor Standard 5 for Speaking and Listening

Make strategic use of digital media and visual displays of data to express information and enhance understanding of presentations.

In Table 5.2, the sixth-grade example, multimedia and visual displays are explicitly mentioned; sixth-grade teachers not only must teach their subject, but also must embed technology by using presentations to meet the standards.

Table 5.2   Sixth-Grade Literacy Speaking and Listening Standard SL.6.5

Include multimedia components (e.g., graphics, images, music, sound) and visual displays in presentations to clarify information.

Table 5.3 explores the writing standards for history, social studies, science, and technical subjects for Grades 6–12. These standards increase with complexity over the years. Creating authentic presentations requires students not only to use the Internet to produce and publish writing, but also to update individual or shared projects with feedback from teachers, peers, and professionals in the field. Students are no longer expected to turn in a *dead* assignment that is meant for only the teacher's eyes. These skills prepare students to create work that matters and that can contribute to the knowledge base of the topic. Graduating seniors who are college and career ready can use collaborative writing and presenting tools like G Suite for Education to meet the needs they face in the 21st century and beyond. Middle school is the grade band that students are first introduced to these types of skills. It is important that teachers mindfully implement them in their lessons. Consider having students develop their own TED Talk-type presentation (see more about that in Resource 5.2 at https://goo.gl/dPIhtA).

Table 5.3   Reading Standard for Literacy in Science and Technical Subjects 6–12

Integrate quantitative or technical information expressed in words in a text with a version of that information expressed visually (e.g., in a flowchart, diagram, model, graph, or table).

Table 5.4 displays writing standards for other subjects. The college- and career-readiness standards hold all accountable for reading and writing. It is clear that using G Suite for Education can meet the challenges set forth in the new learning standards.

Table 5.4   Writing Standards for Literacy in History/Social Studies, Science, and Technical Subjects 6–12

Use technology, including the Internet, to produce and publish writing and present the relationships between information and ideas clearly and efficiently.

Same Great Features

All of the programs in the G Suite (Docs, Sheets, Slides, Drawings, and Forms) have the same great features. This chapter will focus on these programs plus Slides-specific features that make this software ideal for implementing college- and career-readiness standards:

Sharing

Collaboration

Publish to the Web

Embed

Every Doc has a unique URL.

All Docs are stored in Google Drive cloud-based storage.

ACCESSING PRESENTATIONS

All of the G Suite apps share a common pathway to be accessed. Follow the steps here to start working with Slides. When the user is logged into his or her G Suite account, Figure 5.2 will be at the top left of the page. Alternatively, the user may type in any web browser's address bar drive.google.com to access the Documents List. To access Slides, follow these steps:

1. Click on the 9-square icon on the top right of the screen of your G Suite account.

2. Click on the **Drive** icon (alternatively, you can also click on the **Slides** icon to access templates).

Figure 5.2 Accessing Drive

3. Click the blue **New** button on the left-hand side of the page as shown in Figure 5.3 to reveal the drop-down menu displaying all of the G Suite apps.

Figure 5.3 Accessing Presentation Editor

4. Click **Google Slides** to access the editor.

Technology-Infused Teaching Tip

Why not just click on the Slides app in Figure 5.2? It is a good practice to always navigate to the same location to create a Google Drive folder so habits are formed on where files are created and stored.

After clicking on **Google Slides**, the Themes window will appear in the right-hand side to choose a theme for the background of the slides. When working collaboratively on presentations, take note that when a theme is chosen, it is applied to all slides. For example, if a group of students is working on a collaborative presentation, and each student is responsible for a particular set of slides, then if any of the group members change or choose a theme on the shared presentation, it is applied to all slides. Look at Figure 5.4 to see an example of theme choices.

Figure 5.4 Themes

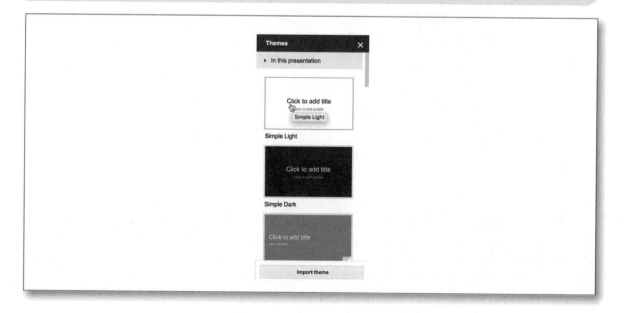

Name the Presentation

The next step in creating a Google Slides presentation is to give the presentation a name. Students need to be aware that naming G Suite files they create ensures that they can easily retrieve the file. To give a Slides presentation or any other G Suite app names, follow these steps:

1. Click on the words **Untitled presentation** as shown in Figure 5.5.

Figure 5.5   Giving the Presentation a Title

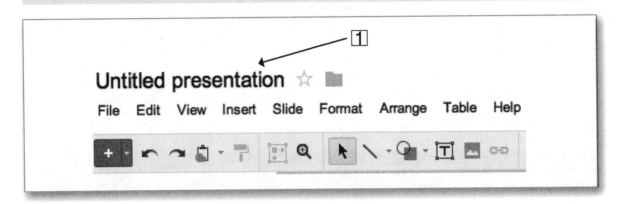

2. Type your new title of the presentation in the box in Figure 5.6

Figure 5.6   Rename the Document

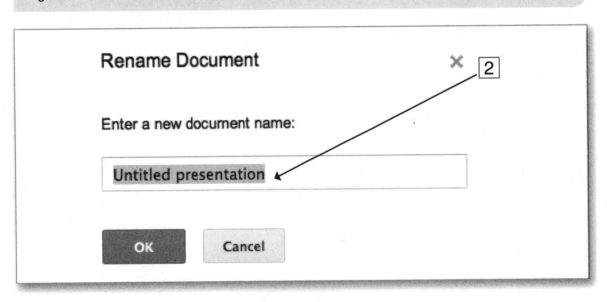

3. Click the **OK** box when finished.

After clicking **OK**, the file will appear in the user's Drive folder with the appropriate name given to it in the Documents List. Notice the star in Figure 5.5 next to the file name. If the user clicks the star, the document is given special significance and will appear in the starred list in Google Drive. The user could star documents that are important or frequently worked on, making them easier to access.

Technology-Infused Teaching Tip

Instruct students to give names to their work based on a predefined formula. Students will create a massive amount of digital content over their lifetimes, and it will most likely be saved in a cloud storage space like in Google Drive. It is important for students to learn how to manage the content they create. Managing students' quality of work over time could be a valuable part of a student's electronic portfolio. It is imperative that the information be easy for the student to recall years later. Giving the documents searchable names that follow a formula will make it easy. For example, student Marcy Tolbert will name documents she creates by defining what type of assignment and adding her name (e.g., "Marcy Tolbert History of NASA Presentation"). Teachers should require this or a similar naming convention to be able to search for Marcy's documents for grading, and later in her school career, she can access these documents to see her progress over time. Students need to be aware that organizing their digital life is an important task. Students who are college and career ready realize that digital organization will be a skill that is in demand in the professional world. A recent *Time* magazine article on learning reports that when students are asked questions, they tend not to think of a particular class. Instead, they think of where the nearest device is located to search for the information. Students and adults alike are thinking in terms of search rather than being able to instantly recall the fact. Learning to search the massive amount of digital content that the user produces or others produce is more important than the futile attempt to memorize it.

Previously Detailed Features

In Chapter 4, many of the same commands were discussed. Please refer back to Chapter 4 to learn how to perform the actions in the following list. This section will focus only on presentation-specific commands, and some may overlap.

Share

New

Rename

Make a Copy

Revision History

Language

Email Collaborators

Email as Attachment

Print Options

FILE MENU

The **File** menu is usually the first menu that computer users come into contact with. Most word-processing programs have similar features, but Google Slides provides some pleasant surprises that other programs can't compete with. Read this section to become familiar with Google's presentation maker.

Import Slides

Import slides is a command that will let the user import slides from any Google Presentation and/or Microsoft PowerPoint files that are located on the user's Google Drive or on the computer's hard drive. Google recognizes the ubiquity of Microsoft Office and wants to make using Google Docs an easy and compatible experience. Teachers will find this helpful with the transition to Google Slides because, just like with Google Docs, users can upload any file type to store in their cloud storage space, Google Drive. Teachers may have created many PowerPoint presentations in the past that are useful for their classes. To use them, teachers can convert them to Google Slides or insert specific slides from Google Slides or Microsoft PowerPoint into Google Slides. Remember, working with Google Docs allows the user to store and edit work from any computer with Internet access. Students in the new economy of the 21st century will most likely not be required to learn only one piece of software. The Common Core State Standards or the Next Generation Assessment consortia have not endorsed any software as of yet, and there is doubt that they will. It is key for the college- and career-ready student to be able to use any software to do the job. That is why Google Docs is so important. It has all of the basic features of the mainstream office packages, but it has the ability to use the Internet to create, collaborate, and share, plus it is free. If a student can be comfortable with Google Docs toolbars, then he or she can master any program the testing companies or their future bosses can throw at them.

Follow the steps below to import slides from other presentations, including Microsoft PowerPoint, from the user's Google Drive.

1. Click **Import slides** from the **File** menu in the upper right-hand corner of Slides to reveal the window in Figure 5.7.

2. Double click the Google Slides presentation or the Microsoft PowerPoint presentation that the user wants to import as shown in Figure 5.7.

Figure 5.7   Importing Slides

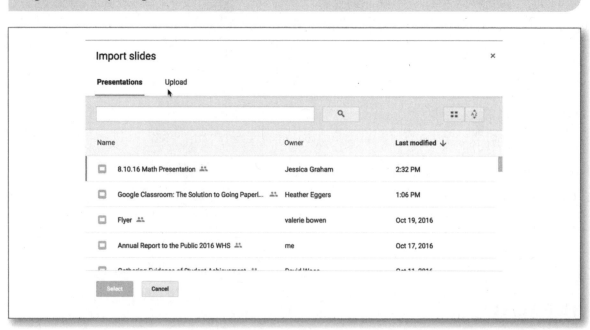

3. Click on which slides to import as shown in Figure 5.8.
   a. Slides selected will appear highlighted like in Figure 5.8.

Figure 5.8 Selecting Slides to Import

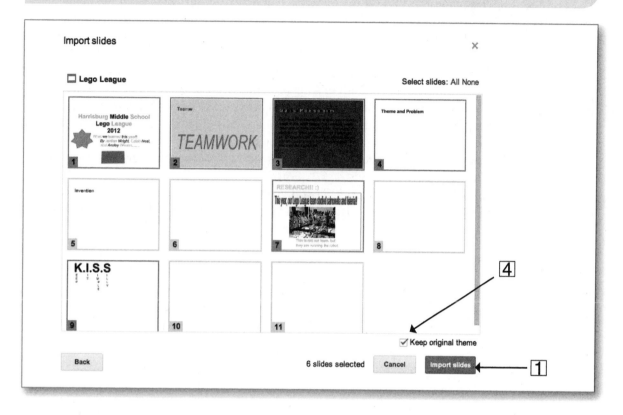

4. Select **Keep original theme** to import backdrop, colors, and other features.

5. Click at the bottom of Figure 5.8.

To upload slides from a presentation that is not in the user's Google Drive, but located on the user's computer, follow these steps:

1. Click **Upload** under Presentations as seen in Figure 5.7.

2. Drag Google Presentation or Microsoft PowerPoint files only from your computer into the box to upload them, or press the button to select files manually from your hard drive to import.

Figure 5.9 Upload Slides From Computer

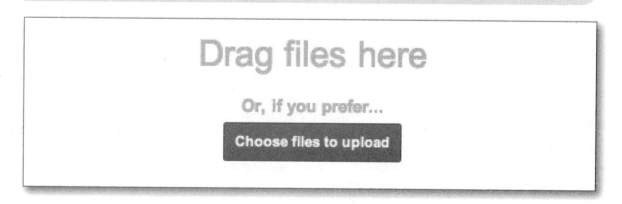

More Reasons Google Slides Works

The G Suite is device neutral. It doesn't matter if the computer lab has iMacs and the mathematics teachers have PCs—no software has to be purchased, and no programs have to be downloaded. Students can move from device to device without the worry of losing information or not having the right program.

Teachers who want to avoid creating "dead" presentations can convert their existing PowerPoint presentations to Google Slides or at least start making presentations exclusively in the G Suite. A dead presentation refers to the information being locked into one saved file on one storage device like Microsoft PowerPoint. Revive presentations by converting them into a Google Slides presentation. This gives life to the work because the information is stored in the cloud: the user can edit the information from any computer or share it with anyone in the world. No longer do teachers and students have to be chained to a physical hard drive.

If users don't want to convert documents but still want to share them the Google Docs way, they can upload the file and click **Share** just like sharing a Google Doc. This is another way that Google strives to make it easy on users.

Download As

Download as is the command that lets the user download the Google Presentations as any of the supported file formats. Presentations supports the following file types for download.

PNG

JPEG

SVG

PPTX

PDF

TXT

Students who want to submit presentations as part of a science fair or other public events may be required to have specific formats other than the G Suite format. Some formats such as PDF are very difficult to edit, unless you have expensive software. This would be ideal for teachers and students who do not want their information changed on the presentation when they share a digital copy with the public.

Publish to the Web

Publish to the Web allows the user to publish the presentation directly to the web, giving it a unique URL. This option will make the presentation easy to share with anyone with Internet access. Teachers may use this option when presenting to a class; they need only to get the presentation's unique URL and copy and paste it into an email to share the presentation with students. When publishing a presentation, the user has the option to auto-advance the slides and create his or her own animated slideshow! When the user clicks on the link, the presentation will appear in the browser. The URL is long and confusing. Use Google's URL Shortener, http://goo.gl, to shorten the link. This makes it easy for the user to share the presentation. This is helpful when the presenter does not have the email of the participants but wants to share the presentation with a group. The participants will type the shortened URL into a browser's address bar to view the presentation.

Another dazzling way to access Google Slides or any documents created in G Suite on the web is through the use of QR codes. QR codes allow the user to access the information on smartphones or tablets without typing in the URL. By using the Google URL shortener, you can access the QR code directly from the shortened URL.

INSERT MENU

The **Insert** menu gives users many options to make their presentations come alive. Read the next section to become familiar with inserting graphic design elements to make your presentations stand out.

Video

Videos can be uploaded from YouTube into Google Slides. There is not an upload from hard drive option for videos. Teachers and students could create a YouTube account to upload videos. Some domain administrators allow students and teachers to link their YouTube and G Suite accounts, allowing them to fully use this feature in presentations. Some districts may not feel that it is in the best interest of their students and faculty to have this option because of inappropriate content. Google owns YouTube, making integration with G Suite easy. The only problem is that the district domain administrator must allow YouTube for Schools to be turned on in the G Suite domain. Contact your domain administrator and ask him or her to allow YouTube for Schools. It is understandable that some schools may opt out of giving students access to the YouTube site. We do not recommend limiting access to YouTube.

Option I: Insert YouTube Video From Search

1. Select **Video** from the **Insert** menu in the upper left side of Presentations.

2. Click **Video search** as indicated in Figure 5.10.

3. Enter a search term into the search box.

4. Press the play icon in the middle of the video thumbnail to preview.

5. Click **Select** to choose that video to be inserted in the presentation.

Figure 5.10   Insert YouTube From Search

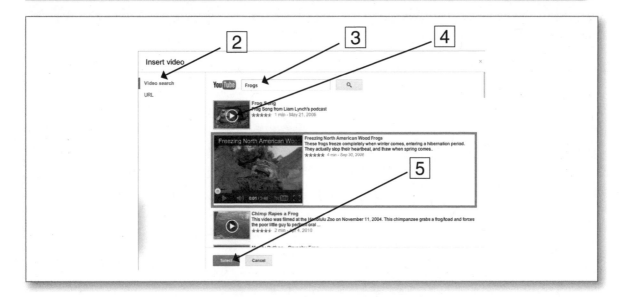

Option II: Insert YouTube Video From URL

Each YouTube video has its own unique URL, exactly like every Google Doc and Google Calendar. To place specific videos into presentations, follow these steps:

1. Select **Video** from the **Insert** menu in the upper left of presentations.
2. Click on the initials **URL** as shown in Figure 5.11.
3. Copy the URL from the YouTube website.
4. Paste the URL into the space provided.
5. Press to insert the video.

Figure 5.11   Insert YouTube Video From URL

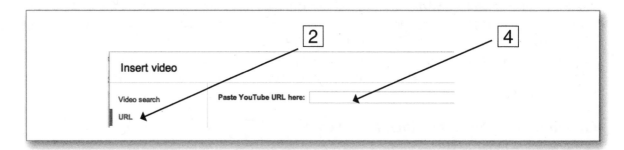

Technology-Infused Teaching Tip

If you or your students have a video that is not on YouTube, you can always take a screenshot of the video of where it is hosted, embed the screenshot image on the slide, and link the image to the video's URL. This will allow the presenter to click on the image while presenting, and the video site will load in a new tab automatically!

Word Art

Word art is a way for students and teachers to add creativity to their presentations. To insert Word Art into Presentations, follow these steps:

1. Select **Word Art** from the **Insert** menu in Presentations.
2. Enter text into the Word Art text box as shown in Figure 5.12.

Figure 5.12   Inserting Word Art

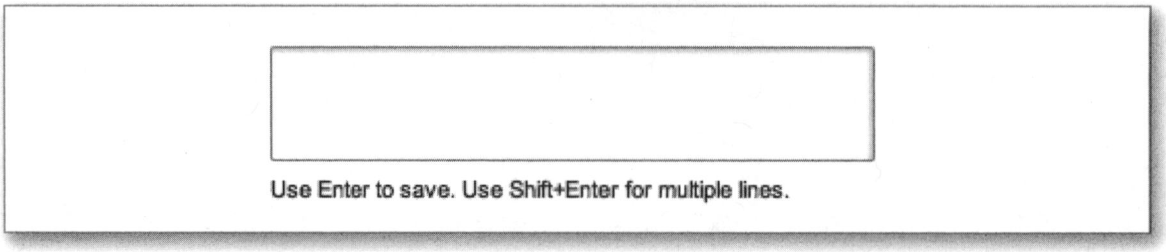

Use Enter to save. Use Shift+Enter for multiple lines.

3. Enter multiple lines by holding **Shift+Enter**.

4. Press **Enter** when finished to insert the Word Art.

Word Art can be edited for the following designs by selecting the drop-down menu when the Word Art is highlighted on the slide.

Fill color

Line color

Line weight

Line dash

Font

Bold, italic, underline

These options allow users to express their unique style. View Google's Demo Slam video in Resource 5.3 to see what is possible with presentations with respect to Word Art, lines, shapes, and other media.

Animations

Animations are a great way to give life to a presentation. The new standards encourage the use of multimedia as detailed in the sixth-grade standard mentioned in Table 5.2. This Common Core standard pushes students to use multimedia components to enrich the concepts being presented. Teaching an appropriate style is essential for college and career success. Students must recognize their audience and present in a style appropriate to the task.

Follow the steps below to add slide transitions in Google Slides.

1. Select **Animations** from the **Insert** menu in the toolbar of Google Slides.

2. Select the drop-down arrow next to the word **Slide** as shown in Figure 5.13 to add slide transition to the current slide.

3. Choose from the list of animations in Figure 5.13.

Figure 5.13   Adding Slide Animations/Transitions

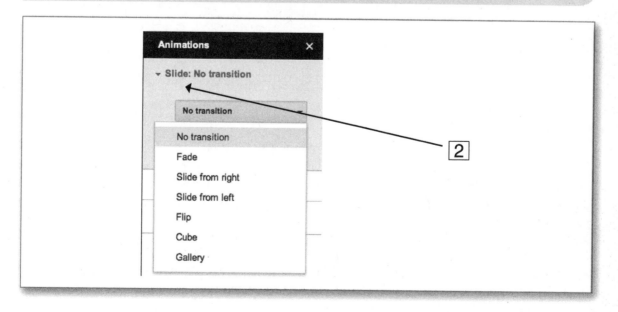

To animate a particular object on the slide, follow these steps:

1. Select **Animate** from the **Insert** menu in the toolbar of Google Slides.

2. Select an object to animate on the slide.
   Graphics
   Images
   Word Art
   Text boxes

3. Click **+Add Animation** to reveal the options located in the drop-down menu in Figure 5.14.

4. Choose which animation style and command to place on the object shown in Figure 5.14.

5. Repeat Steps 2–4 to select additional objects for animation.

6. Select underneath **+Add Animation** to preview animations you have selected.

Figure 5.14 Animate an Object

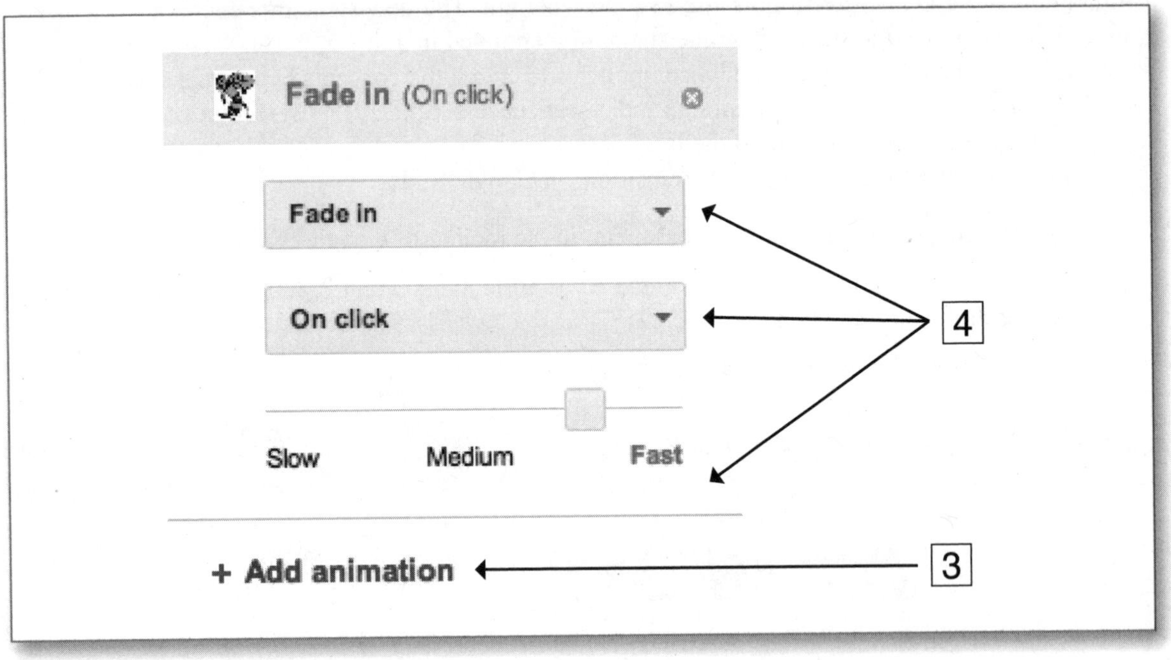

Line

Inserting lines into presentations is a great way for students to express themselves artistically while exploring geometry concepts. For example, the type of line called Polyline is great for learning shapes and their names in early grades math classes. Polylines are used to make polygons. Common Core State Standards for geometry in the middle grades directs students to analyze and create shapes. For example, students could draw polygons on their slides, name them accordingly, and share them with other students. One idea is to create databases of study materials organized in folders stored on the teacher's Google Drive. An example of a database would be slides with explanations and drawings of polygons. These databases (or study guides) could be shared with students when studying a particular shape and its properties. This is a great way to review for a test or send home as a study guide. Once the slideshow is shared with the class, students can access it anywhere they have connection to the Internet. In a perfect world, students would study their materials from their smartphone as they ride home on the school bus. Take this idea one step further by collaborating with other classes or other schools.

To insert lines into Slides, follow these steps:

1. Select **Line** from the **Insert** menu at the top of Presentations to reveal the drop-down menu containing the types of lines that may be inserted as shown in Figure 5.15.

Figure 5.15   Types of Lines

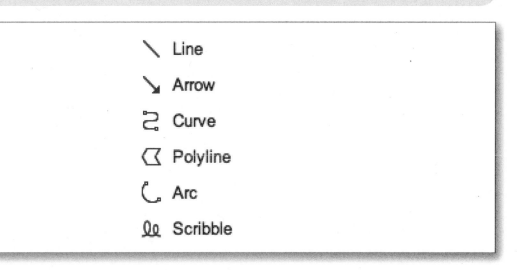

2. Click on which type of line to insert.

3. Edit the line.

4. Highlight the line by clicking on it to reveal the toolbar and drop-down menus that can change:

    Fill color

    Line color

    Line weight

    Line dash

Arrowheads: These are placed at the beginning and end of the line to give it direction.

Technology-Infused Teaching Tip

Students who are college and career ready will be prepared to write in many different mediums. Documents such as Microsoft Word, Apple's Pages, or Google Docs are not the only way to present formal writing. Websites, blogs, wikis, Twitter, Facebook, and countless other not-yet-invented formats in which people consume information will be important. Promote other formats; students who are versatile will be college and career ready. The standard in Table 5.5 seeks to expand students' ability to read and write in diverse media.

Table 5.5   Integration of Knowledge and Ideas Anchor Standard 7 for Reading

Integrate and evaluate content presented in diverse media and formats, including visually and quantitatively, as well as in words.

New Slide

To insert a new slide, follow these steps:

1. Click the **icon** in the left side of Slides.

2. Click the **drop-down arrow** next to the ⊞ to select from the slide layouts shown in Figure 5.16.

The slide layouts shown in Figure 5.16 pertain to what type of text and object boxes will appear on the slide for the particular layout. For example, the Title and Body slide will have a text box for the title of the slide and a separate text box for the body of the slide. If the user wants to create his or her own text and object boxes, select the **Blank** layout.

Figure 5.16   New Slide Layouts

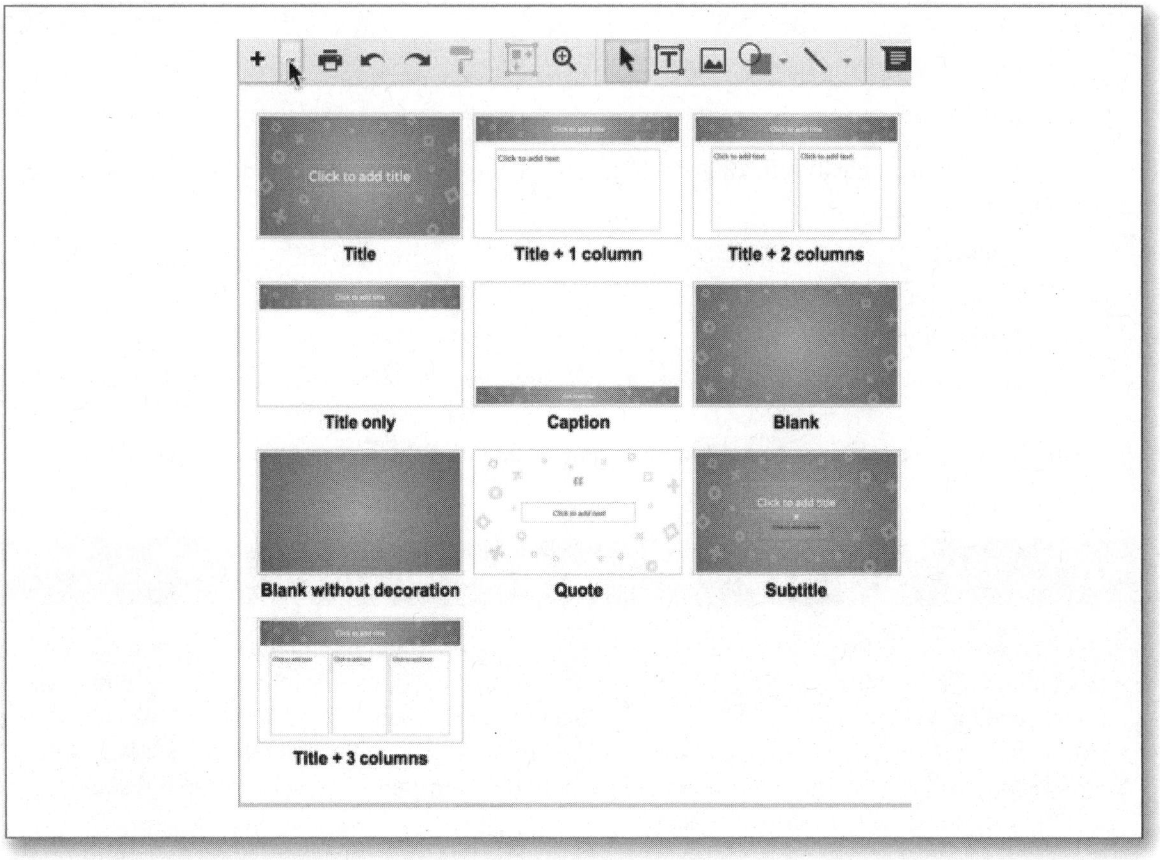

Concerns With Collaborative Work in Presentations

When working collaboratively, students need to be aware of which slides they have permission in which to work. Many times in collaborative presentations, students will be assigned a specific slide number for their contribution. For example, if a student added a slide to the middle of the group's presentation, and every student was assigned a slide number in which to work, then the slide numbers would be changed, causing confusion. If the teacher predefines the slides and does not allow adding slides to the middle of the presentation, then the confusion can be averted. To help avoid the bewilderment, use the chat feature built into every G Suite app. This helps if a small group is working on a presentation project. Users can chat about whatever they need to on the side. This helps collaborators stay organized when unexpected changes occur in the making of the presentation. Google chat is automatically turned on even if chat in Gmail is disabled. This is great because the domain administrator would have to disable all of the G Suite features to keep students from collaborating. Learn how to chat in Slides by reading the next section.

Chat in G Suite

Chat in the G Suite is located in the upper right-hand corner of any G Suite app. When others are viewing, the users can chat with each other. This is helpful when working collaboratively. They are able to talk with each other, discussing the presentation and ideas that they have to make it better. Collaboration is one of the key features of many state standards. Whether the student is working on a math proof in Slides or using the space to create online notecards to study with a friend, collaboration is at the heart of G Suite for Education. The chat feature can make this collaboration a reality. To access chat in G Suite, follow these steps:

1. Click the drop-down arrow denoting how many viewers are collaborating on the document located next to the comments and share buttons as shown in Figure 5.17.

Figure 5.17 Chat in G Suite

a. The names of the viewers are located here with a colored box or profile picture.

b. The colored box represents their cursor color on the document.

2. Type text in the chat box, then press **Enter.**

a. Chat will automatically pop up in the other viewers' windows.

Google Slides for Research Notecards

Consider this Common Core State Standard in Table 5.6 when planning long-term or short-term writing projects with students.

Slides can be used in more ways than a simple performance of conveying knowledge to a formal group of spectators. For example, a student researching information about certain historical figures for a history/social studies research paper would find presentations a useful tool for organization. The student will undoubtedly find many resources in print and digital formats as the many state college and career standards express routinely. Taking notes on traditional note cards does not pave the way into the 21st century. Using Google Slides as research notecards is both efficient and convenient. The content created in Slides is always stored in the cloud and accessed anywhere there is an Internet connection. Students are able to modify their research with their smartphone or home computer. The research will be shared with the teacher so the teacher can give feedback in the form of comments. Comments are used in Docs, Sheets, Slides, and Drawings as a way for teachers to grade or leave feedback on assignments. Slides allow the teacher to guide the student in the writing process from research to final draft.

Table 5.6 Anchor Standard 10 Writing Standards for Literacy in History/Social Studies, Science, and Technical Subjects 6–12

Write routinely over extended time frames (time for reflection and revision) and shorter time frames (a single sitting or a day or two) for a range of discipline-specific tasks, purposes, and audience.

Other Uses for Presentations

Flash cards

Note-taking

Writing projects for elementary students

Teacher presentations for content

Student presentations for content

Game show study guide (follow instructions in Resource 5.4 at http://flippity.net/QuizShow.asp)

Shapes

In Slides, users may insert various shapes, arrows, callouts, and equation elements that enhance the presentation. Look at Figure 5.18 for the full collection of shapes that may be inserted into a presentation. Encourage students to use these transitional elements to make eye-catching flowcharts and graphics. To insert shapes, follow these steps:

1. Select **Shapes** from the **Insert** menu located in the toolbar in Presentations.

2. Hover the mouse over the arrow pointing to the right beside **Shape** to reveal the objects available for insert as shown in Figure 5.18.

3. Click the object to insert and edit it accordingly.

Figure 5.18 Insert Shapes

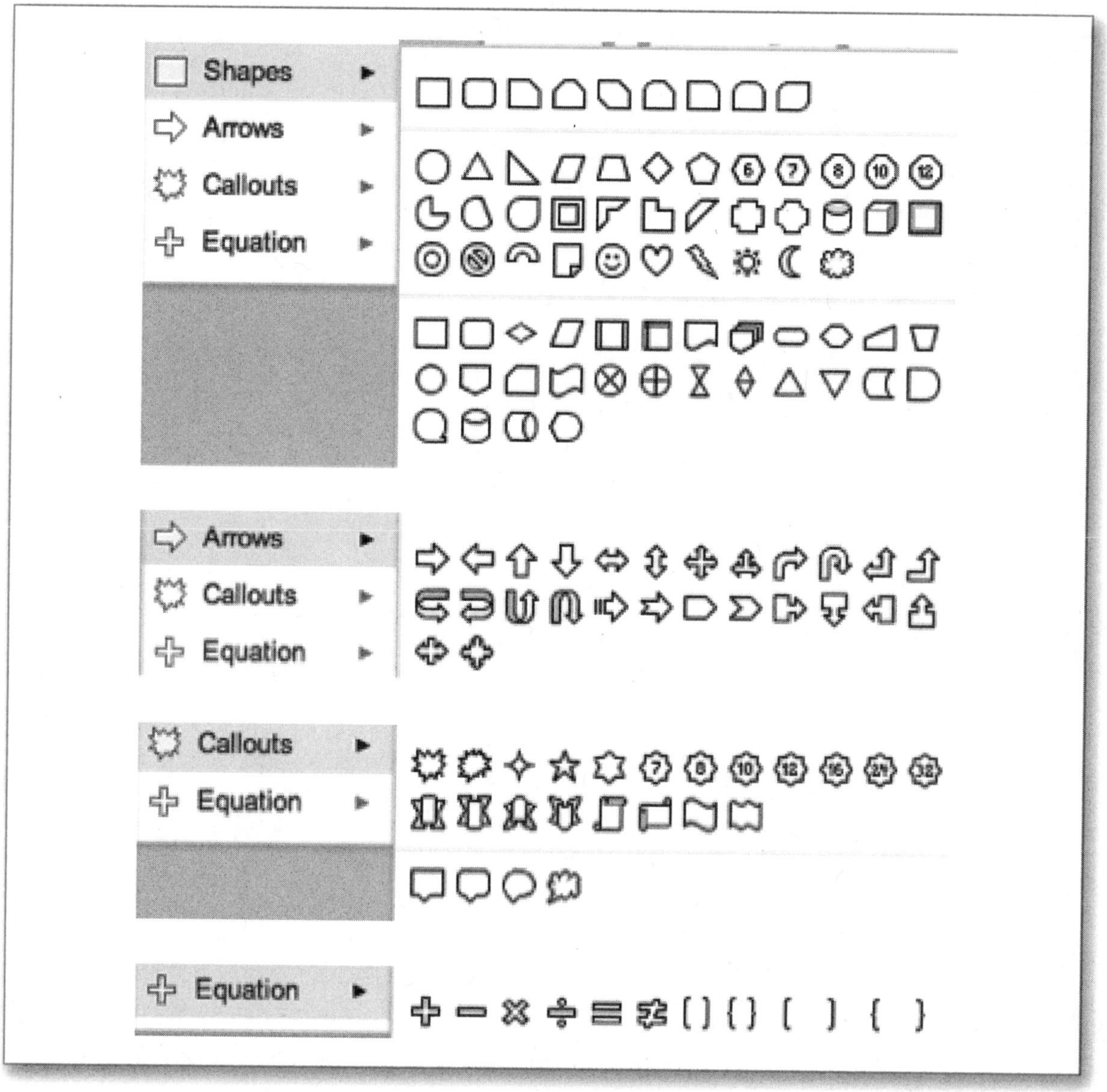

SLIDE MENU

Many of the features in the **Slide** menu are offered in other presentation makers and are self-explanatory. We will learn only about the background option in depth.

Background

Under the **Slide** menu in the toolbar is **Background**. Background is different than theme. The background refers to the color or image on the background of the slide, and it can be applied to all slides or a particular slide. Theme refers to the arrangement of text boxes, titles, and body of the slide. When students are working on collaborative projects, they may change the background color or image to their preference without changing the group's background as a whole. Teach the students to be aware of the **Apply All** button. To change the background, follow these steps:

1. Select **Background** under the **Slide** menu in the toolbar to reveal Figure 5.19.

2. Click the drop-down arrow next to the box to change the color.

3. Click to select an image from your Google Drive, search the web, or upload from your hard drive.

4. Click to reset the theme to default.

5. Click **Done** or **Apply to all**.

Figure 5.19   Change Background

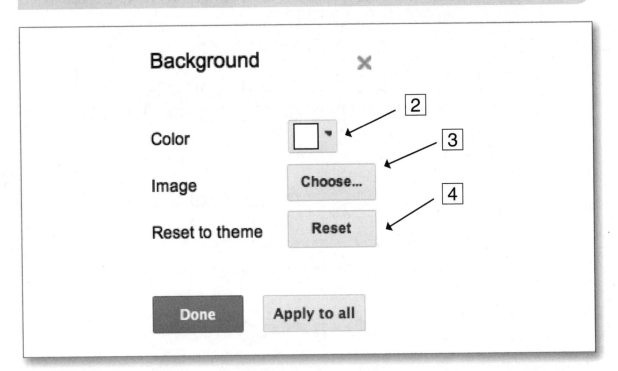

Technology-Infused Teaching Tip

Changing the layout and theme will affect the entire presentation. When working on collaborative presentations, make sure to seek the advice of the group before applying a new motif to the presentation. Use the convenient chat or comment features to consult group members.

FORMAT MENU

Format refers to the style of text, paragraphs, line spacing, and options like bold, italic, and underline. These are common in most office software. One exception in the G Suite that makes it stand out from other presentation- or document-creating software is the **Alt Text** utility. This feature will help students with special needs who have difficulty seeing or reading the text on the presentation. Alt Text works with third-party screen-reader software to deliver text to speech for individuals with text deficiencies. Some of these third-party software programs will work with G Suite to print in Braille. Google Slides can help everyone learn regardless of their learning or physical disability. If you have access to the screen-reader technology, try it for your students. To access Alt Text, follow these steps:

1. Select a piece of text on the slide.

2. Select **Alt Text** from the **Format** menu in the toolbar.

3. Title and describe the Alt Text as shown in Figure 5.20.

Figure 5.20   Alt Text

EXAMPLE OF STUDENT WORK

In this example, students are using presentations to create collaborative slideshows about soil in eighth-grade science class. The teacher, Ms. Jacquie Dubrava, prepared ahead of time a presentation titled "Soil." The presentation she shared had one title page and one individual slide for each student in the class. She shared the presentation with the entire class period easily by using Google Classroom. In the first slide, Ms. Dubrava gave directions and slide assignments to the students. Students were assigned to create a slide covering an aspect of what they have learned about soil within the unit of study. Students were assigned which topics to cover in their slide. Each student was given a particular slide number in which to work. All students in the class were working on the presentation at the same time. By the end of the class period, the students had created a full collaborative presentation covering every aspect of soil that they have learned about. Access Resource 5.5 at http://goo.gl/NJwQ1 to see an example from her seventh-period class.

Classroom Activity With Lines

Students in middle grades must "reason with shapes and their attributes." This mathematics standard wants students to understand that shapes have similarities and differences. For example, a student learning this standard could make a presentation. The teacher may prepare slides in advance that have the names of shapes on them. Follow the steps laid out here to make the lesson a reality in your classroom.

The teacher will

1. Create a Google Slides presentation with each slide containing names of various shapes students are studying

2. Share the premade presentation with the students

Students will

1. Make a copy of the presentation by selecting **File**, then **Make a copy**

This step lets the student take ownership of the shared document. Any further edits that the student makes to the document will not appear on the original.

2. Rename the presentation using the naming convention selected by the teacher

3. Research on the Internet properties of the shapes and their appearance

4. Use Polyline to draw the shapes, then name them appropriately

5. Use the Internet to give research information about the shapes to summarize on the slide

6. Re-share the new presentation with the teacher for scoring

Technology-Infused Teaching Tip

Writing on slides in the middle grades is important. It may be difficult for a middle school student to convey their message with brevity on a single slide or sets of slides with limited text area. Working with slides gives the students a smaller space with a defined area to work in. This is a great way to build presentation skills and assist students in using the slides to enhance their oral presentation instead of just a replica of it.

SAMR IMPLICATIONS—TRANSFORMING INSTRUCTION

Modification	Using Google Slides allows students to transform their own construction of knowledge by allowing them to work collaboratively with students around the world on a presentation. Furthermore, students have the ability to publish the presentation for a global audience.

| Redefinition | Through publishing the slideshow, students can then solicit feedback from field experts. For example, students have the ability to create a slideshow presentation about trends in election results. They can then engage in dialogue and develop a feedback loop with a political statistician/journalist to discuss the points brought across in the presentation. Students can then revise accordingly. |

EVEN MORE

Q&A—Audience Tools and Interactive Presentations

While presenting slides, you or your students can allow for an engaging backchannel of Q&A. Imagine if students are presenting their slideshow, and you want the audience to ask questions during the presentation without interrupting the flow of the presentation. Google Slides is equipped with what they call Audience Tools. These can be used when you are using the extended desktop on the presentation computer (the projected screen acts as one monitor and the computer screen acts as another). You can turn on and off the extended desktop in your display setting on your computer. This is the opposite of mirroring your computer! Figure 5.21 shows how to turn Presenter View on. Simply click the drop-down arrow adjacent to **Present** and select **Presenter view.**

Figure 5.21 Turning On Presenter View

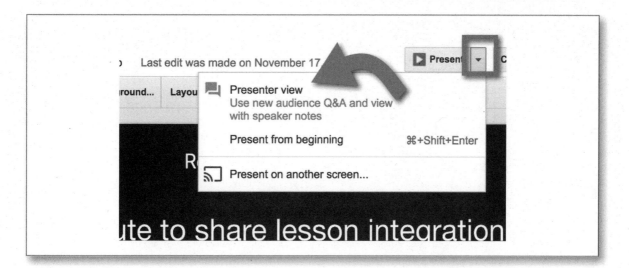

This view also allows you to view your notes and next slides. In Figure 5.22, you can show how you can turn on the question options under Audience Tools. Once turned on, the slideshow will add a header to every slide displaying the URL where the audience can navigate to ask the questions. All questions will be displayed on your Audience Tools screen. The presenter then can present and display the question on the screen when they are ready to address it in their presentation.

Figure 5.22 Turning On Question Option

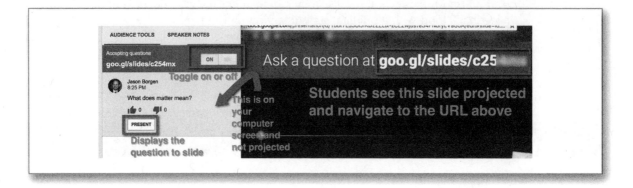

The audience also has the ability to vote on questions and see all the questions being submitted (Figure 5.23) if they want to answer them themselves, allowing for a truly interactive presentation!

Figure 5.23 Submitted Questions

You can get detailed directions in Resource 5.6 on the companion website.

SUMMARY

Slides are one more component of G Suite for Education that will help students and teachers meet the rigors of the various college- and career-readiness standards. The standards addressed in this chapter undoubtedly can be met with the use of presentations. Moving forward, each part of the G Suite will become increasingly familiar. Start to think how you can use these great tools for collaboration in your classroom to exceed the expectations of the 21st century and beyond workplace.

RESOURCES

For more information about G Suite for Education, including

- lesson plans related to chapter content,
- domain setup for tech administrators' videos,
- overviews and Google training materials,
- the authors' favorite websites, and
- testimonials and interviews of schools currently using G Suite,

access Resources from this chapter on the companion website.

Lesson Plans

Lesson Plan Title	All lesson plans and resources can be found on the companion website at: http://resources.corwin.com/googlemeetsms	
Peter Pan by Betsy Davis	http://goo.gl/l9XmX	Resource 5.7

online resources http://resources.corwin.com/googlemeetsms

6 Google Sheets

Key Features

- Collaborative spreadsheets
- Auto fill
- Spreadsheet specific add-ons
- Insert charts, images, and more
- Google Classroom connected

Google Sheets is a fully integrated spreadsheet program that brings data alive in the G Suite of educational apps. Students and teachers can use it for a range of tasks, from kindergarteners making simple T-charts to master's level statistics. This chapter will cover the basic functions of Google Sheets and how they can be used in the classroom to exceed various college- and career-readiness standards, particularly math. Keep in mind that any spreadsheet program is difficult to learn at first. Because Google Sheets is complex, it is best to keep trying new features, and over time, users will gain skills that will help them organize and manipulate data. Google Sheets is the most robust program in the G Suite. The key feature is the collaboration that Google has pioneered. Data collected by Google Sheets users can instantly be shared, modified, and presented in graphically stunning ways with charts and the help of add-ons. Math is the primary focus, but other subjects could use it as well. For example, understanding the 2008 global economic crisis from a history perspective cannot be fully understood if the student has trouble reading graphs, tables, and charts. Furthermore, students need to be able to work with data to convey the information to back up their claims with evidence. A key to learning and working in our data-rich society will be how to collect, analyze, and display data to help us conceptualize complex problems. This is key in the Common Core State Standard for Mathematical Practice 3: "Construct viable arguments and critique the reasoning of others."

Using Google Sheets to integrate mathematics into other classes is important for learning about decision making. Mathematics examples can explain the most complicated parts of history, science, and behavior by disaggregating and displaying data. With Google Sheets, students can unlock the power of information, giving them a way to compute statistical data, present them in the form of graphs, and share and collaborate with the world or class, making real contributions to the understanding of the subject.

All of the G Suite programs operate on the premise of sharing. Many of the same great features are included in Google Sheets that are in the other G Suite programs. This chapter will only cover basic Google Sheet-specific commands that will help the student and teacher begin to understand how to work with and manipulate data.

STANDARDS FOR MATHEMATICAL PRACTICE

The Standards for Mathematical Practice from the Common Core Mathematics Standards are much like the Anchor Standards in the English Language Arts section. They guide the teacher throughout all grade levels to instill into the student certain behaviors and ideas that make them develop critical thinking with mathematics. They are meant to capture the "processes and proficiencies" of mathematics, in other words, how the student uses the mathematics and not just what they acquire as far as knowledge and skill. Students must be aware of these ideas to fully become college and career ready for a world full of data analysis and decision making. That is why Standard for Mathematical Practice 5 is perfect for Google Sheets. Google Sheets will allow the student to collect data in cells and manipulate the data to make charts and graphs that the student can use to explain his or her findings with evidence. The software is not doing the "math" for the student; instead, it is a tool that helps the students explore mathematical concepts and models. Students who can choose the appropriate mathematical tool to help interpret results and critical thinking will become college and career ready. Solving problems in college and career will be messy and most likely not look like the problems in many classrooms today. The boss will most likely not say to the employee, "Sally, if two trains are leaving the station, and one is going 50 miles per hour . . ." Instead of this, bosses will have employees working on complex problems that require deep understanding. Teachers must focus on questions and learning experiences that provide a rich and complex set of problems for students to solve. Students must be able to identify their own problems as well as solve the ones that their professors and bosses identify for them. Students who are college and career ready will have sufficient grasp of mathematical concepts and be able to choose the appropriate tool to conceptualize, share, and present their mathematical understanding. Google Sheets does this by giving the students a full cloud-based statistical package that can help students share, manipulate, and present data.

FILE MENU

The **File** menu gives you access to important commands that will help you create a high-quality spreadsheet. Read the next section to find out some time-savers that will make collecting and sharing data a great learning experience for you and your students.

Import

Import datasets into spreadsheets from any of the compatible formats.

The user can import all or part of the types of datasets displayed in Table 6.1 into Google Sheets. Students and teachers working in other formats can import them into Google Sheets for easy sharing of data. To import data into Google Sheets, follow the steps below Table 6.1.

Table 6.1 Supported Data Formats

Extension	Program supported
.xls	Microsoft Excel 2003 and previous versions
.xlsx	Microsoft Excel 2007 and later versions
.ods	OpenOffice

Extension	Program supported
.csv	Comma-separated value—this format is common as an alternative import/export format to go between large databases and proprietary formats such as Microsoft Excel and Apple's Numbers.
.txt	Text file—similar as a go-between like .csv
.tsv	Tab-separated values—similar to .csv and .txt
.tab	MapInfo TAB format is a dataset that can be used in geographical information systems software.
.xlsm	Microsoft Excel 2007 with embedded macros Macro is defined as a set of repetitive tasks that a user can command a cell or particular set of cells in a spreadsheet to perform. For example, a macro can be set to run a sum of particular cells in a spreadsheet. This may be useful to students and teachers if their spreadsheet calls for some type of automation. Google Sheets will accept macros from Microsoft Excel files when converted to a Google Sheet.
.xlt	Microsoft Excel template file
.html, .htm	HTML files are coded to be displayed on websites. Data created in Microsoft Excel that are saved as an .html file can be uploaded to Google Sheets and edited. If you want to display your data on a webpage, open the **File** menu and select **Download** *as a webpage (.html zip file).*

1. Select **Import** from the **File** menu in the Google Sheets toolbar. This will open the import window as shown in Figure 6.1.

Figure 6.1   Import Window

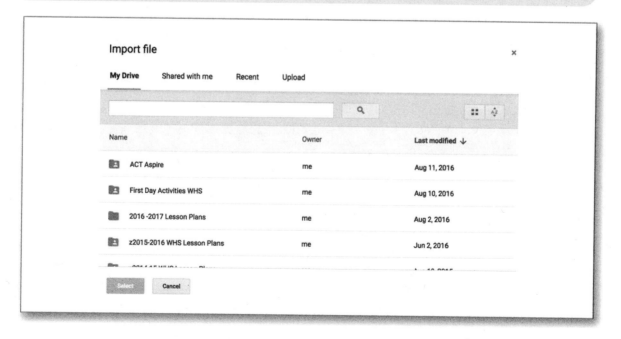

2. Select from **My Drive, Shared with me, Recent,** and **Upload** to upload data from various locations.

3. Choose the appropriate **Import action** as shown in Figure 6.2.

4. Click **Import**.

Figure 6.2 Import Data

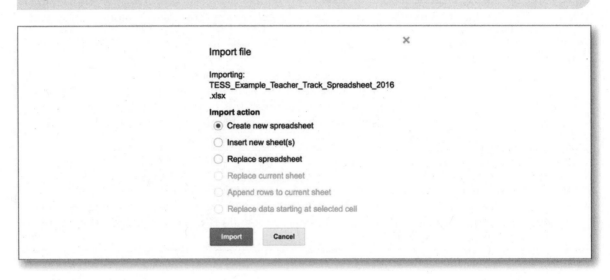

Spreadsheet Settings

Figure 6.3 shows the Google Sheets spreadsheet settings window. Manipulate defaults for currency, time zone, and more with these settings for the particular file only. Spreadsheet settings will affect formatting defaults such as currency, date, and time settings and other country-specific settings. Selecting the time zone will allow the user to have the revision history displayed in their time zone as well as

Figure 6.3 Spreadsheet Settings

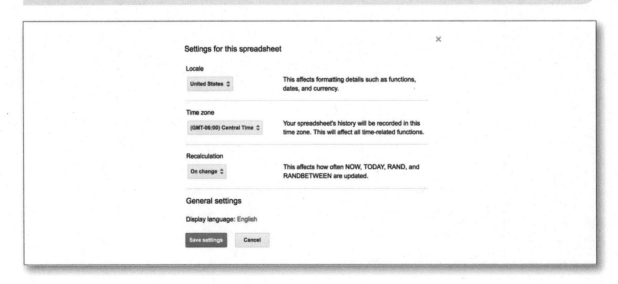

"affect all time-related functions." There are some time-related functions (formulas) that can be inserted into the cells of a spreadsheet. See Resource 6.1 for a full list of functions at http://goo.gl/LBN7R.

See Revision History

It is important to go over revision history once again because of its usefulness in the classroom and particularly Google Sheets. The G Suite programs Docs, Slides, Sheets, and Drawings all have revision history. This is especially important when working with data. Sharing data with other students and teachers presents the possibility of someone in the group making an error that will affect the rest of the dataset. Revision history can alleviate the possibility that a member of the group will make a grievous and permanent error. For example, if a group of students is working on a science fair project, and they are collecting large amounts of data, then that data need to be accurate and secure. Each time an entry is made into a spreadsheet, it is saved along with the time and a note on what was revised. At any point in the project, the students can go back in time and see a previous version of the data to find and correct the errors. For a step-by-step process about how to see the revision history, look in Chapter 4.

Importance of Data and Technology

In the new world economy and because of the college- and career-readiness standards, students will be expected to work with data to help them make decisions and infer possible solutions to problems that they face. Data-driven decision making is an important skill to acquire. It helps students rely on statistics and data to make informed choices. Much like educators must take data into consideration to make decisions about learning and student growth, students need this skill for college and career. Using technology such as Google Sheets can help students and teachers make sense of data and learn how tweaking certain aspects can change the outcomes. Google Sheets is a tool that can quickly generate models for sound decision making. According to the Common Core State Standards, "Technology plays an important role in statistics and probability by making it possible to generate plots, regression functions, and correlation coefficients, and to simulate many possible outcomes in a short amount of time." Tools like this should be used in every class to analyze, predict, and share data that can help mold the understanding of the subject.

Many ideas in mathematics, science, history, and almost every subject taught in school can be explained by observing data and using the data to tell why the event is true. For example, the Common Core State Standards for Mathematics starting in middle school directs students to start to make sense of data and its role in decision making. Consider Table 6.2 for a sixth-grade Statistics and Probability standard.

After the data are collected, students can have rich discussions about the variance and recognize clusters of data points by analyzing the data. Going further the students can make a chart explaining their findings and describing the distribution of the curve. Learn how to make charts from simple datasets later in this chapter.

Table 6.2 Mathematics Standard Statistics and Probability Sixth Grade

Understand that a set of data collected to answer a statistical question has a distribution, which can be described by its center, spread, and overall shape.

Collecting Data: Heights of Students

The teacher will

1. Create a Google Sheet in advance, naming a column: Height in Centimeters

2. Share the spreadsheet with the class via Google Classroom (Sharing via Google Classroom will automatically make a copy for each student giving them rights to edit the spreadsheet.)

3. Instruct students to make a copy of the spreadsheet, taking ownership and renaming the file, or do this automatically when making an assignment in Google Classroom

4. Assign the students a cell number to enter their data

5. Instruct students to take measurements of group members and place their heights in centimeters into the appropriate cell

Download As

Download as is a common command in the G Suite. It lets the user download the file being created as a format other than the G Suite format. The G Suite programs (Docs, Slides, Sheets, and Drawings) have this feature. The only difference among the programs is what type of file is available for downloading. For example, in Google Sheets, only some of the compatible spreadsheet file types are supported. If a teacher were making a Google Sheet that he or she wanted to share with another person that did not use the G Suite, the teacher may **download as** any of the available formats to share with them through an email attachment or other storage device. Being able to **download as** these file formats makes G Suite easy to share with others that do not use Google as their primary document-creating software. Download as PDF is an important feature because sometimes users need to share data without the fear of the data being changed. Downloading a Google Sheet as a PDF creates a file that is difficult to edit. Expensive software is required to tamper with the data. See the list below for available **download as** formats for Google Sheets.

Microsoft Excel (.xlsx)

Comma-separated values (.csv)

Webpage (.html, zipped)

OpenOffice (.opd)

PDF document (.pdf)

Publish to the Web

Publish your spreadsheets to the web as shown in Chapter 4 of the Google Docs section. It may be necessary for the data you collect to be published to a website. This would be great for data collection involving charts and graphs that may change over time. For example, Westside High School has published our school newspaper to an online version using blogger.com (tribaltribune.net). Students often collect data for interesting stories for the publication such as lunch menu likes or dislikes. The data are collected each day by a Google Form that automatically updates a Google Sheet. Each time the form is filled out, the sheet updates, causing a chart to change with the new data. The result is a constantly changing graph that updates automatically to the website.

Email as Attachment

The email as attachment feature enables the user to choose the file type directly from the email as attachment window. In other office software, the user must do the lengthy process of downloading the file to the hard drive, remembering in which folder it was saved, opening an email application, drafting the email, and attaching the document to the email. These steps are cumbersome and time consuming. Within any of the office apps in G Suite, click **File,** then **Email as attachment** to instantly send the file to a recipient. The user can even choose what file type of attachment to send by clicking the drop-down menu denoted by the arrow in Figure 6.4. Notice in Figure 6.4 that any of the Google Suite formats are not listed as a file type in which to email; this is because Google uses a different approach to distributing files, called sharing. Sharing allows the user of G Suite to send an invite to another's email to edit, comment, or view a particular file in the G Suite. There is no need to email as an attachment a G Suite file because the files may be shared. To refresh yourself on how to share files, review previous chapters.

Figure 6.4 Email as Attachment

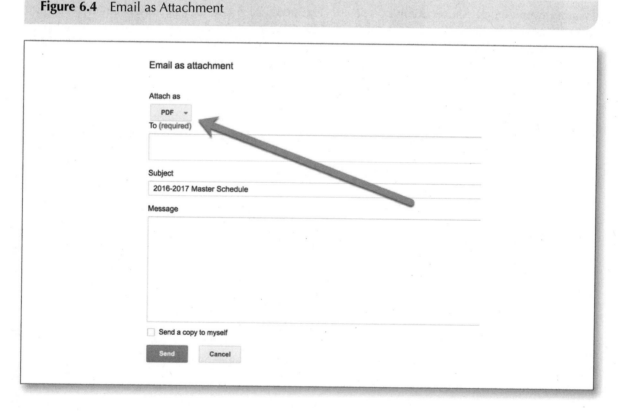

Email Collaborators

In the **File** menu, the command **Email collaborators** will send an email to the appropriate team members that are currently assigned to collaborate on the document. This feature works in all G Suite programs. Figure 6.5 will show you the email template and allow you to choose the collaborators to communicate with. The title of the Google Sheet will become the subject line of the email, as shown in Figure 6.5.

Figure 6.5 Email Collaborators

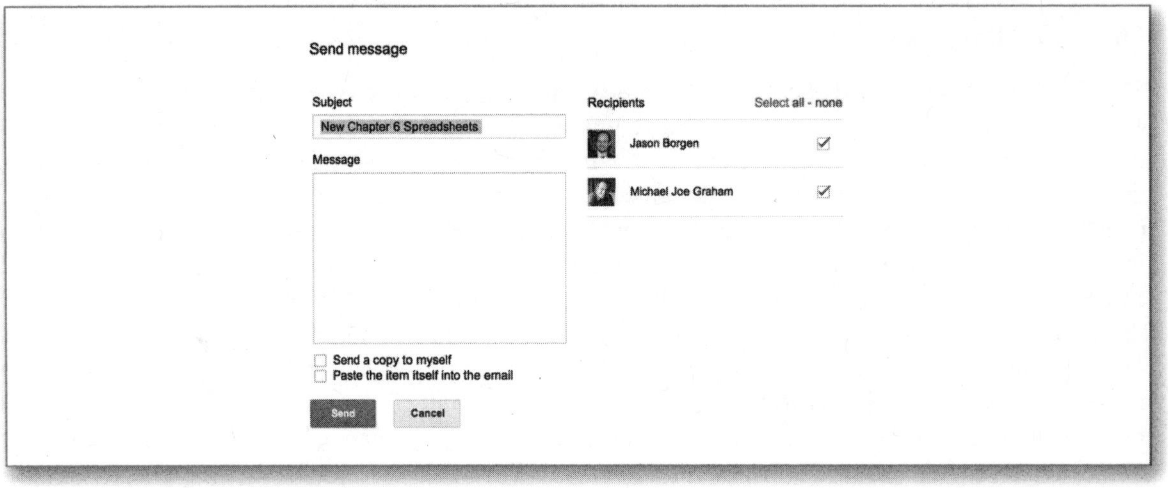

Print

Printing from Google Sheets involves a slightly different procedure than printing from other G Suite programs. Google Sheets has different print settings. For example, the user can have multiple sheets open in one spreadsheet document and print only from the selected one. Also, there are options for printing gridlines, landscape, portrait, and so on. See Figure 6.6 for detailed printing information.

Figure 6.6 Print Settings

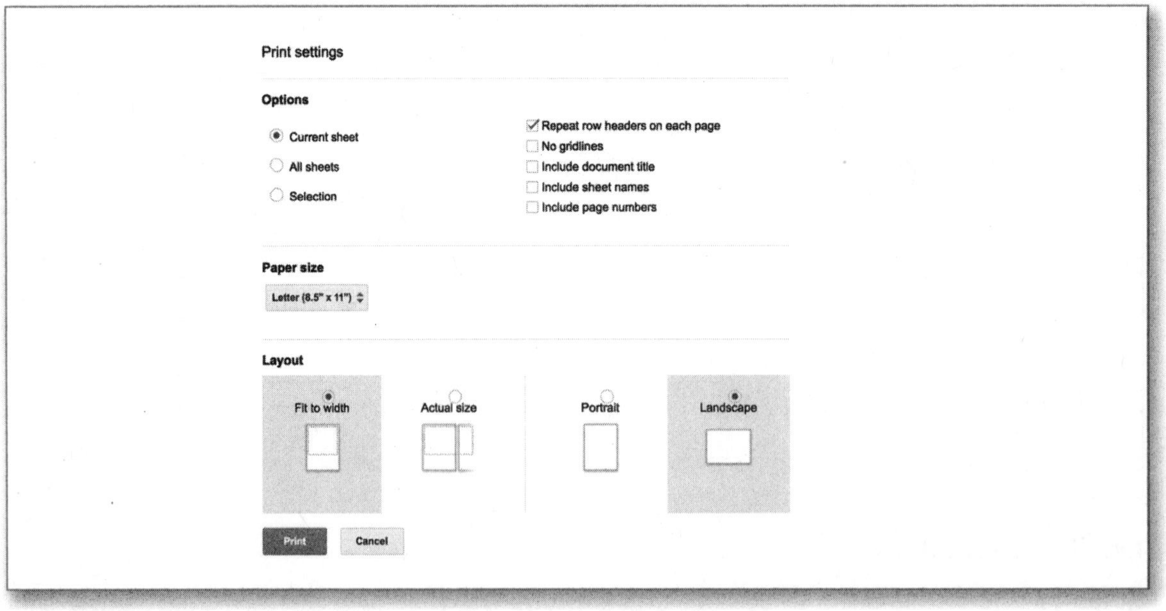

EDIT MENU

Edit buttons are available such as copy, paste, undo, and redo. Chapter 4, "Google Documents," covers these in detail. This chapter will cover the Google Sheets-specific edit commands.

List View and Mobile Devices.

List view is also the default view when editing a Google Spreadsheet on mobile devices. This is useful for students who need to collect data on the go. For example, a fifth-grade class studying data collection and measurement has an assignment that requires them to make 1-square-meter sampling grids on the school's lawn to collect data about plants found there. Students are able to use spreadsheets to collect their data while outside (as long as the Wi-Fi signal is present) on a mobile device such as an iPod Touch, iPad, or Android tablet. Follow these steps to use this lesson idea:

Lesson in Focus

What Grows Where We Play

The teacher will

1. Prepare the spreadsheet ahead of time, making headings for the columns of plants that they may encounter in their class's square

2. Instruct the students to log in to their G Suite account on the mobile device and make a copy of the spreadsheet

Students will

1. Log in to their G Suite account on their mobile device

2. Make a copy of the spreadsheet and rename it or the teacher will share it via Google Classroom

3. Collect data about the plants found in their sampling square

Paste Special

Copying and pasting from cells in a spreadsheet will copy everything in the cell, including text, color, and formulas. Sometimes teachers and students need to copy and paste only particular attributes of cells in a spreadsheet. For example, a student may want to replicate only the cell's background color. To paste special, follow these steps:

1. Copy the cell that has a special attribute you want to replicate.

2. Select **Paste special** from the **Edit** menu in the toolbar.

3. Choose the **Paste special** command from the list in Figure 6.7 and Table 6.3.

Figure 6.7 Paste Special

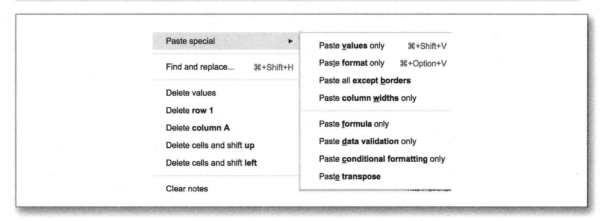

Table 6.3 Paste Special Explanation

Paste values only	*This option only pastes the text within the cell.*
Paste **format** only	Paste **format** will leave all text and formulas out of the cell. Use this option to paste formatting options like center, left and right justified, as well as bold, italic, underline, color of cell, and borders.
Paste all **except borders**	This option will not paste the borders. It will leave formulas, cell formats, and text in the cell.
Paste **formula** only	This option will only paste formulas and will not paste the outcomes of the formulas.
Paste **data validation** only	Only paste **data validation**. Look for the **Data** section for more on **data validation**.
Paste **conditional formatting** only	Only paste **conditional formatting**. Look at the conditional formatting section for more information.
Paste **transpose**	This option will transpose data from a column to a row and/or the opposite. This will allow the user to interchange columns and rows without typing the data again. This is a great way for students to experiment with dependent and independent variables. For example, in a middle school math class, speed vs. time is an important concept in which data are collected and graphed. If a student mixes up the dependent variable speed with the independent variable time, then the student can paste transpose the data to change the graph and interchange the *x* and *y* variables.

Delete Rows and Columns

To delete a row or column, highlight the row or column to delete, select **Edit,** then select **Delete row or column**.

VIEW MENU

The **View** menu helps the user control aspects of the spreadsheet, making it easy to navigate. Choose from show gridlines, formula, and toggle between compact and full-screen views. Read the following section for ways to improve the user experience.

Middle Grades Data Collection

Collecting data using spreadsheets can be a great activity for middle school students. The Common Core State Standards focus in Grades 4–8 on the collection and representation of data on line plots and bar graph and on collecting data with the use of a measurement device. Starting in the sixth grade, students will be asked to "develop understanding of statistical variability" and "summarize and describe distributions." The progression for sixth graders is to analyze the data that they learned to collect in K–5, while grappling with measures of center and how different datasets can have different distributions. This leads to students using data to answer a statistical question. For an example highlighted in the Common Core State Standards, the question "How old am I?" is not a statistical question because the students are not asked about variability of the population. If the question is, "How old are the students in my school?" then students must mathematically reason that some are older and some are younger. This reasoning helps students understand statistics because they are "anticipating the variability" of the ages of the students based on the collected sample. Using spreadsheets to collect and analyze data in the middle grades will help students become familiar with entering data into cells and help them learn how to draw inference from it. Starting in third grade, students will be asked to draw a bar graph representing data that they have collected. Using Google Sheets can help students represent data with tools as mentioned in the Mathematical Practice Standard 5. It will be good practice to have a mix of bar graphs drawn by hand and made with programs like Google Sheets. The good thing about using Google Sheets is that the students will be able to correct errors or change their data and see the bar graph change as a result without having to draw it again. For example, a student in the fourth grade is measuring insects collected on a recent science activity and makes a spreadsheet. Students can use Google Sheets for data collection for data that are easily saved into their Google Drive, and they can use the data to draw their bar graphs and line plots by hand or place the data into charts (see Table 6.4).

Table 6.4 Represent and Interpret Data Sixth Grade

Make a line plot to display a dataset of measurements in fractions of a unit (1/2, 1/4, 1/8). Use operations on fractions for this grade to solve problems involving information presented in line plots. *For example, given different measurements of liquid in identical beakers, find the amount of liquid each beaker would contain if the total amount in all the beakers were redistributed equally.*

Freeze Rows/Freeze Columns

Users can freeze columns and rows while sorting in the spreadsheet. Freezing a column or row will hold some of the data in place as the user scrolls down the page. For example, headings in a spreadsheet that contains hundreds of rows could be held in place, making it easier for users to input information into the correct column. Select **Freeze** from the **View** menu.

Protected Ranges

To protect ranges from being edited or manipulated by editors, choose a range of columns and/or rows by highlighting them. Click **View**, then **Protected ranges** to prevent editing.

INSERT MENU

Choose **Insert** to place a **row**, **column**, a **new sheet**, **comments**, or **notes** about particular cells into a spreadsheet. Comments are an important part of the G Suite. They can be used by collaborating groups to make notes or suggestions to other people managing the spreadsheet and can be used by teachers to give feedback for grading. Teachers that take advantage of comments when giving feedback for grading will decrease the amount of papers to take home. For example, teachers can make comments grading certain aspects of the Google Sheet from anywhere there is an Internet connection. Open the shared spreadsheet, and begin giving feedback and record the score in the grade book. If your school does not have an electronic grade-book application, create your own in spreadsheets. Using Google Sheets as grade-book software provides powerful sharing capabilities. Parents and teachers can stay in constant contact concerning the students' progress through shared spreadsheets. Domain administrators may benefit from giving parents the school's G Suite for Education accounts so teachers, students, and parents can collaborate on students' progress.

Function

Functions allow for the user to perform calculations of the data in a selected cell or block of cells. For example, if a teacher were using Google Sheets as a grade book and wanted to quickly find the average of a particular set of grades, then the teacher could highlight the cells and choose the function called AVE. Another example for the use of functions is performing fast calculations of data that will allow the student to quickly adjust their ideas based on new or updated information. To calculate the datasets, follow these steps:

1. Highlight the block of cells in the sheet in which to perform a function.

2. Select **Insert,** then one of the functions listed in Figure 6.8.

Figure 6.8   Function List

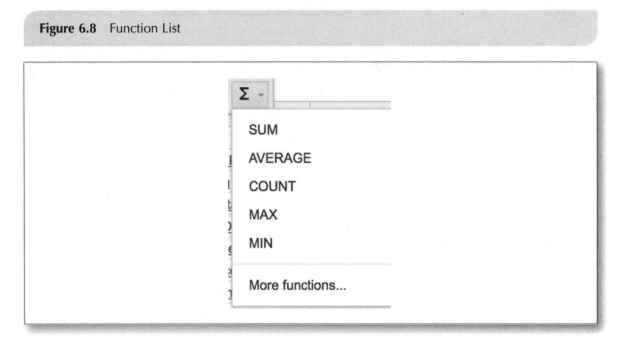

a. Sum, Average, Count, Max, and Min are listed in the **Insert** drop-down menu. However, this is not near the end of the function list. Click on **More . . .** as seen in Figure 6.9 to see descriptions of the hundreds of functions available.

An alternative way to insert functions is to place an equals sign in the cell followed by the first few letters of the function's name as shown in Figure 6.9

Figure 6.9   Inserting a Function Directly in a Cell

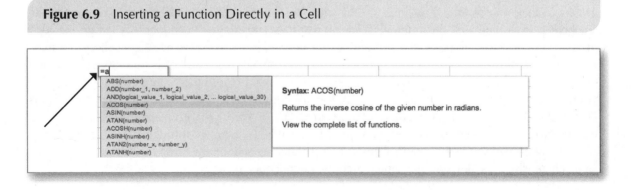

Chart

Inserting charts is one of the most used parts of any spreadsheet program. Taking the data and displaying them graphically can help the students and their audiences conceptualize the data. The Common Core State Standards have a lot to say about data representations. For example, according to the Standards for Mathematical Practice 5 concerning modeling and data, "When making mathematical models, they know that technology can enable them to visualize the results of varying assumptions, explore consequences, and compare predictions with data." Teaching students how to use spreadsheets can help them organize and model their datasets.

To insert a chart, there must be data in the spreadsheet. To create charts, follow these steps:

1. Collect data to display in a chart in a Google Sheet (example data found in Resource 6.2). Lesson plan Paper Airplane Throw #STEM.

2. Highlight the data to be displayed in a chart.

3. Select **Chart** from the **Inset** menu to reveal Figure 6.10.

4. Click on the recommended charts Google provides based on the type of data, or click the **Charts** tab to reveal more types of charts.

   a. Sheets automatically recognizes the data in the sheet and gives the user suggestions for what type of chart may be most appropriate for the data.

5. Click the **Customize** tab to give the chart a title, name the *x* and *y* axes, and changes color options.

The box in Figure 6.10 displays the chart preview. The editor will automatically select all cells that contain data and make a preview of the graph. There are currently 26 chart types, but more are added periodically. Chart types range from bar graphs to maps. If cities or addresses are in the spreadsheet, they can be mapped along with the data accompanying them in the adjacent cell. For example, a middle school class studying weather in science can understand the tendency of temperatures to be cooler in the northern latitudes. Students can create these datasets and make the graph themselves, and overlay that into a map directly in Google Sheets. The student now has an interactive map that contains data about temperature. This map could be exported as a picture file or be embedded live in a website. When embedded, the information is updated or added to the graph or map and will change accordingly. See an example of this interactive map in Resource 6.3.

Figure 6.10 Insert a Chart

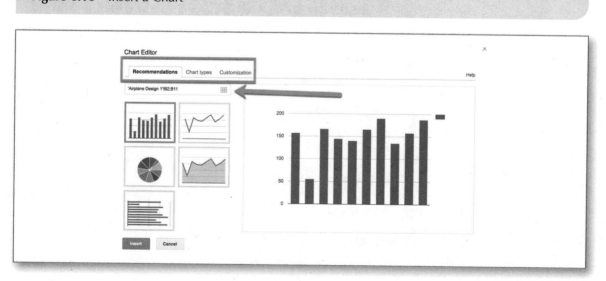

The box in Figure 6.10 draws attention to the chart types and recommendations. When using charts, Google Sheets will automatically create a chart type based on the type of data collected. It will make a fairly reliable guess about how the data should be displayed in the chart. The recommended charts appear as default. To change the chart type, click on the other types listed. For more types, click on **Chart types** as shown in the box. Click **Customization** to edit the chart title, *x* and *y* axes, and color of the lines or bars. It is important for students to label each of the parts of the chart to make it clear to the reader.

When the chart is finished, it is inserted on the sheet containing the data it was made from. After the chart is inserted, it can be manipulated further by right-clicking on the chart and choosing the options shown in Figure 6.12

Figure 6.11   The Inserted Chart

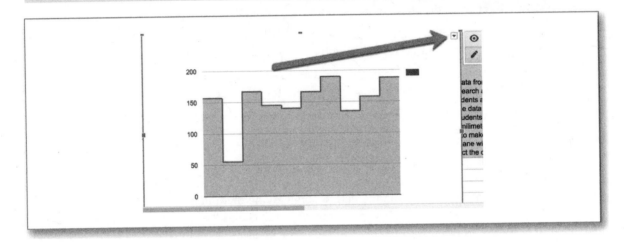

Figure 6.12   Chart Options

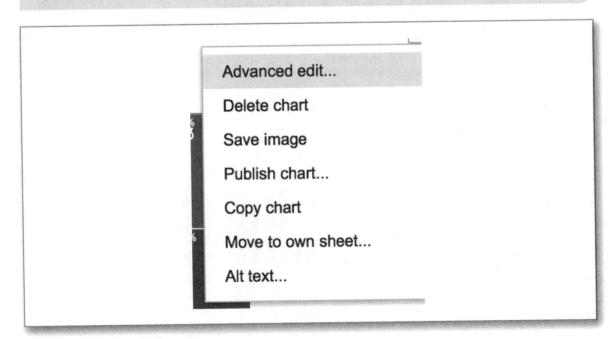

The arrow in Figure 6.11 points to a drop-down menu that is accessed by clicking anywhere on the chart. This will reveal options shown in Figure 6.12. The commands in the drop-down list in Figure 6.12 are common and need little explanation, except **Publish chart.** Publishing a chart is a great way to share the information collected by the students.

Figure 6.13 gives the option to publish the chart as an interactive chart or an image. Interactive charts will change depending on the data entered in the spreadsheet in which it is attached, and the user can hover over data points and see more information. Embed code looks complicated, but all the user has to do is copy and paste it into a webpage's HTML box. Users may choose to publish an interactive version of the chart. This option will automatically update when new data are placed in the corresponding spreadsheet. Also, users may choose to publish the chart as an image as shown in Figure 6.13. That image may be inserted into Google Slides and Google Docs, but this option will not automatically update.

Figure 6.13 Publishing a Chart

Users may also insert images, links, Google Forms, or Google Drawings into their spreadsheets.

Forms

Insert a Google Form directly into the spreadsheet to ask students questions about their data for later assessment. In the example we have provided, the Form asks students to write an explanation of how their design changes affected their distance for each new paper airplane. The Form responses are automatically added to the Form in a new sheet. The responses are conveniently placed in the same spreadsheet so they are easily graded. See Figure 6.14 to find the responses location.

Figure 6.14 Responses Location

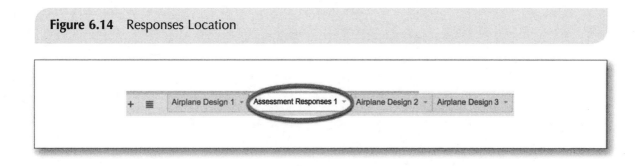

Drawings

Google Drawings may be inserted into a spreadsheet. Drawings can be used to create flowcharts and other graphic organizers to help explain the data on the spreadsheet. Drawings are virtually unlimited in their creative capacity. Encourage students to draw or create graphical representations of the data that are not part of ready-made charts. Students can benefit from expressing the data in their own creative ways.

Consider this excerpt from the Common Core State Standards: "When reading scientific and technical texts, students need to be able to gain knowledge from challenging texts that often make extensive use of elaborate diagrams and data to convey information and illustrate concepts." Use spreadsheets in conjunction with Drawings to create and share data collection information in creative ways.

FORMAT MENU

The Format tab in Google Sheets has many of the same commands as the other G Suite programs. The exceptions are **Number, Conditional formatting, Alternating colors**, and **Clear formatting.** Number relates to how the numbers are displayed in the cells. Look at the box in Figure 6.15 to see the different ways numbers can be recorded in cells. For example, users can choose to have their data be reported in scientific notation using options in the number command. Upon typing in 93,000,000 miles (the distance from Earth to the Sun), the cell would automatically display $9.3E + 7$ if the number command were invoked. Look at the eighth-grade standard in Table 6.5 to gain insight about scientific notation and technology.

Figure 6.15   Displaying Numbers

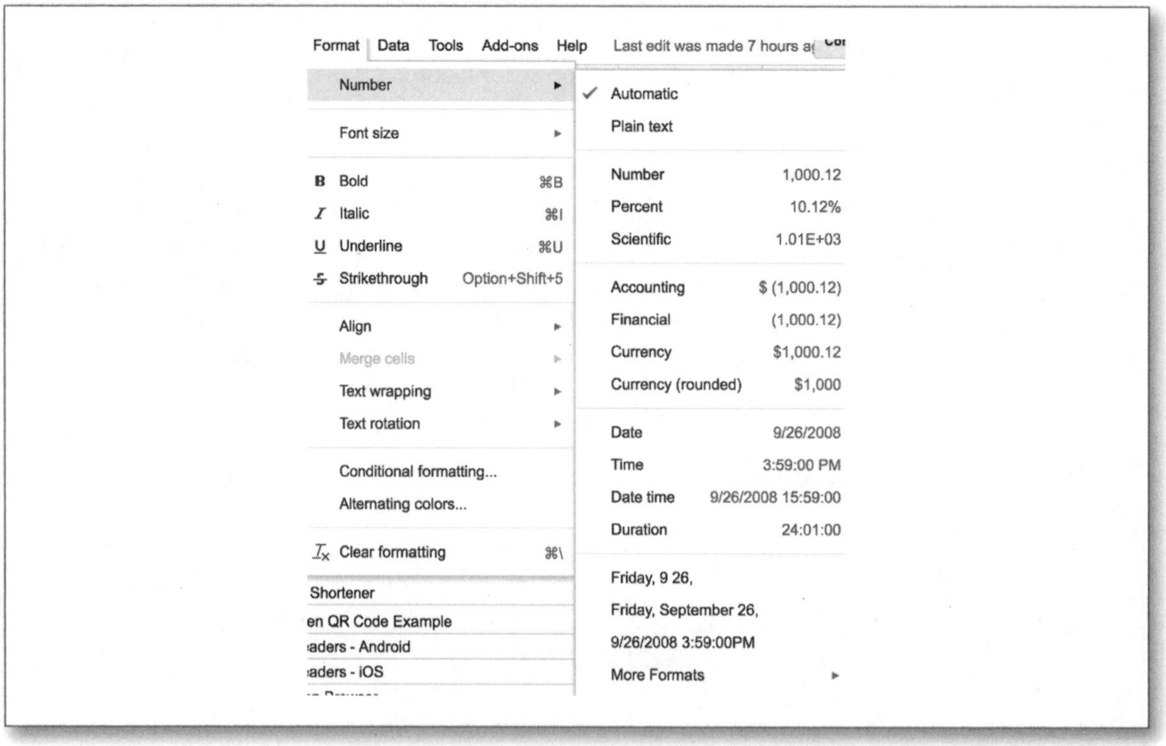

Pay close attention to the last sentence in Table 6.5 about scientific notation that is generated with technology. Students in the digital age will be increasingly reliant on computer technology to display and help interpret data. Students must realize that writing scientific notation with the "E" representing the phrase "times ten to the" is equivalent to the written form of 9.3×10^7. Google Sheets uses the form $9.3E + 7$ to report scientific notation.

Table 6.5 Common Core State Standard: Expressions and Equations Eighth Grade

Perform operations with numbers expressed in scientific notation, including problems where both decimal and scientific notation are used. Use scientific notation and choose units of appropriate size for measurements of very large or very small quantities (e.g., use millimeters per year for seafloor spreading). Interpret scientific notation that has been generated by technology.

Conditional Formatting

Conditional formatting lets the user apply background and text color rules to cells. If the cell contains a particular text or number, the cell background or text will change color among other options.

For example, a math teacher who has assigned homework to be entered into a spreadsheet can look for certain answers in the sheet by applying conditional formatting. Highlight the cells that the user wishes to check with conditional formatting and put in the parameters. Choose a background or text color to make the answers stand out. For example, a math teacher can create self-checking homework assignments by creating a spreadsheet where the students will place their answers to their homework problems. The conditional formatting will be set ahead of time for the correct answer. If the cell matches exactly as the predetermined formatting set by the teacher, the cell will turn a particular color, denoting the answer is correct. If the cell does not turn color, the answer is wrong, and the student needs to try again. Assignments like these could be used as guided practice for homework. Students are using this as a self-check only. In this example, students will be required to turn in their written work along with their shared spreadsheet.

It is important to set the master sheet made by the teacher as a view-only file in share settings; this will force the students to make a copy of the file so their answers do not appear on the master sheet. This way, students can't edit it until they make a copy and name the file accordingly. Use Google Classroom to assign this self-checking sheet to students. Teachers of other subjects can use this feature to create self-grading quizzes. To explore conditional formatting, follow these steps:

1. Select **Conditional formatting** from the **Format** menu in the toolbar to reveal Figure 6.16.

2. The **Conditional formatting** options menu will appear on the right-hand side of the screen.

3. **Apple range:** Highlight a particular range of cells that will respond to the conditional formatting commands or input the range by hand.

4. **Format cells if . . .** is a drop-down menu that will reveal the conditional formatting options shown in Figure 6.16.

Figure 6.16 Formatting Options

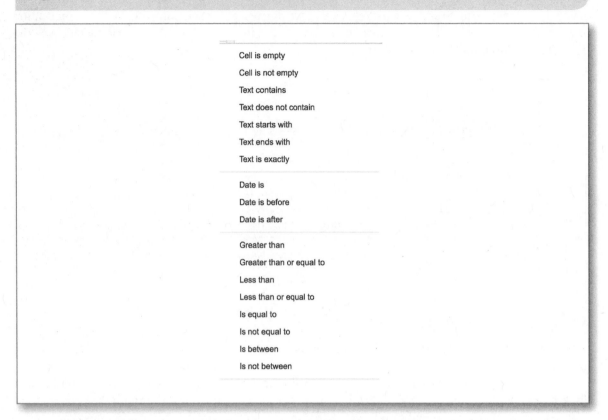

5. Choose from the options in Figure 6.17 and click **Add another rule** to conditionally format more cell ranges.

Figure 6.17 Conditional Formatting

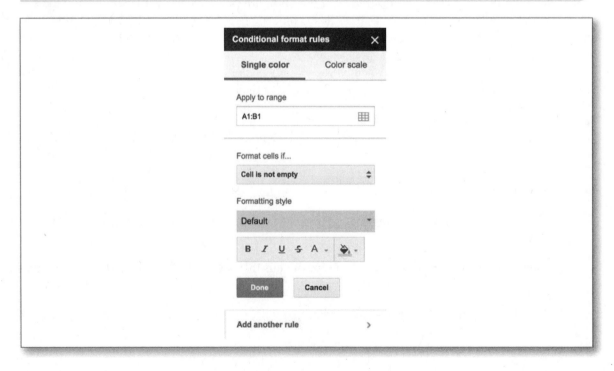

Alternating Colors

Alternating colors is an option to make any boring spreadsheet add some differentiation to the rows by automatically adding alternating colors. This is great to keep students and others organized when reading the data in the spreadsheet.

Clear Formatting

Clearing the formatting is a way to get rid of the fonts, text size, and cell background colors when copying and pasting from cells. When copying a cell from any spreadsheet program or tables on the web, all of the formatting is copied along with the text. To keep the text but remove the formatting, use the clear formatting tool from the **Format** menu. The same feature is available in Docs, Sheets, and Slides. Alternatively look for the I_x symbol in the toolbars or highlight the cell or text, then use the keyboard shortcut **Command+/** (Mac) or **CTRL+/** (PC).

DATA MENU

The **Data** menu holds commands that let the user manipulate data. Sort, Pivot tables, and data validation are discussed here. Use the **Data** menu to make sense of data.

Sort A to Z and Sort Z to A

Sorting by alphabet and reverse alphabet is available. Remember that the cells must be highlighted to sort or filter the data. To sort the data, click **Data** from the toolbar, then click **Sort** as shown in Figure 6.18.

Figure 6.18   Data Sort

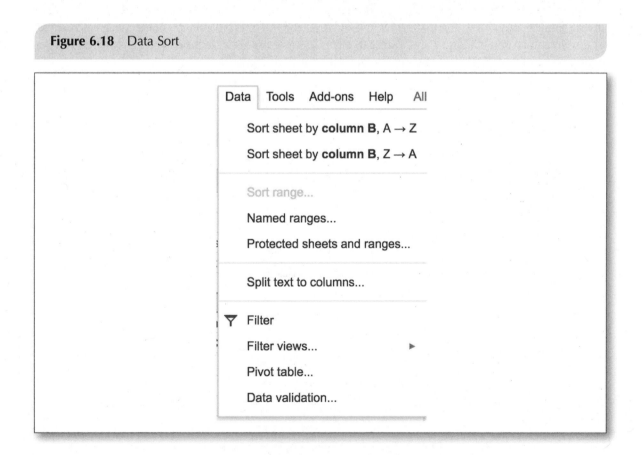

The options in Figure 6.18 not talked about in this book such as **Named ranges, Protected sheets and ranges, Filter**, and **Filter views** are complex and require more time and attention than this book will give. For more information on these options, visit http://support.google.com.

Pivot Tables

Pivot tables allow the user to pull a quick summary from a huge dataset. They are ideal for dealing with large amounts of data and picking out certain aspects to focus on. Teachers and administrators could use pivot tables to disaggregate testing data. See more about pivot tables in Resource 6.4 at http://goo.gl/A5Mqy and in the companion website.

Validation

Validation controls what data are entered into spreadsheets by the collaborators and the user. Validation can help users avoid entering text or numbers into cells that do not match the predefined criteria. Using this tool can allow for a comment to pop up when entering data, reminding the user what type of data are appropriate for the cell. For example, teachers can set validation on cells when assigning students to make spreadsheets that will not allow letters of text to be written in the cell. In this example, numbers are the only valid entry. This can give hints to students about what data type to enter and can help them feel more comfortable with spreadsheets because they will be cued on what type of validation is permitted.

TOOLS MENU

Spelling, Notification rules, and **Protect sheet** are the most used **Tools** commands by educators. Notification rules may be enabled to alert the user when changes are made to a spreadsheet. For example, in large districts, a spreadsheet for technology inventory may be maintained by the building instructional facilitators. The district technology coordinator will need to be made aware of changes to the inventory and manage users' rights to edit. Collaborative spreadsheets are a great way to keep everyone informed. Follow these steps to activate notifications:

1. Select **Notification rules** from the **Tools** menu in the toolbar to reveal Figure 6.19.

2. Choose the parameters that will notify the owner and collaborators of changes to the sheet.

Figure 6.19 Set Notification Rules

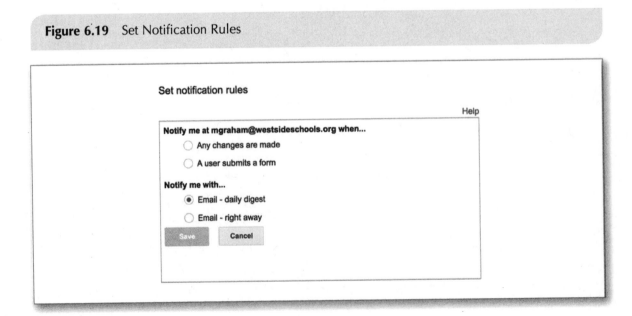

Use **Protect sheet** to determine who can edit the data (Figure 6.20). Follow these steps to protect the sheet:

1. Select **Protect sheet** from the **Tools** menu to reveal Figure 6.20.
2. Select who is allowed to edit the sheet.
3. Type email or names in the box to allow only those people to edit.
4. Click **Save** to set the rules.

Figure 6.20 Protect Sheet

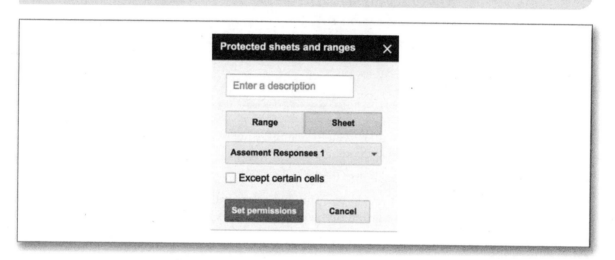

The protect sheet feature will allow you to protect from editing a range of cells or entire sheets. Use a range of protected cells to not allow users to modify important information. For example, oftentimes in data collection in math or science class, the teacher may want to give the first few cells of information to the students as an example, but may want the subsequent cells to be modified by the students as they collect data. Use protect cell ranges to achieve this level of data protection.

ADD-ONS

Add-ons were explained in Chapter 4, but we will highlight a few relevant add-ons specifically used in Google Sheets that will help teachers and students automate their spreadsheets. To insert add-ons into your spreadsheets, follow these steps:

1. Click the **Add-ons** menu located in the toolbar.

Student Excuses Thwarted By Technology

Student: "The dog ate my homework . . . right after I finished my data collection in my Google Spreadsheet, Snoopy, my dog, ate my Chromebook. Sorry teacher . . . I will get it to you tomorrow."

Teacher: "Really? I don't think so, Johnny. I see on the revision history that you started to do your work at 5:51pm, then you stopped at 5:54 pm. When I checked the revision history before I went to sleep last night, I saw that you had only worked 3 minutes. I then called your mom to check on you because I was worried that you may have fallen ill. She said that you started playing video games at 6:00 pm and reported to her that you had no homework."

Student: Utter disbelief.

2. Click **Get add-ons** to open the **Add-ons** search menu as shown in Figure 6.21.

Figure 6.21   Keyword Search

3. The box in Figure 6.21 will allow you to search by keyword for add-ons. Note that available add-ons for Docs are different than the ones for Sheets.
4. Click on the add-on and install it to the spreadsheet.
5. Click the ▆ **+ FREE** ▆ to get the add-on. This will reveal a permissions request that must be approved by the user before the add-on will operate. This is shown in Figure 6.22
6. Click **Allow** to install the add-on.
7. After the add-on is given permission, click on the **Add-ons** menu item again to reveal the installed add-ons.
8. Choose the add-on to start its feature.

Flubaroo is a popular add-on that will automatically grade a teacher-assigned Google Form. Flubaroo will ask a series of questions to get information and generate an answer key to compare student answers for grading. When completed, the add-on may send students automatically generated feedback (or more detailed personalized feedback) directly to students' email. Forward the scores to parents to keep them informed about student grades.

Figure 6.22   Add-on Permission

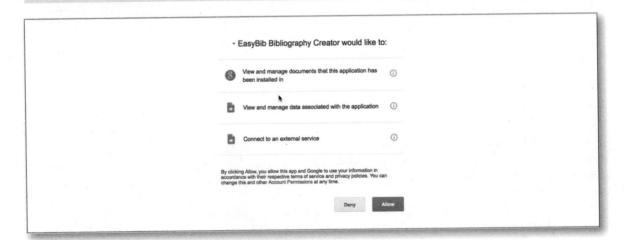

AUTO FILL

Auto fill lets the user repeat the contents of a cell and can complete a pattern in the subsequent cells highlighted. This feature uses Google Search to find patterns in the cells highlighted and will automatically fill in the cells with the pattern. For example, a teacher in fifth-grade social studies class may be studying states and their characteristics. Teachers and students can quickly make lists of common information. Follow these steps to see the magic of auto fill:

1. Type at least three similar items such as states in a column of separate cells like in Figure 6.23.

2. Highlight the text and then click the small blue square in the bottom right-hand corner while holding down **Option** for Mac and **Alt** for PC.

3. Select the cells that you would like to populate and then release the buttons.

The result is that the list is automatically populated within the cells that were highlighted. If the user does not hold down **Option** or **Alt,** the contents of the cell are repeated for the selection, and then the pattern will not appear.

Figure 6.23 Auto Fill

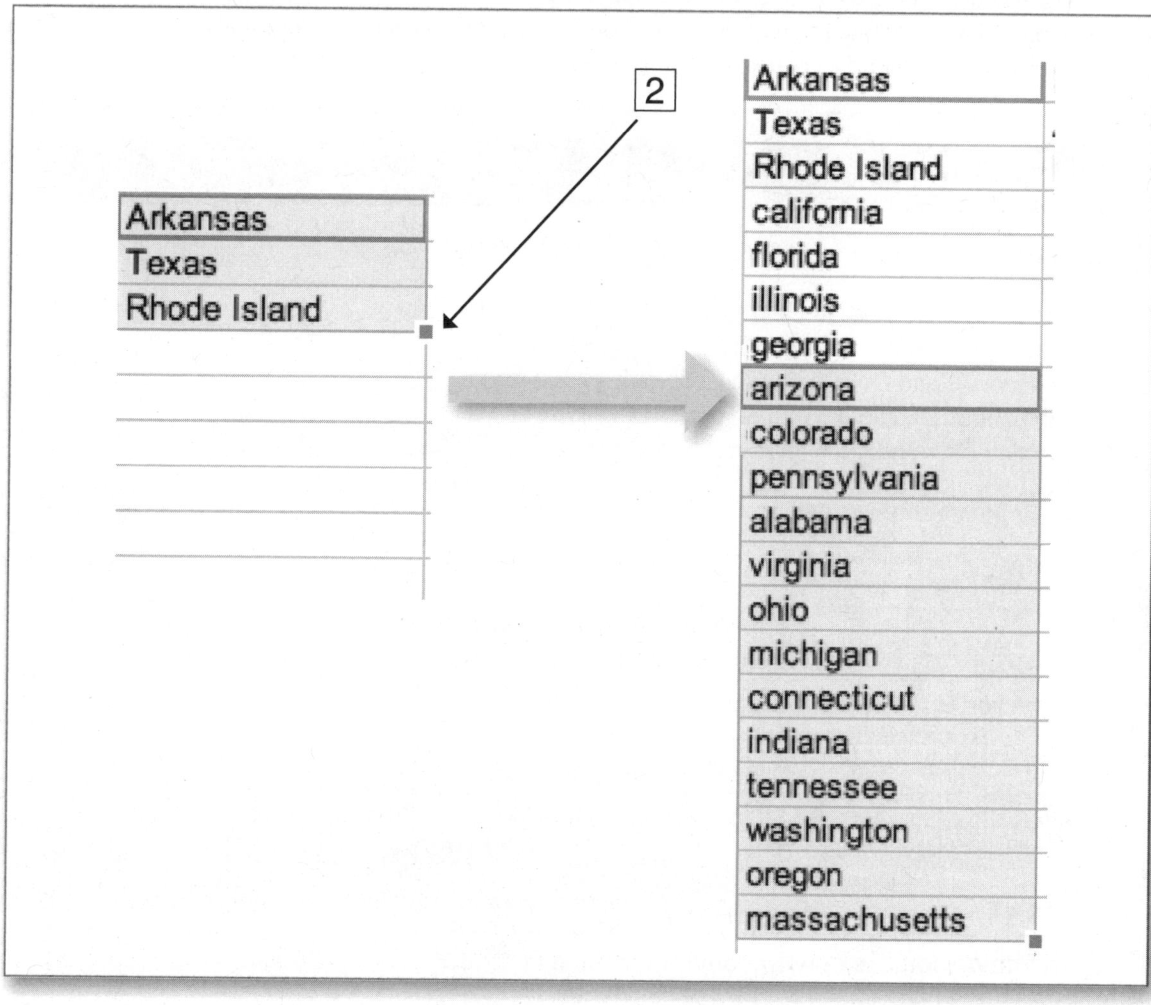

SAMR IMPLICATIONS—TRANSFORMING INSTRUCTION

Modification	Allowing students to share data and information in real time on the same spreadsheet creates options for students to access, analyze, manipulate, and discuss the data anytime/anywhere. This instructional continuity creates real and ongoing dialogue about the relevant data.
Redefinition	Consider having students create shared datasets with students all over the world to increase the relevancy of the information. This will allow students to compare and contrast their work with others in different locations and learn how cultural, geographic, and tools can affect the study.

SUMMARY

Google Sheets is the most complex program in the G Suite. It houses a powerful spreadsheet program that can rival any statistical package with user-friendly tools that people have come to expect from traditional office software. The difference is in the collaboration. Google Sheets can share and collaborate on data projects from within the room or around the world. Use tables, charts, and add-ons to publish real-time data to websites and other spreadsheets to make student findings real and authentic in purpose. The many college- and career-readiness standards push students to use appropriate tools when thinking mathematically. When students take the time to collect, analyze, and report findings with data, they become better decision makers. Google Sheets gives the student one more tool to become college and career ready. Keep reading to explore another data collection and student assessment device: Google Forms.

RESOURCES

For more information about G Suite for Education, including

- lesson plans related to chapter content,
- domain setup for tech administrators' videos,
- overviews and Google training materials,
- the authors' favorite websites, and
- testimonials and interviews of schools currently using G Suite,

access Resources from this chapter on the companion website.

Lesson Plans

Lesson Plan Title	All lesson plans and resources can be found on the companion website at: http://resources.corwin.com/googlemeetsms	
Introduction to Scientific Method Mary Fran Lynch	http://goo.gl/WtCm6	Resource 6.5
iTravel Vacation	http://goo.gl/KZul5	Resource 6.6
Collaborative Lab Experience Cheryl Davis	http://goo.gl/LzaTz	Resource 6.7

7 Google Forms

Mrs. Martinez asked students in her eighth-grade science class to log in to their Chromebooks and navigate to Google Classroom. Awaiting there was an assignment that said "Newton Quiz." Students clicked the link and were taken directly to a five-question quiz. One of the questions was, "Inertia of an object is directly related to what?" Mrs. Martinez could tell students were struggling with this free-response question. Mrs. Martinez was able to look at Google Classroom to see who completed the quiz in real time. Students were able to receive their results and knew questions they got wrong immediately. Mrs. Martinez spent about 25 minutes building the quiz, setting the answer key, and posting to Google Classroom. Google Forms provides streamlined formative assessment, allowing Mrs. Martinez to give students immediate feedback.

Google Forms is a G Suite app that can deliver data for decision making. This tool is ideal for gathering data from students and the community, as well as delivering online assessments to students. To collect data using Google Forms, share the form's (questionnaire's) unique URL in Google Classroom on a handout, email, embedded in a website, on Learning Management System (LMS), or on social media. The data collected from Google Forms goes directly into a Google Sheet, where it can be analyzed, organized, and displayed in charts. There are two main parts to a form: the front-end (what you send to students/respondents) and the back-end (the area in which the data are stored that is only available to the form creator). You can choose from many themes to create a professional-looking front-end form with nine question types:

Text

Paragraph Text

Choose From a List

Checkboxes

Multiple Choice

Scale

Grid

Date

Time

In this chapter, we will discuss Google Forms and its ability to gather information efficiently. The information collected can be anything that the user needs to know. For example, you might use forms for the following purposes:

- Self-grading student quiz
- Student survey for use in data collection
- Beginning of the year student information form
- Collect interests, phone numbers, addresses, and other information that may help the teacher
- Faculty meeting sign-in form
- Discipline form that automatically emails parents, team teacher, and principal
- Parent contact log
- Parent information collection from a beginning of the year open house or through email.
- Creating a role-playing, Choose Your Own Adventure, game

ADVANTAGES OF FORMS

Google Forms offers an easy way to connect with the public's concerns by gathering relevant data from the community. School administrators can create questionnaires and surveys to obtain information about the community to inform decisions made by school officials. For example, many schools send home a parent survey to gather information from the parents about certain aspects of school life. A Google Form could be created and posted on the school's website, Facebook page, Twitter feed, and other communication channels. Posting these forms on public virtual spaces allows for easy data gathering. If the parents do not have access to a computer, provide it at school or suggest that they access the Google Form from their mobile device or direct them to the local public library. Alternatively, at public events such as fine arts performances or sporting events, students or a group of volunteer parents and/or teachers could man a table with laptops or tablets. The workers would cue up the Form's link on the device, hand it to the patron, and gather information from the community.

Teachers also need to gather data, but in different ways. Educators in the classroom are bombarded with collecting data concerning student performance. For example, teachers are responsible for managing parent contact logs, students' grades, and teacher documentation about discipline and good behavior. This information can be emailed directly to the parents and shared with other teachers. The data collected in Google Forms give teachers and parents powerful insight about how their student is performing. Start by focusing on struggling students. Create forms that can track concerns raised by parents, teachers, and other school professionals, and share the information with other teachers on the team to craft a better educational experience for the child.

Technology-Infused Teaching Tip

For advanced users, research Google Forms Add-ons to find out how to automatically email the parent the information gathered by the teacher. Every time the form is submitted, the program will automatically email parents or anyone who might find the information useful from the user's school Gmail.

Managing Forms

Every Google Form is given a unique URL. When the URL is typed into any web browser, the live form is ready to be taken. Save the URL as a bookmark or a favorite in your web browser to get access to forms that are frequently used. Another option is to create a desktop icon linked to the form that automatically opens the form when clicked. For example, at my school, teachers have icons on their computers, smartphones, or tablets that are linked to the discipline referral Google Form. Another example is Mrs. Casey Kocher, a special education teacher. She uses Forms to track her students' progress. She has eight special education students that she teaches all day. She is very busy throughout the day with her teaching duties, and she wants to collect data on her students' progress on certain skills. She has created a personalized Google Form for each of her students so she can track their progress daily. Instead of filling out the form on a laptop or desktop computer, she uses her iPhone. She has made a folder on her home screen that contains an app icon with the students' names that, when tapped, opens the particular student's form using the web browser on the iPhone. She is able to quickly collect students' progress with the mobile smartphone because all Google Forms can be taken anywhere there is an Internet connection. Android phones have the same shortcut feature. The data are automatically populating a Google Sheet, where they are kept safe and ready for review.

Use Form Data in PLCs

Monitoring students' progress and collecting data with Google Forms is ideal for professional learning community (PLC) meetings. PLCs need this information to accurately assess problems and successes students are facing. Use the time to accurately discuss student's strengths and weaknesses and to formulate a path for success with other teachers on the team. A PLC without data is less effective. Use data from forms like in the example of Mrs. Kocher to talk about the student objectively, based on the data, and to make better decisions to improve the child's educational experience.

Students and Forms

The Common Core State Standards provided in Table 7.1 and Table 7.2 are good examples of why forms are important to get students college and career ready. According to the standards, students will "present information, findings and supporting evidence." They can authentically gather real information from peers, parents, and the community using Google Forms and use that information to make decisions and form conclusions about a given topic.

Gathering the information about real events and attitudes and presenting it, making "strategic use of digital media and visual displays of data," is vital for college and a career. For example, eighth-grade student Mark is working on a joint research project for English and mathematics classes. Mark wants to research school safety. In addition to using appropriate print and digital sources such as primary sources of informational text, Mark needs information from his peers and teachers to compare with his research. He wants to investigate how local attitudes of school safety compare with the nation as a whole. Mark should use Google Forms to create an attitudes survey to collect real data from his school community. After the information is collected, Mark can draw inferences with his knowledge of statistics and spreadsheets learned in mathematics class. This is done without printing one sheet of paper or counting tally marks of responses from paper forms. After the form was created, Mark emailed his participant sample the link to the form. After the participants took the survey, all of the responses were collected in the attached spreadsheet. Giving students assignments that use technology will prepare them for life after high school.

College and career professionals are asked to perform analyses like this in their work or place of higher learning. Society asks these skills of the citizen. For example, choosing political candidates to support requires analysis of primary sources and the ability to make sense of peers' opinions to help form their own. The technology in G Suite for Education connects information and people in a way that allows for deeper understanding of what is learned. That is one of the most important challenges the Common Core State Standards pose to educators. Teachers must have the courage to slow down, delve deeper into understanding, and explore concepts thoroughly.

Table 7.1 displays two Anchor Standards for Speaking and Listening.

Table 7.1 Presentation of Knowledge and Ideas Anchor Standards 4 and 5

4. Present information, findings, and supporting evidence such that listeners can follow the line of reasoning and the organization, development, and style are appropriate to task, purpose, and audience.
5. Make strategic use of digital media and visual displays of data to express information and enhance understanding of presentations.

In addition to the Anchor Standards in Table 7.1, consider Table 7.2 standards for middle school writing in Ryan's scenario. To become college and career ready as defined by the Common Core State Standards, Ryan will need to focus on data gained from others to aid in making assertions in writing. In addition, data management that he will learn through the use of Google Forms and Google Sheets can help him with his writing. Citing relevant data in writing only improves the work. The standards push students to take lessons from all disciplines in the completion of a project. The standard in Table 7.2 will also be tackled in mathematics, science, as well as English language arts. Seek out ways to bring in other disciplines when planning projects.

Table 7.2 Middle School Writing Standard

W.7.8, W.8.8, and WHST.6-8.8
Gather relevant information from multiple print and digital sources, using search terms effectively; assess the credibility and accuracy of each source; and quote or paraphrase the data and conclusions of others while avoiding plagiarism and following a standard format for citation.

CREATING A GOOGLE FORM

The previous sections contained some ideas about how to start thinking about forms and how they could be used with students, faculty, and the community. The next sections are devoted to learning the processes to create forms and distribute them. To create a Google Form, follow these steps after opening Google Drive:

1. Click the **New** button to reveal the list of Google Docs.

2. Click **More.**

3. Choose **Google Forms** as shown in Figure 7.1.

Figure 7.1 Create a Google Form

EDITING A GOOGLE FORM

Start creating questions immediately using the steps in the following section. This is where the user can create the form and customize it to meet the needs of the project.

To edit a Google Form, follow these steps:

1. Title the form by clicking on **Untitled form** like in the box in Figure 7.2. Underneath the title box, include any directions or help statements that will guide users to provide relevant information.

2. Type a question into the **Untitled Question** box.

3. Select an appropriate **Question type** from the drop-down menu. (*Note:* you can add images as answer choices for multiple choice and checkbox answers.)

4. Click **Required** to force the user to answer the question. When this is checked, the user will not be able to submit his or her answers to be collected if he or she has not marked an answer.

5. Click **Done** to finalize the question.

6. Click the **+ icon** to add another question or you can add text, images, videos, and/or page breaks depending upon your need (e.g., you may want students to watch a video about Abraham Lincoln prior to answering the next question).

Figure 7.2   Edit Form Window

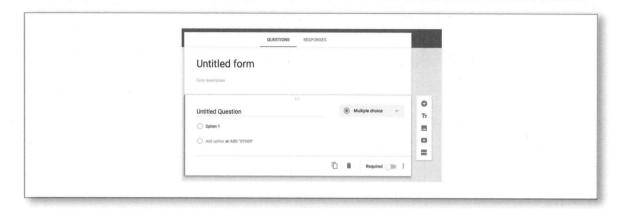

Technology-Infused Teaching Tip

Copy long lists of multiple rows of text or answers to a form question, and paste them into the first box of the possible answers. This will automatically make each line of text a possible answer to a form question. Teachers use this when converting old quizzes to Google Forms. Watch the video found at this link to see it in action in Resource 7.1 at http://goo.gl/Eoa1s.

SETTINGS

Prior to administering any form, you will want to verify and customize any specific settings including the ability to automatically collect users' email addresses, limit responses to only one response, shuffle the question order, customize the confirmation message after they complete the form, and/or enable the quiz functions. Use the gear in the top right of the form to access the three areas of the settings: General, Presentation, and Quizzes, as shown in Figure 7.3.

Figure 7.3   Settings—General

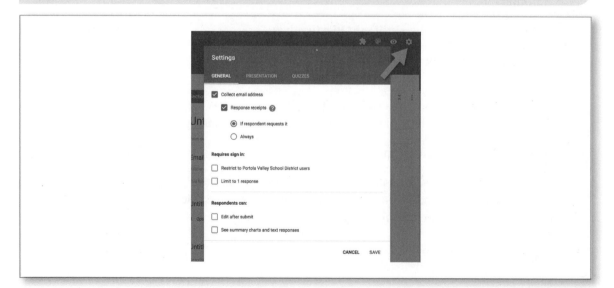

General

There may be times when you are administering a quiz and you want to be sure the student who completes it does not type someone else's name in the Name question. Or, if you are using Add-ons to send emails to the user completing the form, you can save the user time by automatically collecting their email address so they do not need to type it in. Select the checkbox for **Collect email address**. If you check the next checkbox, you can also send the user's responses an email with the data they submitted. You can also invite users to edit their results after they submitted their responses. If the **Edit after submit** checkbox is selected, users will see a link on the final confirmation page to edit their responses. They can save this link and edit at any time! For instance, middle school students can easily track their progress on assessments throughout the year on a Google Sheet. They can submit each assessment score to a Google Form you create. If they bookmark the link to edit their response, they can continue to add new scores to the form and you as a teacher will have one spreadsheet that continues to update the students' scores. This will help build student agency.

Presentation

The presentation section of settings allows you to change the display for the students. You can show a progress bar if you have multiple pages. You can shuffle the questions if you don't want students to see the same order of questions for quizzes. You can also update the confirmation page they see when they complete. For example, once students complete the form, you can give them instructions on the task you want them to complete, add links to relevant articles to read, or simply remind students to read quietly.

Quizzes

This is a fabulous feature of Forms. You can simply turn this on and allow students to view their results immediately and allow or disallow students to see correct answers. If you have constructive response questions, you have the option to wait to send grades as well. This may be beneficial if you have or administer the quiz in multiple classes so students do not share correct answers. (See Figure 7.4.) Once you turn this on, you can go back to the form, and each question will now have an answer key link. Once you click on it, you can set the point value and select the correct answer(s). You can learn more about quizzes in Forms in Resource 7.2.

Figure 7.4   Answer Key

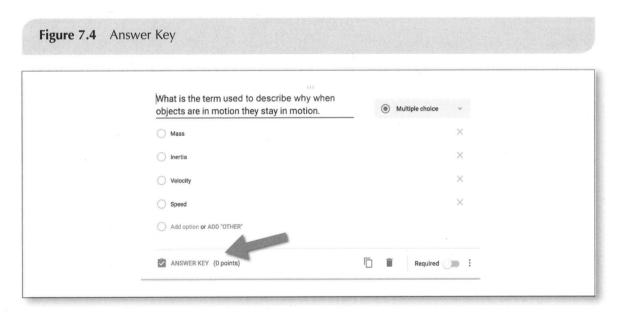

ADMINISTERING THE FORM

Once you have updated the look and feel of the form, you are ready to send the form to your respondents. There are several ways to administer the form. (See Figure 7.5.) If you are using Google Classroom, you would simply create a post and click on the **Drive** icon to share the form. If you do this as an assignment, once students click **Submit**, the assignment will automatically be marked as done for that student. If you want to administer to others or you do want to use Classroom, you can click on the **Send** button on the top of the form editor. You have the options of sending via email and accessing a link. If emailing, you can embed the form in an email by checking the box or just email your respondents a link to complete. The latter is recommended as different email clients will display the form differently, so all users would not have the same experience.

Figure 7.5   Send Form

Technology-Infused Teaching Tip

Quick-response (QR) codes work well with Google Forms. Create the form and shorten the URL with http://goo.gl. Click on **Details** after it is shortened to reveal the QR code for the link to the form. The uses are limitless with the QR code. The code is an image file that can be copied, emailed, faxed, or printed on anything. When the code is read by a smartphone or tablet, the user will be taken directly to the live form. Print the code on T-shirts, coffee mugs, or letters to parents. Get the word out with QR codes!

RESPONSES IN GOOGLE FORMS

After administering a form, you may be ready to view responses. There are several ways to review response as shown in Figure 7.6. You can view the data in the form file itself, which will display charts and graphs. You can also review each respondent's result, but probably the most useful view will be in a spreadsheet that can be created with all the data. To access the results, simply click on **Responses** in the form file. The **Responses** tab allows you to review the data and will automatically create charts and display quiz results if you enabled the quizzing functions. You can also delete data and access other options by clicking on the three vertical dots.

Figure 7.6   Responses

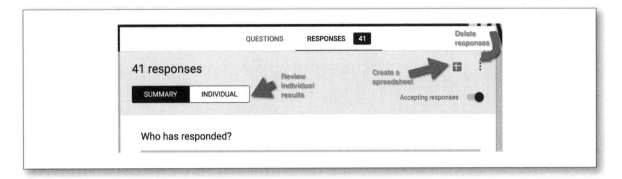

Accepting Responses

If **Accepting responses** is turned on under the **Responses** tab, then the form will allow respondents to submit data. If this is toggled off, the respondent will get a message saying that the form is no longer accepting data.

Doing More With Responses

You have the option to clear the form responses from the summary-of-response report. This is great because when teachers are giving the same test or quiz to multiple class periods, the teacher can make a copy of the accompanying spreadsheet, saving those answers as first period's, then clear the form for second period's answers. Simply click the three vertical dots on the **Responses** tab and select **Delete all responses**. (See Figure 7.7.) You also have the option of getting an email notification when forms are submitted, downloading the data, and printing the data!

Figure 7.7   Delete Responses

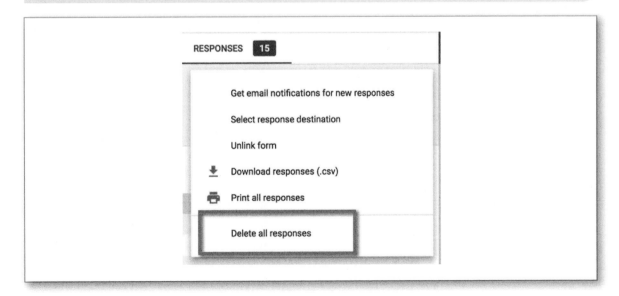

There may be times where you want to pre-fill an answer response for students if, say, you want to give them the correct answer, or you would like for them to view the answer and either correct it or verify its correctness. You can also create a study guide for students using this method! You can create a pre-filled form, add collaborators on forms, and make copies of forms by clicking on the three vertical dots on the very top of the form as seen in Figure 7.8. Alice Keeler, a Google Forms guru, discusses how to create custom pre-filled links for individual students. See more in Resource 7.3 on the companion website.

Figure 7.8 Send Command

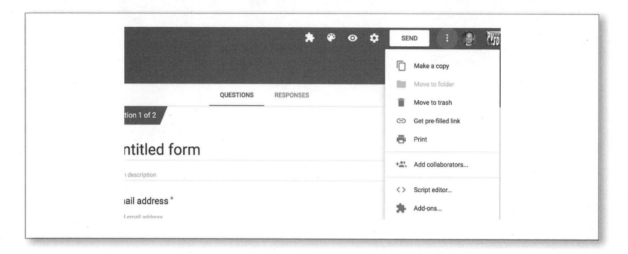

GOOGLE FORMS MENU IN GOOGLE SHEETS

If you elected to create a spreadsheet to view, access, and manipulate the data, you can always access any of the Form features within the spreadsheet directly. If a Google Sheet is connected to a form, you will see a **Form** menu (as in Figure 7.9) to be able to access many features of the form, including a link to edit the form, send the form, go to the actual form, access embed code to embed in a website, show a summary of responses that will display graphs and charts, and unlink the form to the spreadsheet if you no longer want the spreadsheet to record responses.

Figure 7.9 Responses in Sheets

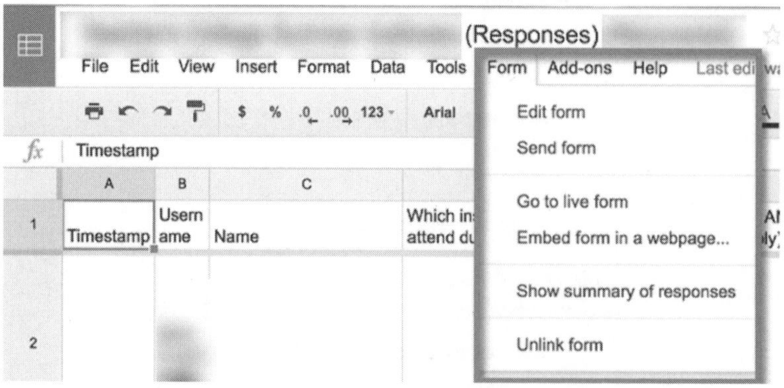

Summary of Responses

Responses from participants who completed the form are continuously being collected into the form in real time. Click **Show summary of responses** to view the responses to the form—you can even publish the summary document to share with students to engage them in data interpretation. Summary view automatically creates simple charts and graphs that describe the data in the spreadsheet. Students and teachers do not have to learn how to create charts and graphs in spreadsheets to see the data graphically. This is great for students who need immediate results without having to learn complicated spreadsheet commands. To see the data in the spreadsheet, open Google Drive and search for a spreadsheet that has the same file name as the form. Use the commands learned in Chapter 6 to create visually stunning charts. The Common Core State Standards Mathematical Practice Standard 5 calls for students to use appropriate tools wisely. Also, Anchor Standard 7 for Reading states that students should "integrate and evaluate content presented in diverse media and formats, including visually and quantitatively, as well as in words." Using forms and spreadsheets is good practice with relevant meaningful data.

USES FOR FORMS

Forms are especially useful in the day-to-day management of school information. Once the user is comfortable with the creation and deployment of Google Forms, it becomes easy to collect and sort data. Use the next section as a starting point for form creation, but remember Google Forms can collect any information you need.

Special Education

Collecting data and making them work for the teacher is one of the best strategies that special education educators can employ to identify weaknesses and find solutions. Knowing the difference between incremental changes in ability to comprehend is a great indicator of successes. Teachers have a hard time objectively knowing without measurable data. Forms could be created to include certain skill sets desired by the successful special education student. It may be hard to define goals for the students with special needs, but it is imperative to actively assess where they are and where they are going skillwise. Forms can make tracking students' progress a reality. For example, a teacher could create a form that is designed with the particular student in mind. Review individualized education plans, accommodations, and other learning goals before creating the form. Begin with the end in mind. Ask these questions when making forms for student skill data:

What benchmarks should this individual student strive for?

What is appropriate developmentally for this particular student?

What skills are coming soon in the teaching plan that will help students reach their specific goals?

Create a form that assesses this information so that it is easily discussed in meetings and that has the validity of data to back up the assertions made by the educators. An example form is located in Resource 7.4.

Parent/Student Communication Log

Regular communication with parents and students is key to a successful partnership in learning—especially in the middle school years. Sometimes you communicate with the same parents on a weekly, or even daily basis. It is always important to log these calls/emails/texts so you have a record of the conversations. You never know when a parent may come back to say, "You never did tell me that!" or, "Why didn't I know?" You probably have had many of these experiences already and have a method for logging your communication. Google Forms makes it easy and simple as it will time-stamp when you submitted the log and organize everything in a sortable spreadsheet! Use this template in Resource 7.5 at https://goo.gl/eUZsWX (click on **Form** menu and **Edit Form** to add/modify questions) or make your own.

Dean/Disciplinarian/Assistant Principal

Discipline forms are perfect for Google Forms because they reduce cost of paper, time, and clutter. Create teacher-friendly discipline forms that can expedite the process. All data are secure and are immediately incorporated into a spreadsheet for easy data analysis by the person who created the form. The spreadsheet is safe and data are secure because, unless told otherwise, Forms does not let participants see the results. Depending on the contents of the form, disciplinarians can filter or sort offenses by time, class period, teacher, and student. Use your knowledge of spreadsheets to make data color-coded for easy viewing. Take a look at Form 7.5 Lunch Detention Form on the companion website. Encourage teachers to make shortcuts to forms for discipline and other types. You can even make shortcuts on mobile devices like those that Mrs. Kocher did earlier in the chapter.

Counselor

Counselors need to be contacted by students for a variety of reasons. Counselors could create forms that are accessible by students. For example, the counselor will create a form in Google Docs, copy the link, and shorten it using http://goo.gl. Students need easy access to important forms that they are required to use. The principal or their designee should be "keeper of the forms." In this role, the keeper of the forms will create a Google document that has the links displayed under a heading for the purpose of the form. Share the document with every student, keeping it in his or her documents list. When students need a form, they are able to log in to their account, find the forms list, and fill out the form. For examples of forms, go to Resource 7.6 at http://goo.gl/8NyVq. This link provides a sample of what a Student Form Bank would look like. Feel free to take and modify the forms to make them appropriate for your school. Find the forms and more at the book's companion website, http://resources.corwin.com/googlemeetsms.

Response-to-Intervention Progress Monitoring

Monitoring student progress is an important part of a teacher's role in differentiating instruction for the individual student. Forms are an easy way to collect such data that could make a difference in the way a student is taught. For example, students identified as performing below expectations should be monitored. PLCs that meet during or after school could look at the data and help teachers make better decisions about instruction or remediation. Data should drive decision making, and Google Forms can provide a modality for collecting and sharing that data.

Tests or Quizzes

Google Forms is perfect for assessment. Ask questions pertaining to the subject in a form and wait for the responses to fill into the spreadsheet for grading. Students will be engaged while taking the quiz because of the use of technology. Teachers will be happy because the responses do not have to be printed. No more carrying home stacks of papers to grade. To grade the assessments, log on to Google Drive and grade from anywhere there is an Internet connection.

Self-grading quizzes are also a possibility using the free script Flubaroo. To learn more about Flubaroo, go to www.flubaroo.com to see a short demonstration.

Choose Your Own Adventure

Forms do not have to be limited to teacher or staff creations. Students can also create forms such as sample quizzes, data gathering in science, progress monitoring, and the creative Choose Your Own Adventure stories. According to Wikipedia,

> **Choose Your Own Adventure** is a series of children's gamebooks where each story is written from a second-person point of view, with the reader assuming the role of the protagonist and making choices that determine the main character's actions and the plot's outcome.

Students can use Google Forms with branching pages that will go to a different page based upon a multiple-choice selection. Students can retell literature stories, create their own narratives based upon historic events, and/or tie into any content to these. Again, this allows students to write with meaning by using diverse media including text, video, and/or images.

Other Ways to Use Google Forms

Getting-to-know-you first day of school icebreaker

Maintenance request forms

Computer technician request

Teacher evaluation

Principal can gather data about classroom during a class visit

---

Lesson in Focus

Student Collaborative Study Guide

The teacher will

1. Create a Google Forms quiz with three simple questions related to content that students have been studying

Students will

1. Review and then make their own quiz relating to more questions that may be on the test

2. Create at least 20 questions of varying forms of questions (e.g., multiple choice, free response)

3. Share the front-end of the quiz with a partner and grade their partners

4. Discuss the incorrect answers with the partner and what they should look at to improve

5. Regive the quiz to see if improvement was made

Students can repeat with different partners if time is available.

Modification	Through the use of Google Forms, you can get a response from every student both extrovert and introvert almost immediately on any given topic. Students can then view and interpret class results after submitting the form that will then help drive classroom discussions for the rest of the period. You can also refer back to our initial student responses at any point in the lesson to emphasize or clarify an idea.
Redefinition	Google Forms provides the ability to survey and/or share data with people all over the world. Imagine students administering a survey about food interests in a seventh-grade history class to schools in Egypt. Or, imagine students collecting real-time data about weather with schools in a different state or country. Students, in this case, would have real-time relevant data to draw conclusions. Being able to collaborate using the Internet is key to CCSS.

EVEN MORE

Add-ons—Automate Your Form

Google Forms offers some advanced features. You can use Add-ons in Forms to add math-based equations, automatically remove answer choices once selected, and send email notifications to respondents with the data they submitted. To browse the Add-ons, simply click on the three vertical dots on the top right of the form shown in Figure 7.10 to access and install.

Figure 7.10 Add-ons

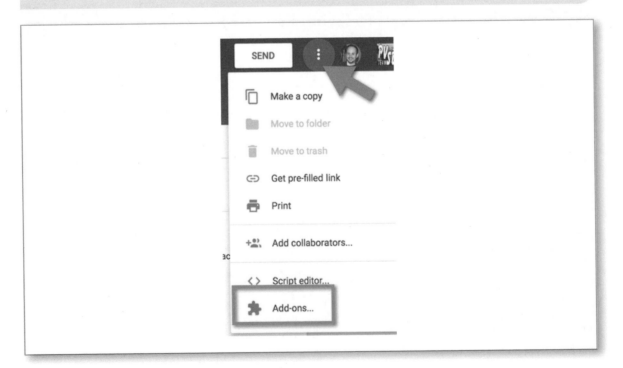

Data Validation

When collecting data, sometimes you want to limit the response to a three-digit number. Or, maybe you want to limit students to only selecting two answer choices on a multiple-answer type question. Or, maybe you want to limit a narrative response to 500 characters. You can validate the submission to be sure you get the results you intend. To view and set up validation for the different question types, click on the three vertical dots while editing the question and select **Data validation** shown in Figure 7.11. Depending on the type of questions, there are different types of validation. To learn more about data validation, access Resource 7.7 at https://goo.gl/jOca8R.

Figure 7.11 Data Validation

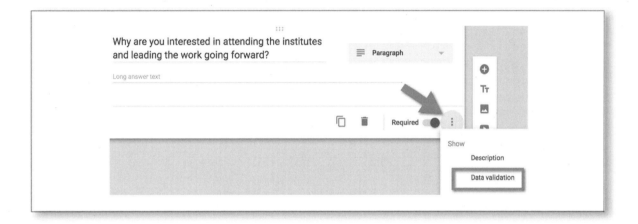

SUMMARY

Forms are great at gathering and organizing data into spreadsheets. These can help students be more responsible and self-directed, especially in the middle grades. Students can create surveys gaining authentic data they can use in research, math class, or for organizing a club event. Teachers can create self-grading quizzes and monitor student progress with ease, making real impacts on students during PLC meetings. Google Forms supports the effectiveness of the Common Core State Standards by getting technology into the hands of students, allowing them to analyze their world and help them make better decisions. In the next chapter, find out how Google Drawings can help students be creative to explain what they are learning in the form of art. Also, students can organize information in show-stopping drawings that can be inserted into any of the Google Docs or simply shared online.

RESOURCES

For more information about G Suite for Education, including

- lesson plans related to chapter content,
- domain setup for tech administrators' videos,

- overviews and Google training materials,
- the authors' favorite websites, and
- testimonials and interviews of schools currently using G Suite,

access Resources from this chapter on the companion website.

Lesson Plans

Grade Level	Lesson Plan Title	All lesson plans and resources can be found on the companion website at: http://resources.corwin.com/googlemeetsms	
Middle School	Slow Down!	http://goo.gl/XnXki	Resource 7.8

online resources http://resources.corwin.com/googlemeetsms

8 Google Drawings

Key Features

- Design organizational charts, flowcharts, and graphic organizers
- Publish work directly to the web or insert into other Google Docs
- Work collaboratively on drawings
- Create charts, diagrams, and graphic organizers
- Chat in the margin to guide collaborators
- Express what is learned visually

Seventh-grade students Mike and Sam had to develop a diagram of a microscope. They learned about the various functions of each of the components in class and wanted to find a way they both could work on a diagram at home. Mr. Powers recommended they use Google Drawings. Mike and Sam went home that night, went online, and Mike created a Google Drawing. He shared this with Sam, and they worked collaboratively over the next hour to build their diagram. Figure 8.1 on the next page represents the finished product.

Google Drawings offers something other office productivity suites cannot compete with. Google Drawings is the only drawing program that allows users to share their work with colleagues in real time. Users can share creations that connect meaning in real time by drawing flowcharts, custom graphs, informational posters, and graphic designs. These can be published online using the document's unique URL. Insert these creations into presentations, spreadsheets, or documents to make visual connections to text. Add images to drawings from your hard drive or the web, or add text and other annotations. Google Drawings has "snap-to" alignment guides and auto distribution to keep objects on the drawing canvas precisely spaced. These features make it easy to create professional-looking graphic designs with this free Google app.

Google Drawings can help students with writing by helping them organize their ideas. Students can make their own graphic organizers, use templates found online or in a book, or use a specific teacher's template. For example, a teacher could create a custom graphic organizer designed for organizing ideas obtained from text. The Common Core State Standards Anchor Standard 1 for Writing wants students to "read closely" to understand the text and make analytical conclusions from it, as shown in Table 8.1. This type of close reading should be taught throughout the reading standards, as well as reading in the content areas. Teachers who create graphic organizers give students a chance to organize their thoughts and facts gathered from text to prepare for writing.

Figure 8.1 A Google Drawing Diagram

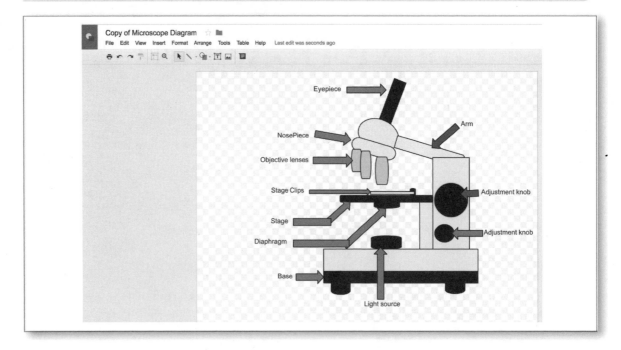

The teacher may create the graphic organizer using Google Drawings and share it with the class. The class will make a copy of the organizer and use it to prepare for their writing about the text.

Table 8.1 Anchor Standard 1 for Reading

Read closely to determine what the text says explicitly and to make logical inferences from it; cite specific textual evidence when writing or speaking to support conclusions drawn from the text.

GRAPHIC ORGANIZERS

Use the graphic organizer in Figure 8.2 made for organizing complex text. The reader can have full access to this graphic organizer by going to Resource 8.1 at https://goo.gl/H0gI1S.

Creating graphic organizers that are saved in the user's Google Drive account will help the students and teachers transition to a paperless classroom. The standards are clear that college- and career-ready students will need to be organized when writing. Take advantage of Google Drawings to provide digital organization that can be accessed by any Internet-ready device. Access Figure 8.2 Graphic Organizer for Writing by visiting the companion website. Then follow the directions in Figure 8.2 to make a copy of it. Once a copy is made, rename it to become the owner and then edit or share the document with anyone. Readers can have full access to this graphic organizer for use with their students by going to Resource 8.2 at https://goo.gl/H0gI1S.

Figure 8.2 Graphic Organizer for Writing

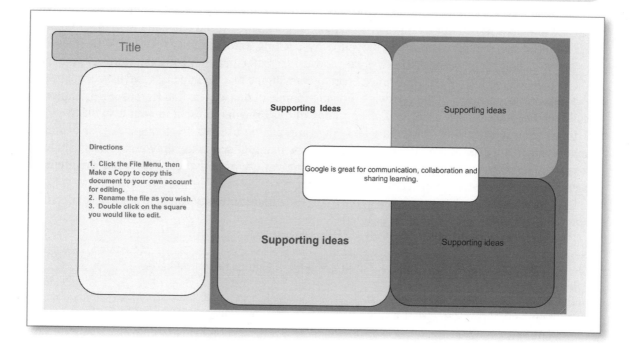

Technology-Infused Teaching Tip

Notice in Figure 8.2 that the drawing has objects (directions) outside the canvas area. Use the whole area to create the drawing. When publishing the drawing, only the objects on the canvas will be seen. However, objects outside the canvas will be seen during sharing. Teachers can create objects off-screen for students to use while making a drawing; sometimes limiting their options increases their creativity.

SHARE VERSUS PUBLISH

Sharing a Google Drawing allows it to be viewed, edited, or commented on by the person it is shared with. Collaborative drawings shared with students allow them to create the work together in real time like any of the other document programs. They can work on it at the same time, or they can contribute at any time they choose and the work will be saved along with the revision history. Publishing the drawing, conversely, will publish the work that is on the canvas only. That means if the user has placed directions or other objects off the canvas, then that content will not show up in the published version. When publishing drawings, the URL given to the drawing will automatically download the drawing as a .PNG picture file. This downloaded file will not change with subsequent versions of the work. However, if the user clicks on the published link again, this will download the new and most current version of the drawing.

Using Google Drawings for Exploration of Math Concepts

Look at Table 8.2 to see an appropriate Common Core State Standard for using Google Drawings to explore geometry. For example, teachers who want students to investigate shapes could create a drawing that has the shapes placed outside the canvas region. The students would click on the shapes to manipulate them on the canvas. Shapes can be edited by clicking and dragging, rotating 90 degrees, and flipping horizontally and vertically (also great exposure to mathematics vocabulary words). Have them add color and text to liven up the drawings. Share them with the teacher and class and have the students explain their understanding of their drawing. For an example of this lesson, find Resource 8.3, Exploring Shapes, on the companion website and make a copy of this drawing to use it in your own class.

In addition to exploring shapes, the Drawings app can be used to create puzzles. For example, teachers can create a set of digital tangram shapes to be manipulated in the drawing. Instruct students to explore the shapes using flips, slides, and turns in a variety of activities. Freely use the premade tangram set, Resource 8.4 on the companion website.

Exploring shapes and using lines to make triangles with technology can help students understand how graphic design could be used as a career.

Table 8.2   Draw, Construct, and Describe Geometrical Figures Seventh Grade

Draw (freehand, with ruler and protractor, and with technology) geometric shapes with given conditions. Focus on constructing triangles from three measures of angles or sides, noticing when the conditions determine a unique triangle, more than one triangle, or no triangle.

FILE MENU

The **File** menu in Google Drawings contains commands that will help the user with the creation of the drawing. The following section only describes Drawing-specific commands. For more on the other **File** commands, see previous chapters.

Download As

Download as will download the file that the user has created in another format other than a Google Docs format. Each document type has its own set of Download as options (see Figure 8.3). The least common of the file types in this figure is .SVG. That extension is used in high-end graphics and can easily be imported into graphic design programs such as Adobe Illustrator for further design. PDF, PNG, and JPEG are very common image file types and will work on any platform (PC, Mac, iOS, or Android).

Figure 8.3   Download As

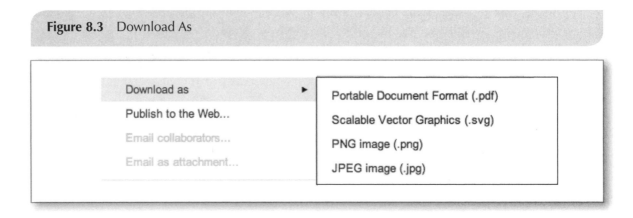

Technology-Infused Teaching Tip

The default canvas size can be changed to form any rectangle. Click and drag the lower right-hand corner of the canvas to make it a different size and shape. For example, to make a square canvas, click on the sizing handle and shrink it to its smallest size, then hold down **Shift** and enlarge it to make a square. Holding down **Shift** while resizing objects keeps the proportions of the sides the same. For example, if the default canvas ratio is 4:3, then holding down **Shift** while resizing will keep the 4:3 proportion no matter how large or small the canvas is resized.

VIEW MENU

The **View** menu is pictured in Figure 8.4. It has some of the same features as other **View** menus in previous chapters. Read the next section to see Drawing-specific commands.

Figure 8.4   View Menu

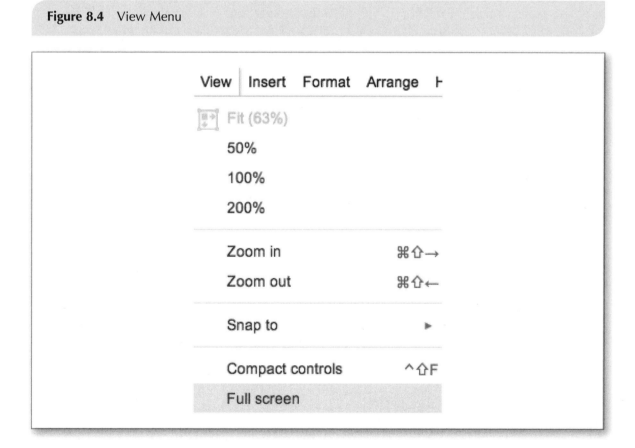

Fit Zoom

Fit zoom fits the drawing to the size of the screen. While editing a drawing, the user may zoom in many times to get a detail just right. Click **Fit zoom** to go back to show the entire drawing. For example, a student making a flowchart for chemistry class explaining how to balance a chemical equation may need to add specific detail in certain parts of the drawing. Use the zoom feature to zoom in on a particular part of the equation, then click **Fit zoom** to go back to see the whole drawing.

Snap To

This feature helps align objects to the canvas of the drawing. Choose from **Snap to grids** or **Snap to guides**. Snapping to grids aligns the objects to the coordinate plane. For example, objects such as squares will appear straight, forming 90-degree angles with the borders of the canvas. The downside to this is that having to align two shapes in similar size proportional distances from the vertical and horizontal will be difficult because it will have to be done by sight. **Snap to guides** aligns objects to guide lines that keep objects equidistant from each other and from the canvas borders.

FLOWCHARTS

Creating flowcharts in science and math is a great way to take the information of processes and make it graphically appealing. This is a great differentiation tool for students. Have students use Google Drawings to take a complex set of steps and make a flowchart. For example, students studying the scientific method could create a custom graphic organizer outlining the steps. For an example of a flowchart illustrating the scientific method, view Resource 8.5 at http://goo.gl/qkCMb. In Table 8.3, the Common Core State Standard describes the importance of using various forms of visuals and media to explain writing. Students can use drawings to make timelines or animations to explain text or gain information from these informational objects. Using technology can improve the access of these visual displays because they can be shared with the class or the world using share settings.

Table 8.3   Writing in History/Social Studies, Science, and Technical Subjects Grades 6–8

Introduce a topic clearly, previewing what is to follow; organize ideas, concepts, and information into broader categories as appropriate to achieving purpose; include formatting (e.g., headings), graphics (e.g., charts, tables), and multimedia when useful to aiding comprehension.

Technology-Infused Teaching Tip

While making drawings, especially flowcharts, use copy and paste to make copies of the shapes. In some flowcharts, it is great to have the same size shape for each of the objects in the flowchart. Use copy and paste instead of inserting a new shape and trying to draw the shape the exact size.

DRAWINGS AS ASSESSMENTS

Teachers can use Drawings as an assessment tool. For example, use Drawings to assess what the student knows about the scientific method. Assign students to create a flowchart of the scientific method and then share it with the teacher for grading. Another way Google Drawings can be used as an assessment tool is by creating posters. Common Core State Standards for Mathematics Eighth Grade address the Pythagorean Theorem. Students should be able to "Explain a proof of the Pythagorean Theorem and its converse." Use drawings to create an informational poster describing the proof of the theorem and its converse. Students should be graded on presentation of the poster for speaking and listening standards as well as the mathematics content. Insert drawings into presentations to give students the valuable experience of presenting to groups. Raise the ante by inviting mathematics experts to grade the posters and the presentation along with the teacher's rubrics. Use Gmail's video chat feature to let experts chat with students from far distances. Exposing students to professional science, technology, engineering, and mathematics careers and having them interact will have a positive impact on them.

GRAPHICAL TOOLBAR

The graphical toolbar featured in Figure 8.5 is located at the top of the screen in Google Drawings. The commands listed here are also available in the **Insert** menu. Google places them at the top with graphics to make them easier to access.

Figure 8.5 Insert Menu

Undo and redo. Undo and redo are familiar commands. Keyboard shortcuts for these commands are **CTRL/CMD+Z** and **CTRL/CMD+Y**, respectively (CMD for Mac, CTRL for PC).

Copy to web clipboard. Web clipboard is an innovative feature Google has developed. Instead of using the computer's clipboard that allows users to copy and paste only on the physical computer, Google Docs can copy and paste from computer A to computer B. This is done by using Google's cloud technology. With Google Docs web clipboard, students are becoming device neutral even with copy and paste.

Paint format. This feature is much like conditional formatting used in spreadsheets. The command will copy the formatting rules for the selected region and paste them in a particular area on the drawing. The word *paint* is used figuratively to describe pasting the formatting. For example, select a region that has a particular style or font and paint format that style or font into another region of the drawing without pasting the content.

Fit zoom and zoom. This is detailed in the View section.

Select. This icon is important because it allows the user to grab and move objects on the drawing. The icon must be selected before the user clicks on the drawing to perform a task. If this is not done, then whatever command is selected, such as insert a line, will be performed. Avoid making unnecessary errors by being aware of the select tool. Students new to drawings will be inclined to not pay attention to which icon is selected and will most likely become frustrated not knowing why there is a problem.

Select line. This icon is a shortcut to inserting lines. Click the drop-down arrow to choose from six line types to give the drawing a unique presence. Look at Figure 8.6 to see what line types are available.

Figure 8.6 Line Type Drop-Down Menu

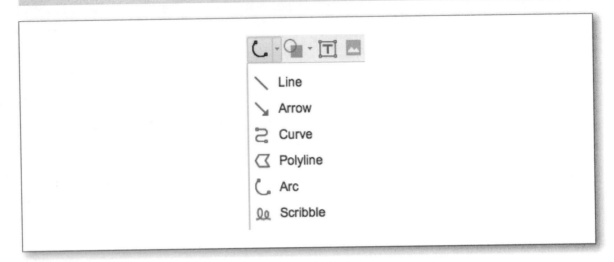

Shapes, Arrows, Callouts, and Equations

Click the drop-down menu to insert a shape, arrow, callout, or equation symbol. Add text to any of these by double-clicking inside the object. Students can create graphic designs that aid in their understanding of the concept. Creatively exploring concepts is an important differentiation tool and should be used with students of all ages. For example, when using shapes, students learning early-grade geometry lessons could practice manipulating shapes in the drawing program. To manipulate shapes, follow these steps:

1. Insert a shape by clicking on the drop-down menu in the toolbar.
2. Resize the shape by clicking and dragging one of the white, square resizing handles.
   a. To maintain proportion, hold down **Shift** while resizing.
3. Rotate the object about its axis by clicking on the shape's white, circular handle above the object as shown in Figure 8.7.

Figure 8.7 Rotate an Image

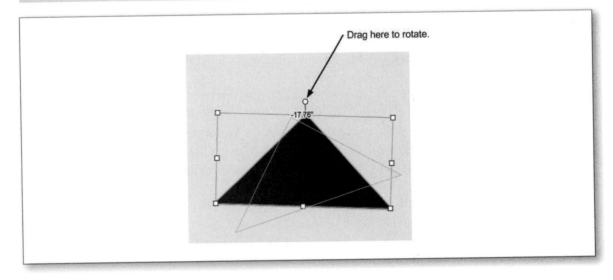

Callouts. Make it possible for students to construct comics with their drawings by inserting callouts. Use callouts to give inanimate objects a voice. For example, when explaining the layers of rock in a photograph, insert callouts to make the rock "say" something clever about its composition. Create comic strips by inserting comics made in drawings into presentations; set the timing of slide transitions to create animation.

Equations. Equations are perfect for math. Create easy-to-read equations that can help students understand a particularly hard concept. For example, create a flowchart on how to use the distributive property. In each object, insert equation symbols showing the steps in order.

INSERT MENU

The **Insert** menu has many of the same commands as other programs as seen in Figure 8.8. Insert will be the most used feature, but also remember to use many of these same commands from the graphical insert menu located in Figure 8.5.

Figure 8.8   Insert Menu

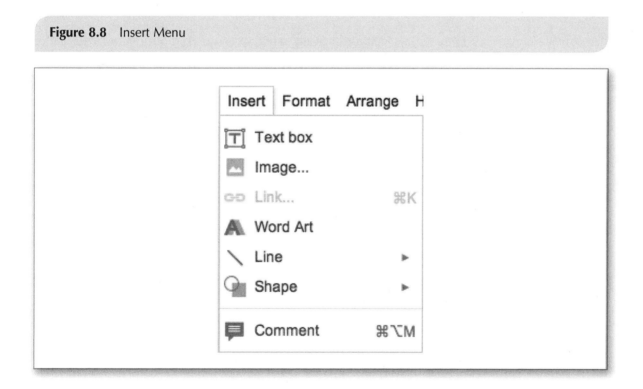

Text Box

Insert text boxes into drawings by following these steps:

1. Click **Insert,** then **Text box** or select the icon in the toolbar menu.

2. Size the text box accordingly by clicking and dragging the white resize boxes.

3. Fill the text box with color or change the color of the font using the edit buttons shown in Figure 8.8.

Image

Insert images exactly like previous chapters by clicking on the icon in the toolbar menu. Inserting images into the Drawings apps gives the user more creativity. For example, students can insert images that they have taken themselves or have permission to use to explain a set of ideas. Students can edit the photo by annotating with text, adding arrows, shapes, callouts, and equation symbols to add meaning. Creativity is up to the student. Insert these modified images into presentations, embed in a website, or publish them with the unique URL. Students can tell a story about what they are learning with their artwork, meeting vital speaking and listening standards.

Link

Insert live links into drawings by following these steps:

1. Select a portion of text to be linked with a web address.

2. Click on the icon to reveal Figure 8.9.

3. Type the URL for the link into the box.

4. Click **OK** to link the object.

When a user clicks on the link, a web browser will open, directing the user to more information about the object. For example, a flowchart describing the scientific method could have links directed to more information on the hypothesis step. Students can create Google Docs that are linked to the drawing, detailing the concepts within the flowchart for further study. Create living drawings.

Figure 8.9   Linking Objects in Drawings to Web Addresses

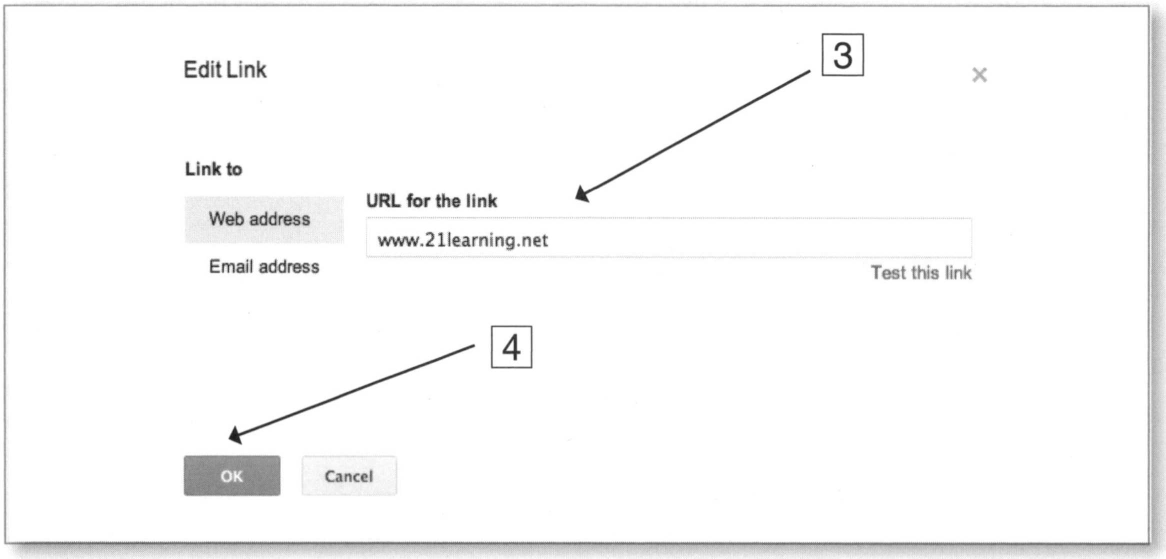

Word Art

Inserting word art gives an artistic feel to text in drawings. Inserting text boxes alone is limiting because the font is somewhat standardized. With word art, users can select edit options, including color fill, line color, border weight, and border type. Insert word art by following these steps:

1. Click **Insert,** then **Word art** to reveal Figure 8.10.

2. Type text in the box.

3. Use **Shift+Enter** to insert multiple lines of text.

4. Press **Enter.**

Figure 8.10   Insert Word Art

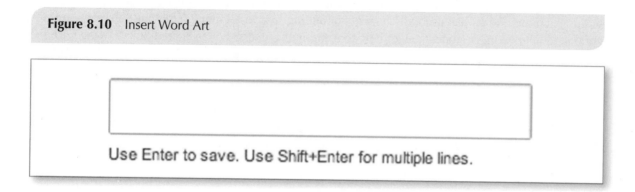

Use Enter to save. Use Shift+Enter for multiple lines.

Comments

Comment on certain aspects of the drawing by right-clicking on the object you want to comment on. This is great for grading students' work. Insert comments that will be constructive and make the students' project better. Grade for content and style from any Internet-connected computer. Comments will be seen on the drawing, but will be off of the canvas region and will not be published. Click the object that the drawing is attached to resolve. Use the comment stream to review conversations about aspects of the drawing. Also, use the chat feature to collaborate on drawings. To insert comments, see that section in Chapter 4, "Google Documents."

EDIT ICONS

Edit icons become visible when the user clicks on an object. If the object can hold text like shapes, callouts, arrows, and equation symbols, then the text edit buttons will appear. If the objects cannot contain text, only the fill color, line weight, and so on will appear. Look at Figure 8.11 to see the edit icons as they appear in the graphical toolbar in Google Drawings.

Figure 8.11   Edit Icons

Adding Text

To add text to any drawing, use text box, word art, or double-click a shape, callout, arrow, or equation symbol. Click the object, and the following edit buttons will appear:

Color fill and color lines of any object in the gallery.

Choose font size for any object.

Choose font style for word art only.

Change the color of text, underline, make bold, or italicize.

For an example of actual student work from sixth-grade student Fallan Harper, look at Figure 8.12. In this example, Fallan has used all elements of adding text to a Google Drawing to create an infographic to help younger students learn how to open their lockers. Fallan shared this drawing with the entire middle school as part of a school community service project. Students now have this information in their Google Drive.

Figure 8.12 How to Open Your Locker

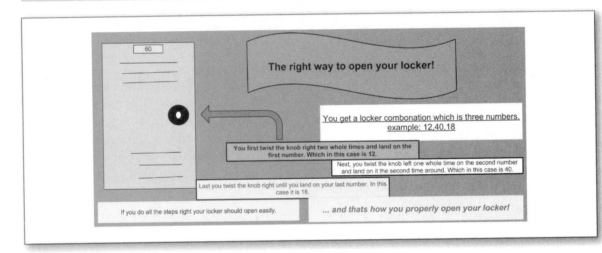

Lesson in Focus

Pre-writing Strategies

The teacher will

1. Create or use a template to be used for planning students' narrative writing; use the template referenced in Figure 8.2 or use Resource 8.6 at https://goo.gl/2BiKnJ for more advanced students

2. Share the drawing so everyone gets a copy in Google Classroom as an assignment—Pre-writing

3. Ask students to identify key components of their narrative with words or phrases along with supporting details

4. Provide students feedback on their drawings by using the commenting feature

5. Ask students to revise and share their ideas with another student

Modification	Google Drawings can be used collaboratively and allow for students to work with other students both in and out of the classroom. Students can create linkable images in different parts of the drawing to provide an interactive document. See this example of the different resources relating to Life in a Spanish Mission for an interactive drawing in Resource 8.7 at https://goo.gl/dAOj4X.
Redefinition	Google Drawings allows for students to collaborate with students from different geographic areas in real time. Imagine students in five different states in the United States who work together to build an interactive map where students in each state add links to images they have taken around their state. Students can save all the images in a public Google Drive folder and link to each individual image. Students can then use the commenting function to ask questions and share feedback on the images from the different states.

EVEN MORE

Students have the ability to not only build their own images in Google Drawings, but they can design headers and footers for their websites (teachers can do this too) using Google Drawings. Simply have students resize the canvas to the header of their websites (typically 990 pixels wide by 180 pixels high) by clicking on the **File** menu and selecting **Page setup**. They can then select the **Custom** option from the drop down and then change the point size to pixels. See Figure 8.13 for more details. Students can then design their custom website header.

Figure 8.13 Customizing Image Size: Website Header

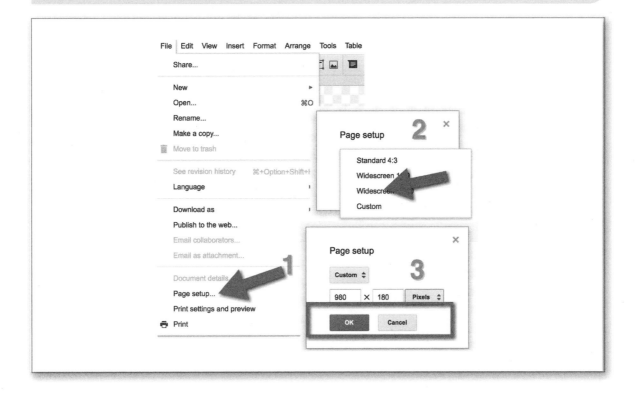

SUMMARY

Google Drawings is a dynamic graphic design program that uses G Suite for Education signature collaborative features. Students and teachers can create collaborative drawings that explain meaning in visually stunning ways. Students are able to express their learning in creative ways using art, while learning an important skill of graphic design. Insert drawings into other Google Docs to add creativity to presentations or documents. Teachers are able to assess Common Core State Standards of speaking and listening by allowing students to present their ideas depicted in their work. Students are able to create informational posters, flowcharts, and custom graphs that can be published to the web and contribute to the world's understanding of the topic in new ways.

Google Drawings is a great differentiation tool that can urge students to create, collaborate, and share their work with parents, peers, or the world. It is the final app in the Google Docs suite, but the collaboration is not over.

RESOURCES

For more information about G Suite for Education, including

- lesson plans related to chapter content,
- domain setup for tech administrators' videos,
- overviews and Google training materials,
- the authors' favorite websites, and
- testimonials and interviews of schools currently using G Suite,

access Resources from this chapter on the companion website.

Lesson Plans

Content Area	Lesson Plan Title	All lesson plans and resources can be found on the companion website at: http://resources.corwin.com/googlemeetsms	
Math	Tangram Square	http://goo.gl/ehls8	Resource 8.8
ELA/Science	Persuasion and Ecology	https://goo.gl/Clid0y	Resource 8.9

online resources http://resources.corwin.com/googlemeetsms

9 Google Drive

The G Suite for Education have collaborative power to help students become ready for college and careers. Google Classroom organizes all content, and Google Docs, Sheets, and Slides provide a world-class office suite for users to create, collaborate, and share. The last piece of the puzzle is storage. Google Drive is a cloud-based storage solution that gives access to all of the user's files in an online cloud-based drive that can be accessed from anywhere there is an Internet connection. This means that students and teachers can store unlimited files of any type in Google Drive. Google Drive lets users upload files or whole folders and gives the option to share any file type with others. Access Google Drive on tablets or smartphones, including Android, iPhone, and iPad, with easy-to-use mobile apps. Google Drive is not necessarily an instructional tool, but a management and organizational tool.

Google Drive is important to the use of technology in the classroom because it moves students into the cloud for working, learning, and organizing their digital learning profile. These traits are evident in the ISTE Standards for Students in Table 9.1.

It is imperative that students have access to their files and creations across many devices from anywhere in the world. Device-neutral learning and working environments are the gold standard for 21st-century educational systems. Students and teachers today must have quick and easy access to their content from any device. It is the norm. Many schools and businesses rely on a wide variety of devices to access the Internet and their work. For example, my school has a mix of Apple, Microsoft, and mobile devices that are all compatible with the G Suite of educational applications. Google works on any device. When students are exposed to the tools that are used in

Table 9.1 ISTE Standards for Students

ISTE Standards for Students: **(1) Empowered Learner:** Students leverage technology to take an active role in choosing, achieving and demonstrating competency in their learning goals, informed by the learning sciences.

1b: Students build networks and customize their learning environments in ways that support the learning process.

1d: Students understand the fundamental concepts of technology operations, demonstrate the ability to choose, use and troubleshoot current technologies and are able to transfer their knowledge to explore emerging technologies.

college and in a career, they will be better prepared when they are thrown into that world. In this chapter, we will learn how Google Drive supports the college- and career-readiness standards, unifies the G Suite, and can increase digital literacy across the middle grades to help the early adolescent face the challenges brought upon them by the ever-increasing digital working and learning life.

ACCESSING DRIVE

Google Drive simplifies storage. For example, a student no longer has to be on the same computer that he or she started working on to access a file. Storage becomes easy because files are stored in the cloud on Google's Drive servers and can be accessed, edited, or shared with anyone in the world from any device. For example, as soon as a student creates a Google Doc, the Doc is saved every 2 seconds in the user's Google Drive. A deadly computer virus could completely kill the student's computer, and nothing would be lost. The information does not save to the computer, but it saves to the cloud-based storage application. There are several ways to access your Google Drive:

1. Go to www.google.com in any web browser (preferably Google Chrome Web Browser).
   a. Sign into your G Suite account (if not signed in already)
   b. Click on the ⚏ apps icon as shown in the arrow in Figure 9.1

2. Go to http://drive.google.com in any web browser

3. When already signed into your G Suite account, you can open the ⚏ apps icon from Docs, Sheets, Slides, and Gmail.

4. In the **File** menu of Docs, Sheets, Slides, and Drawings, you may access Drive files by clicking on **File**, then **New.**
   a. Use the Search bar, then **Shared with me, Starred**, **Recent,** or **Upload** a file from your computer's hard drive.

Figure 9.1   Accessing Google Drive

MANAGING DRIVE

Google Drive gives users access to all of the G Suite and any other file types they have uploaded to Drive. It is like the documents folder that is stored on a computer, but it can be accessed from anywhere. Files can be stored, shared, and organized in the cloud, giving the users the ability to have their files on demand no matter where they are. Students and teachers will find that managing their files in the cloud-based storage platform will greatly increase their productivity. For example, students may create folders for each class and place documents, research, or other classroom materials into the specified folder for easy retrieval and sharing. When a teacher uses Google Classroom, student work assigned through the learning management system (Google Classroom) is automatically saved in that class's Drive folder.

Technology-Infused Teaching Tip

Students live in a mobile computing world. It is natural for digital natives to share photos and ideas using other cloud-based social media platforms such as Facebook, Twitter, Instagram, and Snapchat. Look for ways to incorporate sharing and communicating ideas about classroom topics on social media. Teachers can use Facebook and Twitter as discussion forums connecting content from their subject areas to learning experiences online. Google Drive makes it easy to supplement the conversation with class materials such as links to documents and videos because it allows the user to share files easily. Share a file about a classroom topic, copying and pasting the unique URL that Google Drive gives every uploaded file. This is the new lifelong learning. Give them opportunities to engage in conversations that will inspire learning in online spaces that they already are involved in.

Click on the blue **New** icon to reveal a drop-down menu that the user will select to create a new Google Sheet, Slide, Drawing, Form, or More, as shown by the arrow in Figure 9.2.

1. Click on **Folder** 🗀 to create a new folder in Drive.

2. Click on **File upload** ⬆ to upload a file from your computer's hard drive.

3. Click on **Folder upload** ⬆ to upload an entire folder from your computer's hard drive. Note that Drive works from any device. For example, you may upload a file or folder from your work computer, then go home and upload a file or folder from your personal computer to Google Drive. All of the files end up in the same place.

4. Click any of the G Suite file types to create a new file.

   a. Click **More** as shown by the arrow in Figure 9.2 to reveal more file types.

   b. Click **Connect more apps** to open the file types shown in the box in Figure 9.2. (*Note: The file types in the box may be third-party apps that will save their files to your Google Drive for online cloud-based access.*)

Figure 9.2   Drive Menu

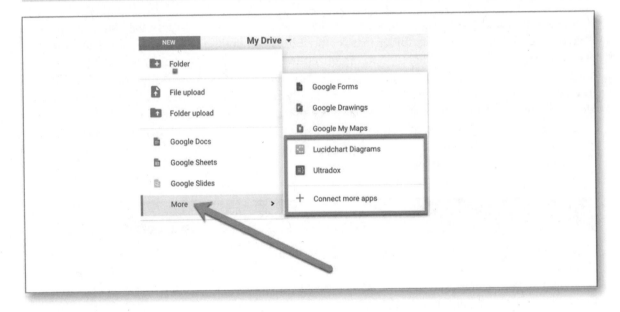

Drive Menu Options

Under the **My Drive** section in Figure 9.3, the arrow points to a drop-down arrow to show folder structure that the user has created. The My Drive parent folder stores all of the files that the user owns, has created, or uploaded in addition to the subfolders. See how the folders are displayed in Figure 9.1. Files are displayed in a similar fashion, but icons represent documents, sheets, forms, slides, drawings, etc.

When clicked, the **Shared with me** option in Figure 9.3 displays the documents list items that are shared with the user. These files are not part of My Drive because the user does not own them. Sometimes it is possible to accidentally search My Drive when one is actually looking for a file that someone has shared. In that case, any keyword that matches the document would not find any results. Make sure to also search the **Shared with me** tab as well. You just might have forgot if you created the document, or you are collaborating with a student or colleague.

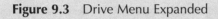

Figure 9.3 Drive Menu Expanded

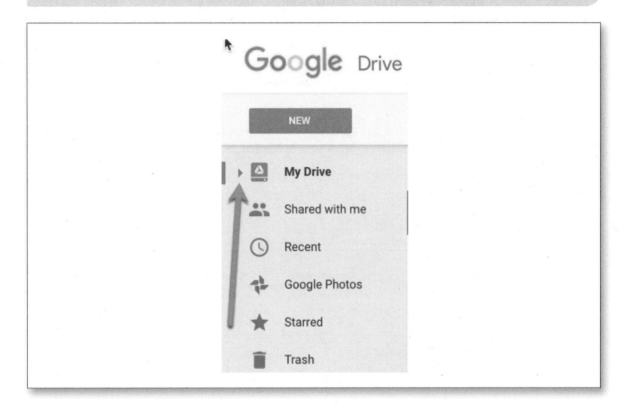

The **Recent** menu shows a chronological order of documents that the user has accessed or edited. This is the first place we look to start working on a file, because it gives us a list of our most recent projects.

The **Google Photos** menu opens the photos that you have uploaded to Google Drive. In your G Suite for Education, you have unlimited storage for photos and all types of files. There is even an iOS and Android app called Google Photos that can upload your photos taken from your smartphone camera automatically to your Google Drive. Please remember that your Google Drive on your school G Suite for Education account is not your personal storage. Anything in the school's account may be discoverable in a freedom of information request. Open another personal Google account to store your photos and docs that have nothing to do with school.

The **Starred** menu automatically lists the important documents and files that you have given a star. This is a feature to mark certain files as important. To give a document a star and to have it appear in the starred list, follow the steps.

1. In any document type, next to the filename of the document as shown by the arrow in Figure 9.4, is an outline of a star.

2. Click on the **star** to "star" the document, and it will be added to the important list under the **Starred** menu.

Figure 9.4 Star a Document

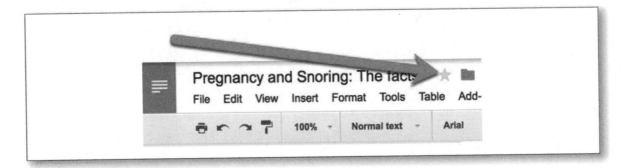

Trash shows the files that the user has deleted. Google never deletes files unless the user empties the trash. It is like the old school recycling bin found in Microsoft operating systems.

Figure 9.5 Documents List Sorting

Name ↓	Owner	Last modified	File size
Tech Notes and Docs	me	May 22, 2013 me	—
WHS Tech PD	me	Aug 10, 2014 Jason Borgen	—
WeVideo_folder.	me	May 15, 2012 me	—
WeVideo	me	Oct 1, 2014 me	—
YouthCouncil	me	Feb 15, 2013 me	—
VideoNot.es	me	Feb 6, 2014 me	—
transferred from district	me	Jun 10, 2014 me	—
spring retreat work	me	May 18, 2013 me	—

Figure 9.5 shows the documents list in Drive. You may sort by the categories in the boxes by clicking on the word. The **File size** in Figure 9.5 does not register because Google does not measure the size of the folders compared to each other, just file types. All of the things listed in the figure are folders.

SEARCH

Google's search power does not stop with www.google.com. It is incorporated into everything it does. This includes Google Drive. Use the search bar at the top of the page in Drive to search for any file type that you own or is shared with you. There are three main types of searches. The first, **Keyword search**, is the simplest and most efficient. Google reads each word of the document and the title, and when you search for something that Google's search algorithm thinks it is what you are looking for, it gives you **Instant search suggestions**. The instant searches are shown in Figure 9.6. If your item appears in the instant search, you are done searching. For a slightly more detailed search, click the **magnifying glass icon** to reveal more files and file types that the algorithm suggests. The search suggests files before you are done typing.

Figure 9.6   Google Drive Search

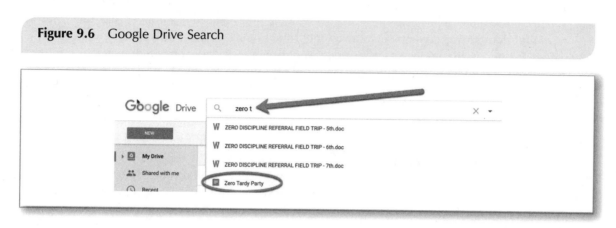

The second search type is accessed by clicking **Search Drive** in Google Drive. This reveals the list of file types shown in Figure 9.7 that the user may search. When you click on a file type, the keyword that you use will only search the chosen file type. This is great because you may have related spreadsheets and text documents with the same or similar names. Students and teachers can differentiate with their searching.

Figure 9.7   Types of Searches

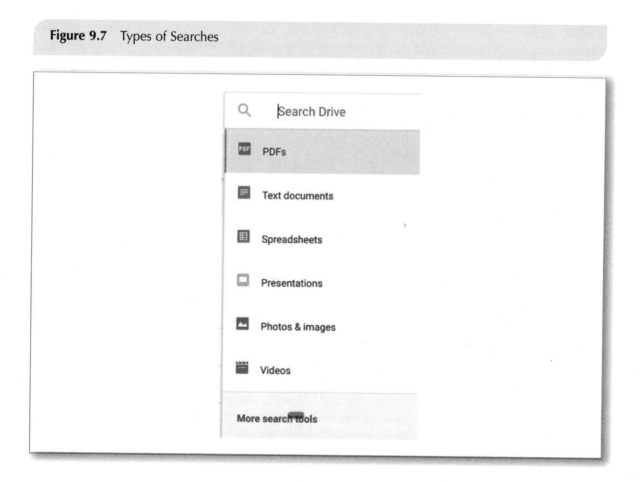

The most advanced way to search Google Drive is with the **More search tools** option, shown in the bottom of the menu in Figure 9.7. This is also accessed by clicking on the **down arrow** in the search bar in Google Drive, as shown in Figure 9.8. Advanced search will allow the user to pinpoint specifically what they are looking for in Drive. If your Drive is set up like ours, this will become invaluable. We do not treat our Drive like a clone of My Documents (PC) or Finder (Mac). With their file systems, it resembles a physical filing cabinet where a file is placed in a drawer (like the C: Drive, F: Drive) and that drawer contains certain folders (documents, photos, downloads) and the file is somewhere located in the folder. Once you go through this maze of cabinets, drawers, and folders, time is lost and you might not actually find what you are looking for. In Michael's drive, there is just too much content to place into a system of folders. In fact Michael has been storing every piece of content he has created since 1995 in his Google Drive. Google Drive's search feature will search everything you have ever created or uploaded to the Google Drive simultaneously with its best in the universe search algorithm. No need to create a system of drawers and folders. Just search it with the three tools to maximize the chances you will find what you are looking for. In Michael's case, he is a digital hoarder. He went to his mother's house and got his hands on all of his old 3.5in disks that his middle school and high school work was saved on. In 2005, just before 3.5in drives were eliminated, he uploaded everything to his Google Drive. He literally has everything he has ever created digitally stored on his Google Drive. He can find anything with these great searching tools.

Figure 9.8 Advanced Search in Drive

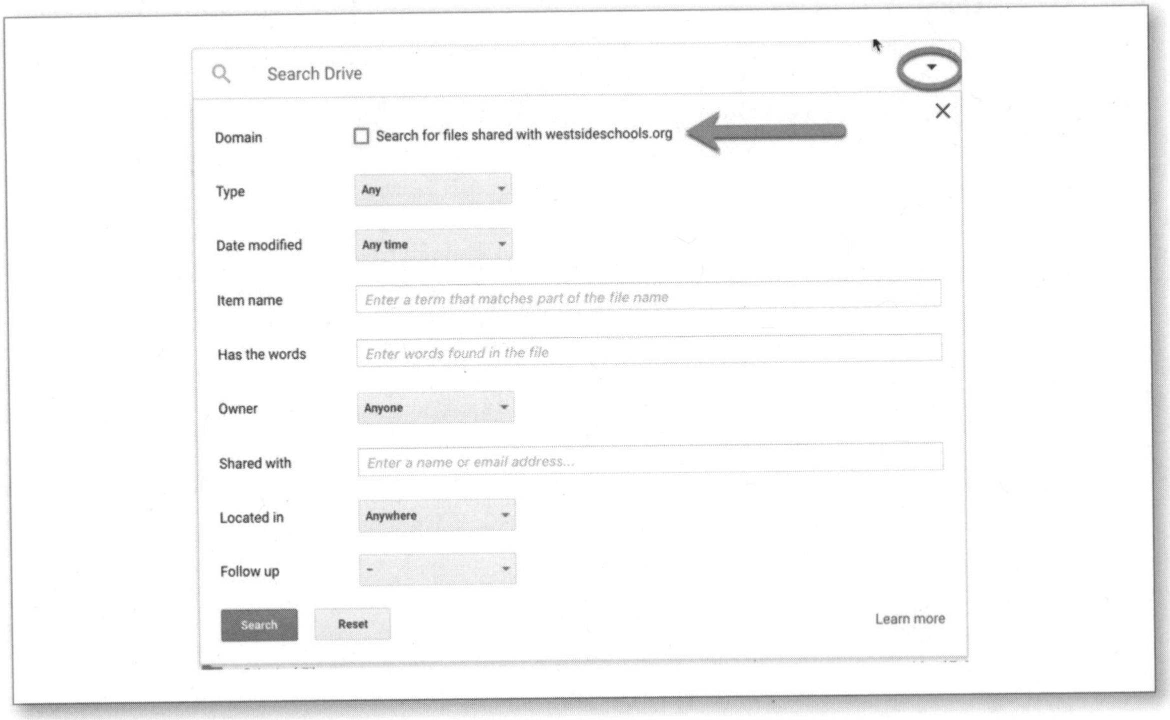

The arrow in Figure 9.8 denotes searching inside the school's domain. For example, the central office may have official documents shared with the entire staff to access such as personnel leave forms or lesson plan templates. The owner of the document may give access to view or comment to the entire school domain. This is great for templates and district documents that are uniform for the entire system. Technology professionals love this feature because it does not take up space on district servers, and it can be accessed from anywhere without complicated virtual private networks.

Clicking in Drive and Mouse Maneuvers

Getting around in Google Drive is very similar to regular computer commands in Mac and PC systems. The following rules apply:

- **Right-click on any file or folder**: This will open a menu of options, as shown in Figure 9.9. Many of these are self-explanatory. We will highlight the important notes about the menu items.

Figure 9.9 Right-Click Menu

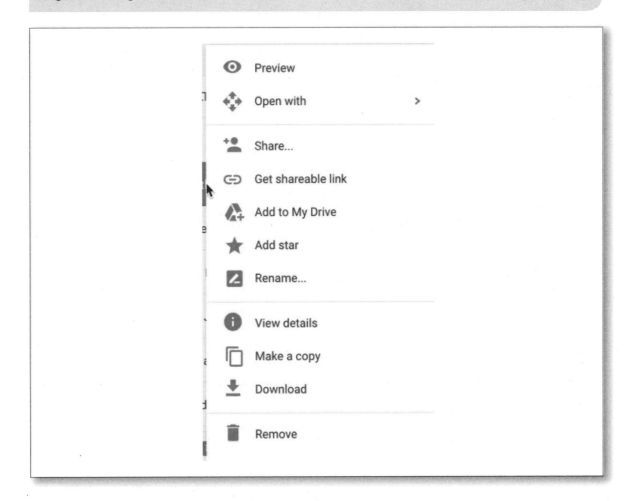

- **Open with:** When you right-click on a file that is not a G Suite file, you may open it with your associated G Suite application. For example, if you have uploaded an Excel spreadsheet to your Google Drive, then you may upgrade the file to a Google Sheet that will be collaborative and stored in the cloud.
- **Get shareable link:** This option will give you a shareable link. The link may be copied and pasted into any social media application or emailed. This is great for sharing projects with parents.
- **Add to My Drive:** Remember that if something is shared with you, it is not in your Drive. You have access to it with the **Shared with me** menu, but it is not located in your My Drive folders. Click on this menu item to put it in your Drive so you can organize it anyhow you wish.

- **Add star:** Star important files that can be accessed with the **Starred** Google Drive menu on the Drive homepage.
- **View details:** This option will open a small window on the right-hand side of the Drive to show **Details and Activity.** This will allow you to see who last edited the document, and the type, size, and owner of the work. Look at the bottom of Figure 9.10 for the **Add a description** button to make notes.

Figure 9.10   View Details and Activity

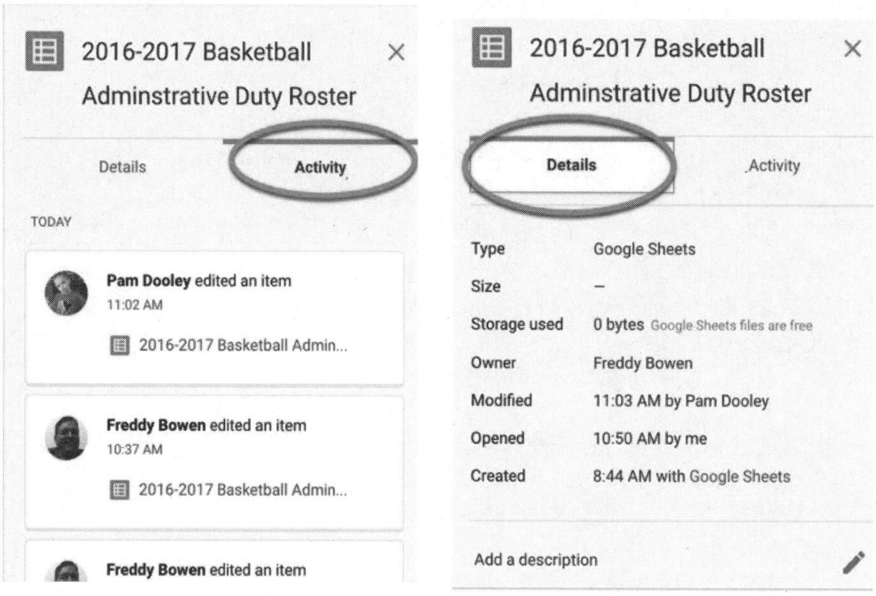

- **Download:** This is like the **Download as** feature in the **File** menu in Docs. This will download the file to your computer in the corresponding Microsoft format.
- **Remove:** This is the delete option. It moves the file to the trash.

Shift+Arrow keys and **Command/CTRL+Click** are just like Microsoft programs and Mac computers commands when in any file window such as Downloads, My documents, or Finder. **Shift+Arrow** keys will allow you to highlight consecutive files together to perform some action. The **Command/CTRL+Click** option will allow you to click a list of non-consecutive files and perform some action.

Icons of Drive

Google Drive houses files and folders and offers ways to organize the huge amount of digital content that is encountered from day to day. Drive has many organizational options to choose from that can benefit teacher and student. Students in college and career will be exposed to a large amount of digital information that they create, consume, and share. Look at the following steps and lists to learn more about how to retrieve and organize files in Google Drive. Figure 9.11 shows a list of icons that can be used to organize and search for files.

To **Get shareable link**, **Share**, **Preview**, **Delete**, **Add to my drive**, **Organize**, or perform more actions, click on the three dots in Figure 9.11.

Figure 9.11 Organization Icons

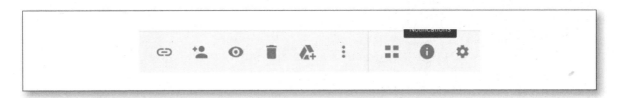

Click the **Get shareable link** icon to copy the link and share.

Click the **Share** icon to share the clicked/highlighted file or files with others using the share settings.

Click the **Preview** icon (the eye) to reveal a detailed overview about the file including (see Figure 9.11):

Image of the file

Who it is shared with

Description

What folder it is in

Click the **Remove** icon to move the checked file or files to the trash.

Click the **Add to my Drive** icon to manage files and folders.

Click the **Sort files icon** ▓ to create list views or thumbnail views of documents in your drive.

Click the **Details icon** to see the details and activity of certain documents.

Click the three-dots icon to manage additional options to the checked file, such as changing the color of a folder, as shown in Figure 9.12.

Figure 9.12 Three Dots Managing Files

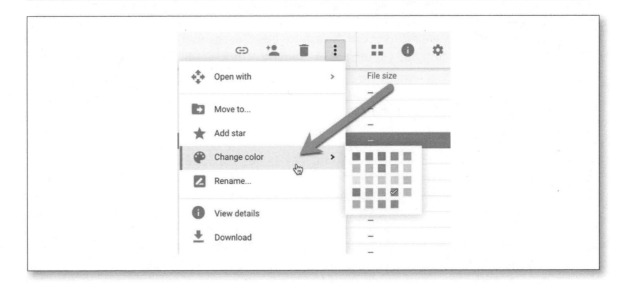

Figure 9.13 Settings

Clicking any one of these options will display the files in the documents list with the particular format. For example, the **Storage** view will show the user how much space is taken up in their Google Drive. Do not worry—G Suite for Education accounts have no storage limits. Unlimited storage!!! Clicking the **Convert uploads** checkbox will automatically convert files to their corresponding file type in the Google Suite.

Convert uploads settings will set how the user wants to upload files into Google Drive (Figure 9.13). These options are important to consider because if the user is uploading a file from another format such as Microsoft Word, the user cannot edit it with the Google Documents program. The file must be converted to a Google Docs format before editing can occur using the online collaborative tools. Alternatively, do not convert the file and leave it as a .doc format to simply store the information and download it to a device where Microsoft Word is available to edit the document.

Keyboard shortcuts are quick commands that are ideal for experienced users. Some examples include **Command+C** for copy and **Command+V** for paste. Click **Keyboard shortcuts** for a list.

DOWNLOAD GOOGLE DRIVE

Mac and PC users may download the Google Drive folder to their computer. This installs a folder on the computer similar to other folders like the My Documents folder on a PC. When a file is saved into the folder called Google Drive, the file is synced into the user's My Drive folder in the cloud. This allows the file to be accessed from anywhere with an Internet connection and syncs any changes automatically to Google Drive. The user can drag and drop files into the drive for instant access across all of the users' devices. Files that are too big to email can easily be saved in the My Drive folder for sharing. Share them in Drive instead of using attachments. Sharing creates a unique URL that allows users to download the file to their computer or start editing right away if it is a G Suite file. To share a non-G Suite file with the Google Drive app, follow these steps:

1. Install the Google Drive folder onto your computer by clicking on the **Download Google Drive** link from the settings gear in Google Drive.

2. Save any file type into the folder called Google Drive on your computer.

   a. This will automatically upload the file to the My Drive folder in the cloud. For example, when working on a Microsoft Word document, you could save the file into the Google Drive folder on your computer and later download the file again to a different device. When editing from another device, save the file to Google Drive again, and the most recent version of the file will be saved in the cloud. This reduces multiple versions of files that were saved on many different devices.

3. Click on the **My Drive** folder in Google Drive to see the documents list.

Technology-Infused Teaching Tip

In Google Chrome Web Browser, you may open the last tab that was closed by using the keyboard shortcut **Command+Shift+T** (Mac) or **CTRL+Shift+T** (PC). This is great when you accidentally close a tab that you were working with.

Lesson in Focus

The teacher will

1. Ask students to create an organization system to their Google Drive that includes creating a folder for each course and color code them appropriately

Students will

1. Create folders named Notes, Assignments, Projects in each course folder

2. Begin to add their files to the appropriate folder

3. Share these folders with their teachers so teachers can monitor the organization

SAMR IMPLICATIONS—TRANSFORMING INSTRUCTION

Substitution	At the lowest level of SAMR Google Drive simply allows students to organize their content digitally—from photos and digital articles to multimedia projects and documents.
Redefinition	In the redefinition level of SAMR, Google Drive allows students to share entire folder content to experts and peers around the world. As students work on an in-depth project (e.g., science projects), it may include multiple files like documents, spreadsheets, and presentations. This folder can be shared with an outside-approved expert to provide feedback and advice for revisions. The experts can drop their own research and articles into the folder for possible inclusion in the student's project. This allows for real-world, global collaboration! *Note: Your G Suite for Education administrator must allow for outside domain sharing in order for students to share outside your school/district.*

Google Drive does not just support Google file editing, but many other well-known Google applications and third-party programs can be worked on and organized directly in Google Drive! From photo-editing apps and whiteboard creation to Google Maps and graphic organizing tools, Google Drive is truly your one-stop shop for organizing and accessing tools for learning. To access and add these applications to Google Drive, simply do the following as shown in Figure 9.14:

1. Click on **New** in Google Drive.

2. Select **More**

3. Access the defaults applications such as MyMaps allowing you and your students to create their own maps and Google Sites, which will also allow your students to create their own websites and digital portfolios (more of which will be discussed in the high school book).

Some other Google Drive apps that work well with middle school students are LucidChart and VideoNot.es.

Figure 9.14 More in Google Drive

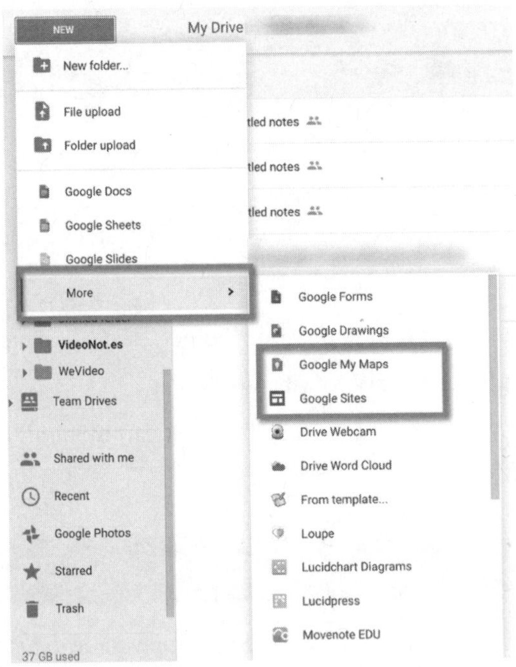

LucidChart

LucidChart is a graphic organizing tool that provides templates such as Venn diagrams and other relevant tools to assist students in visualizing and organizing content. It is extremely intuitive, collaborative, and efficient. All files are available in Google Drive. Consider having students plan their writing sequence with this tool or build timelines and other visual representations of content. As of early 2017, students and educators can sign up for a free upgrade by accessing Resource 9.1 at www.lucidchart.com/pages/usecase/education.

VideoNot.es

VideoNot.es is a great note-taking tool that works directly with YouTube videos. Students use this tool to take notes as they watch a video. Every single note is time-stamped aligned to the video. Students can at any time click on any note, and the video will play at the time that specific note was taken. See Figure 9.15 to see how it is laid out. Especially in middle school, students sometimes need to review what the context of a specific note references. This makes it simple for students to better understand the content and become more self-directed. All these notes are saved in Google Drive in a VideoNot.es folder that is automatically created.

Figure 9.15   VideoNot.es

SUMMARY

Google Drive is the storage solution for G Suite for Education that provides unlimited storage for users to store any file type. Students and teachers can share, manage, and upload files and folders easily to their online hard drive, which gives them flexibility to work anywhere. With Google Drive, students can create folders and organize their digital content creating student progress portfolios that can track their academic record. For example, students entering college may be required to submit a writing sample from their high school work. With Google Drive, students can access all of their work from any grade level and not worry about where they saved it. Similarly, teachers can create their professional learning folders where they can store information found online and share it with coworkers through share settings.

Wherever the users go, so do their files. Google Drive is the final piece of the puzzle for storage for the G Suite, giving the user mobility. College and career will increasingly rely on mobility of its students and employees to get work done on the go. Although this chapter highlights the last of the official G Suite for Education, the next chapter will explore an array of supportive tools produced by Google to make G Suite for Education even better.

10 Even More Google

Throughout the previous chapters, we have been learning about the G Suite. In the G Suite of applications, students and teachers have access to world-class cloud-based applications. These apps are not the end of the story when learning and working with Google, but they are just the ones nicely packaged and controlled by the school's domain administrator. Other apps exist that are not part of the G Suite for Education service, and they can be accessed with ease and have high educational value linking to the college and career standards. This chapter explores other free Google products that can supplement the G Suite for Education package to help students and teachers thrive in a technology-based learning environment.

SEARCH

Search is Google's most popular product. It is so popular that it is now part of the English language. USAToday.com reported as early as June 2006 that the word *google* was added to the *Merriam-Webster's Collegiate Dictionary* as a verb (Resource 10.1). To google means to do a web search for something. Google frowns on this use of the word because it may take away from its brand if people start to use it generically as *any* web search and not specifically a Google web search. Xerox faced this problem.

Search is Google's first priority. Google's familiar search bar is in every part of the G Suite, where it can help users find what they have created in Google Drive, emailed in Gmail, or can help users search for appointment details in Google Calendar. Most people's first experience with Google is using the search engine www.google.com. Google has a clean look with no advertisements on its front page. The crisp, clean backdrop clears the mind and reminds the user to think simply when searching. Simple search terms are often the best. For example, when a user wants to find websites that contain information about how to cite using American Psychological Association (APA) style, type the search term *APA citation example* in the search box and press **Enter** to reveal websites that Google has ranked based on its search algorithm. The simple approach using the fewest words possible will reveal the most relevant results. The most relevant websites are found near the top of the search results. This directs the user to a webpage that may contain the information the user seeks.

Search is difficult to teach. It requires trial and error and attention to precision. The user should learn from the first few searches and tailor subsequent searches to acquire information that is useful. Students who do not find what they are looking for in the first few results that Google provides tend to give up and report their findings with incomplete or inaccurate information. Google provides online courses for anyone to learn how to search better. Sign up for Google's Power Searching Course by clicking on the link in Resource 10.2 on the companion website. It is student friendly, and it is a required part of our middle school technology classes. Use the following tips to help students avoid misinformation in searches.

Use quotes. Placing quotes around a specific word or phrase will signal Google to only provide search results that contain the exact spelling and order of the words in quotes. For example, when searching for *education technology,* the search results will give the user content that has the words *education* and *technology*. By placing quotes around the two words "*education technology,*" Google will provide search results that have the words *education technology* exactly as it appears in the quotes. This will narrow down search results and save the user time.

Search a specific site. Search a specific website by typing the word **site** followed by a colon. For example, *site:www.nytimes.com education technology* would return results that only come from www.nytimes.com that have to do with education technology.

Use the minus sign. Use the minus (−) or the dash sign to eliminate terms from the search results. For example, a student wants to know about King Tut, but the teacher explicitly does not want the information to come from www.wikipedia.org. To exclude search results that originate from www.wikipedia.org, place a minus sign in front of the website like in the following example: *King Tut − site:www.wikipedia.org.*

Use the calculator. Every Google search bar is a calculator. Place common or complex math in the search bar, and Google will give you the answer. For example, students are able to type into the Google bar *2 * 8 + (sqrt 64)^ 3* and Google will calculate the expression and display the result. It even recognizes functions such as $y = 2x + 4$ or $y = x^2$. Google will graph the function as the first search result (see Figure 10.1). For an example of higher level math, watch the YouTube videos on the companion website to see amazing three-dimensional graphs and explanations of their −functions. It is a must see for any math teacher!

- Resource 10.3
- Resource 10.4
- Resource 10.5

The box in Figure 10.1 below the search query, $y = x^2,$ notes that there are more search results than just the graph. Google ranks the graph of the function above the other search results because it thinks that the graph is the most useful for the query. In case the user was looking for more information about the function, he or she can scroll down below the graph, and Google will provide webpages associated with that search.

Figure 10.1 Calculator in Search Bar

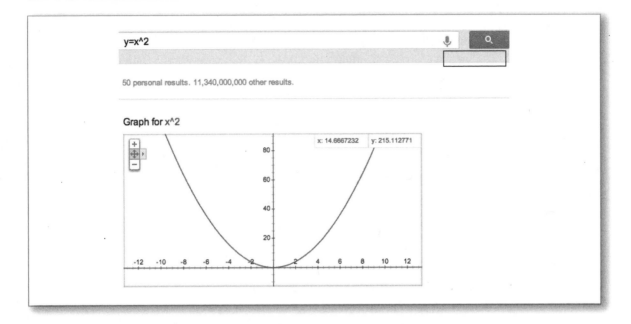

Search public data. Users may search the public data provided by the United States, World Bank, United Nations Economic Forum, and others. The data are searchable through Resource 10.6. Search through several databases and take advantage of the charts generated by Google for stunning visualizations. For example, popular data are displayed in the form of graphs and charts that are interactive. Students can interact with the information by changing variables based on different views. Motion charts are a great example of this. In these charts, the data are shown on the graph with a **Play** button in the bottom left-hand corner. Clicking **Play** shows how the data move in response to time. One of the best examples of this is the public data of births per woman versus life expectancy of the nation in which they live. Clicking **Play** will show how the data have changed over time. Find this example at Resource 10.7 on the companion website. An example of a simpler use of public data is U.S. population. Search from the Google bar *population of United States,* and it will yield a graph of the nation's population over time. In addition to this information, the user can select specific states to compare (see Figure 10.2).

Figure 10.2 State-by-State Comparison of Population

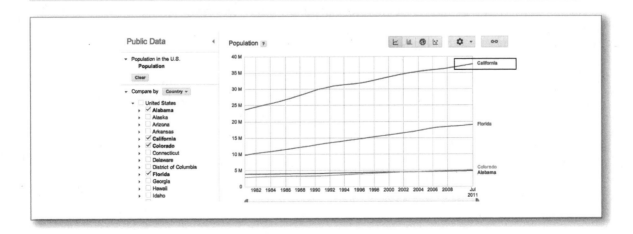

Convert units. Users can convert any comparable units of measure, including but not limited to length, volume, weight, and time. For example, students can easily convert fathoms into feet by searching for *20,000 leagues to miles*. This query will yield the answer as shown in Figure 10.3. The graphic in the box in Figure 10.3 next to the answer lets the user know that the answer came from the Google Calculator rather than regular search results. For instance, you would cite Google itself with the information, not a website Google brought you to. We are not sure what planet Captain Nemo is on, but over 69,000 miles is a pretty deep part of the ocean.

Figure 10.3 Fathoms to Miles Conversion

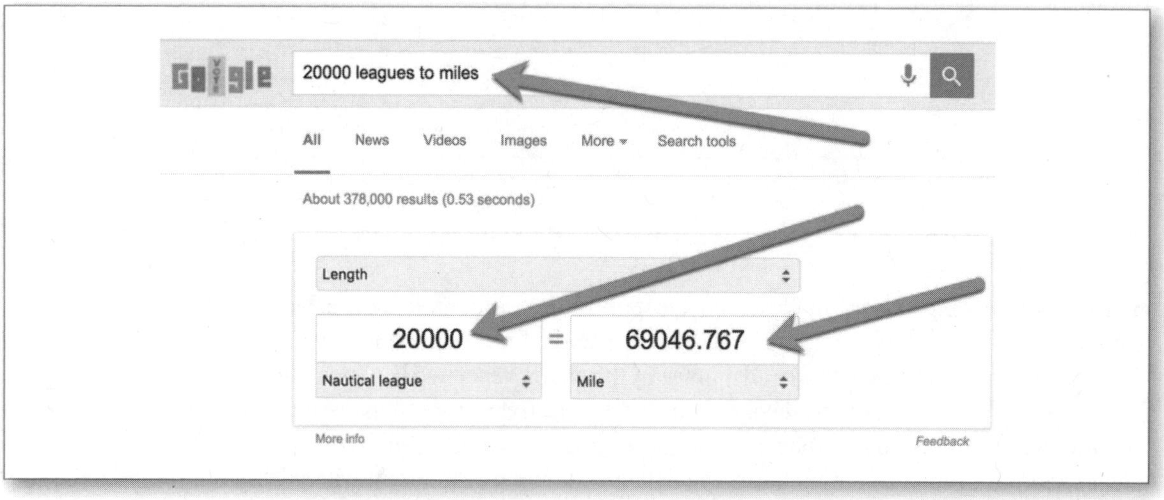

Knowledge Graph

Google has developed the Knowledge Graph to make it easier to find important information about a topic being searched. Simple and clear searches with few words, like names of places, people, or things, yield the Knowledge Graph located on the right side of the regular search results. The Knowledge Graph contains facts, pictures, maps, and informational highlights about the query. Look at Figure 10.4 for an example of a search for *Memphis, TN*.

The Knowledge Graph will be different depending on the search term. Memphis, TN, is a place, so located in its Knowledge Graph is the population, area, and current weather conditions, among other items. If searching for a person, then the graph will contain different information such as birthplace, age, contributions to society, etc. Students and teachers can use the Knowledge Graph as a starting point for research. It is fantastic for middle school searchers because of the quick facts that it provides the users without having to wade through webpages for information.

Figure 10.4 Knowledge Graph

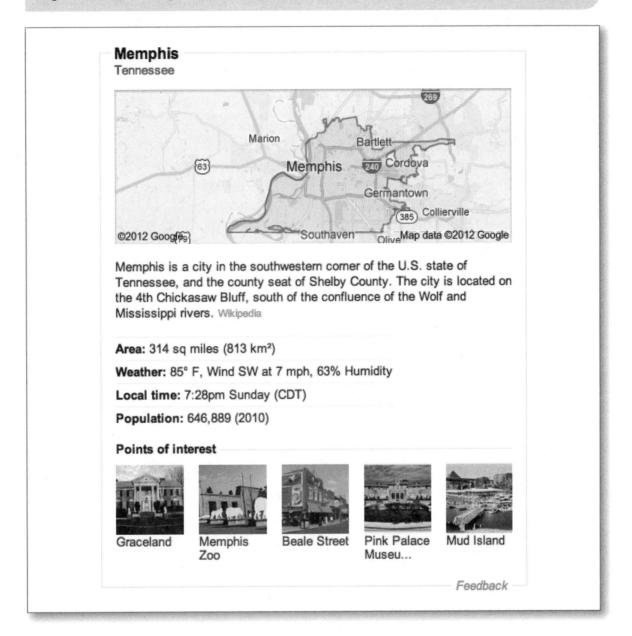

Memphis
Tennessee

Memphis is a city in the southwestern corner of the U.S. state of Tennessee, and the county seat of Shelby County. The city is located on the 4th Chickasaw Bluff, south of the confluence of the Wolf and Mississippi rivers. Wikipedia

Area: 314 sq miles (813 km²)

Weather: 85° F, Wind SW at 7 mph, 63% Humidity

Local time: 7:28pm Sunday (CDT)

Population: 646,889 (2010)

Points of interest

Graceland   Memphis Zoo   Beale Street   Pink Palace Museu...   Mud Island

Feedback

Special Search

Google provides many ways to get information. The most common way is to type a query in the search bar, and Google will provide the user with webpages that contain the information. Sometimes, the information given is too broad. Google will perform specialized searches that can narrow down the results to the user's specific needs. For example, students in science class may be researching current science news for a project. But, every time the student searches for the *Large Hadron Collider*, news results are buried deep in the search results that may contain off-topic content. The student would then perform the search and click on **News** search shown in the circle in Figure 10.5 to access only news articles about the topic. This list is located on the left side of the search results. Specifically search the Internet using the filters in Figure 10.5 to maximize searching efficiency.

Figure 10.5 Special Search

All searches everything on the web and does not exclude any of the other specific searches on the list in Figure 10.5.

Images will search any image file from the web, even search for a particular color in the images.

Maps searches Google Maps and provides driving directions if the search query follows this example: *Portland, OR, to Little Rock, AR.*

Videos searches videos related to the query from across the web.

News searches news-related websites and provides results accordingly.

Shopping searches various web and brick-and-mortar stores, including amazon.com and Wal-Mart, to provide pricing and ordering of products.

Books searches the books.google.com database providing samples or in some cases full copies of books.

Flight information can be searched using this filter. Flight search includes:
Departure/Arrival times
Prices
Map of flight

A GOOGLE A DAY

Being good at search takes experience and knowledge of how the search engine operates. Googling something without giving it thought may lead to results that do not yield the best information; experience is necessary. Google's algorithm that ranks pages and web content based on the search query is constantly evolving, and staying up-to-date can be challenging. To gain experience, teachers and students can play the game *A Google a Day*. This trivia game asks players to use their search skills to find the answers to questions posed by Google. The game is a great way for teachers to implement a little fun in the classroom, while teaching the students a lot about search skills. The many college and career standards do not specifically address using computerized search algorithms like Google's to find digital information. Although search is not a skill demanded by the some standards, it will be an imperative skill for the college- and career-ready student. Practicing search skills and becoming competent in finding information will be one of the most important skills for life after high school. The Internet has given us valuable information, but using search skills and developing them will help you become an expert searcher of information. If the teacher is asking questions that Google can answer with a quick search, then she is asking the wrong questions. It is important that we can search and conceptualize the information to be a better decision maker. Have students try it at www.agoogle-aday.com. This will make excellent bell work or a class starter to get students warmed up for learning. See Figure 10.6 for a screenshot of the game.

Follow these steps to play:

1. Enter Resource 10.8, www.agoogleaday.com, into a web browser's address bar.

2. Click on the **Start playing** link as shown in Figure 10.6 to reveal the page in Figure 10.7.

3. Read the question in the box as shown in Figure 10.7.

4. Use the Google search bar above the question to search for the answer.

   a. Answers may take longer than one query; be diligent and remind students of Standard for Mathematical Practice 1: *Make sense of problems and persevere in solving them.*

5. Click the box to answer the question.

6. Press to check the answer. If correct, points will be awarded based on speed.

Figure 10.6   A Google a Day

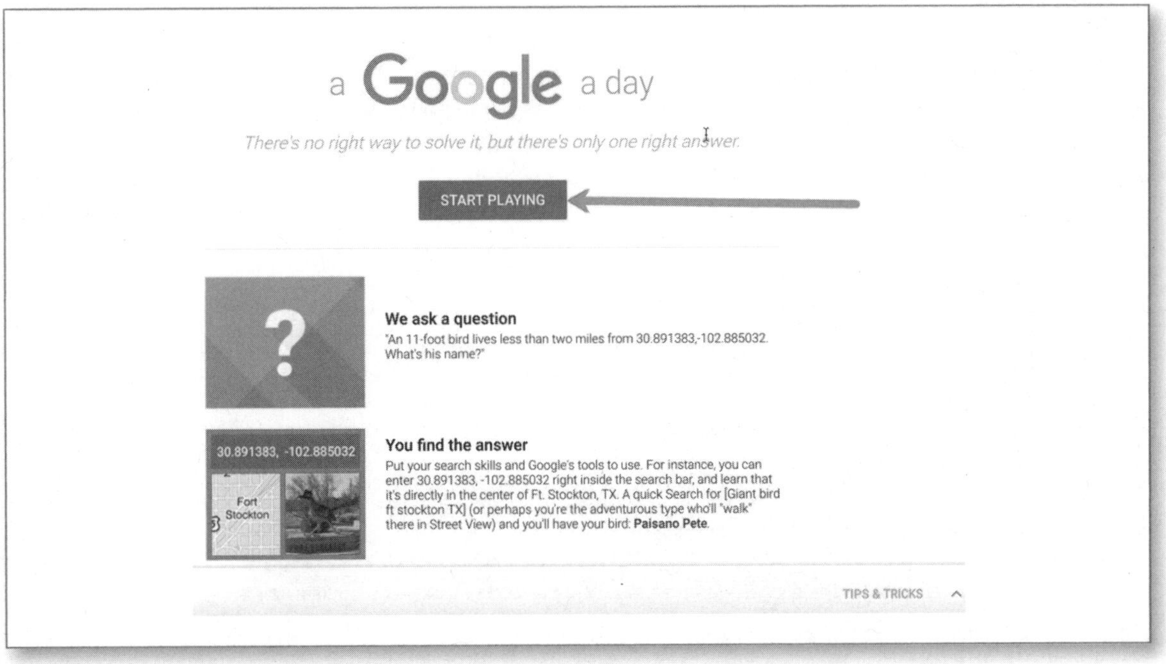

Figure 10.7   Search Game

GOOGLE URL SHORTENER

Long, complicated URLs are cumbersome to students and teachers. Long URLs can make it very difficult for students or teachers to type the original URL into the address bar to be directed to a website. Google provides a service that shortens the URL and gives it a new manageable link. For example, the URL for a document a teacher wants to share with students is https://docs.google.com/document/d/1TNd9xj4hVWiiz7VHTfmSX7JZVnYd_tOJJ-oYcBRrDRs/edit. Imagine typing this entire URL in the address bar; it is difficult to get it right because every character in the URL must exactly match for the web browser to find the page. The teacher can use the Google URL Shortener to shorten the URL. For example, the URL above now turns into http://goo.gl/mZP6T. This new URL will direct the user to the exact same document or webpage as the long URL but without the confusion. Follow these steps to create a shortened URL:

1. Enter Resource 10.9, http://goo.gl, into a web browser's address bar.
2. Copy the long link to the computer's clipboard (right-click, then copy).
3. Paste the long link into the box shown in Figure 10.8 (right-click, then paste).
4. Click the icon.

A new shortened link is now created. The user is limited only by his or her imagination of how to use the shortened link. If the shortened link is a Google Doc or a file from the user's Google Drive, then the user can share the file by providing the shortened URL. Share the URL through Twitter, Facebook, email, or print it out on a flier or parent newsletter. If it is a document that is used by the class regularly, have the students memorize the shortened link, or have them write it down in their notebooks.

Figure 10.8   Shorten the Links

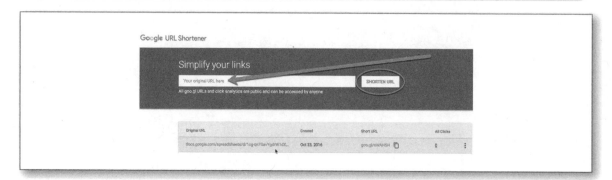

QR Codes and goo.gl

In addition to shortening URLs, http://goo.gl automatically creates QR codes. QR codes are like traditional barcodes found on library books or at the supermarket, but they can hold many times the information a regular barcode can hold. The most frequent use of QR codes in education is to make accessing URLs easy on mobile devices. With the QR code, the user does not have to type long URL into his mobile device's address bar. Instead, he can snap the QR code with his QR code reader application and have instant access to the link that is encoded into the image. Figure 10.9 depicts an example of what a QR code looks like. Snap this QR code with your reader to see a lesson where middle school students learned about watermelons.

Figure 10.9 QR Code Watermelon

Technology-Infused Teaching Tip

Use your phone's QR code reader application to snap the QR code in Figure 10.9 or go to this link if you do not have a QR Reader (Resource 10.10, http://goo.gl/YbSN6). This code is attached to a link of a Google Document. The Google Doc is an informational sheet made by a student to inform readers about items in our school garden. The codes were printed and laminated, then placed on stakes next to the plants. The codes serve as extra information to the people who visit our garden and for our classes that go to the garden to research the produce grown there.

Technology-Infused Teaching Tip

Visit the links below for a list of free QR Readers for iOS and Android.

Android: Resource 10.11, http://goo.gl/yCA3D

iOS: Resource 10.12, http://goo.gl/xccVu

To create a QR code from http://goo.gl,

1. Follow the steps to shorten a link located near Figure 10.8.

2. Click on the **three dots** as shown by the arrow to reveal the QR Code option.

3. **Copy** or **save** the QR code image

(Continued)

(Continued)

   a. This allows the user to print on paper, post to social media, or print on a t-shirt the QR code that was created. This may be read by any tablet or smartphone to directly take the user to the link encoded in the image.

Figure 10.10 Access QR Code

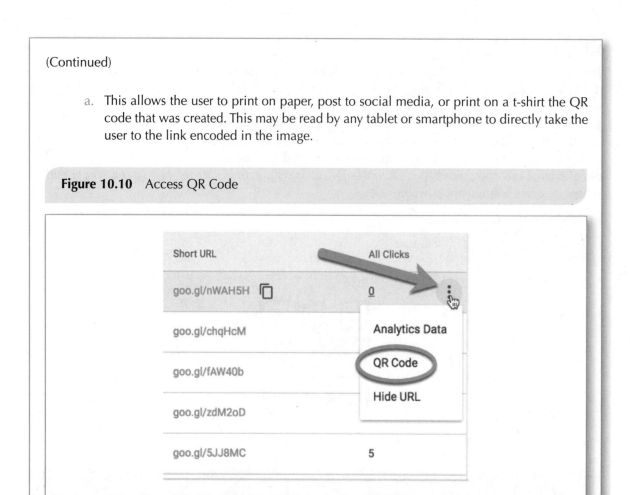

In Figure 10.11, valuable statistics and information about the link are recorded. Access the **Analytics data** page by clicking on the three dots as shown on Figure 10.10.

Figure 10.11 Google URL Shortener QR Code

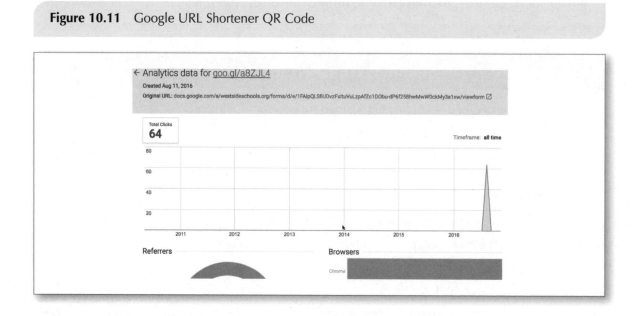

GOOGLE CHROME

Mashable, an online tech magazine, reported in May 2012 that Google Chrome is the number-one portal to the web in the world, outranking all other browsers, including Microsoft Internet Explorer, Mozilla Firefox, and Apple Safari in number of users (Resource 10.13). It is a web browser developed by Google that offers users a complete Google experience when interacting with Google's apps and features. Other browsers like Microsoft Internet Explorer, Apple Safari, and Mozilla Firefox are designed to access the web differently than Google. It stands to reason that using Google Chrome will work better with Google tools. The other browsers do work with Google tools, but they may not have all the features that are available in Google Chrome. These tools that the Chrome browser provides are scaffolds to assist students (and all individuals) in productive sharing, organizing, creating, and prioritizing their web-based content. For example, Ben is a seventh-grade special needs student. He was asked to read a CNN article discussing climate change. Ben already has some attention issues. When he navigates to an article on CNN, there are advertisements, suggested news stories, and other content that does not directly relate to the article—of course, he is considering clicking around to view the other pieces of content surrounded by the article. His teacher has him install the Mercury Chrome Extension (Resource 10.14) and now he can read the online article without all the overstimulation! See Figure 10.12 to see the transformation.

Figure 10.12   Mercury Extension—Article Comparison

Chrome Web Store

The Google Chrome Web Store is the application, extension, and theme store for Google Chrome. Here users can install specific applications and extensions that make the Google Chrome experience better and more efficient. Many educational apps and extensions are available free to help students learn and teachers be more productive. Visit https://chrome.google.com/webstore/ to search the database.

To search and download apps from the Chrome Web Store, follow these steps:

1. Download the Google Chrome Web Browser at www.google.com/chrome.

2. Install the program on your computer.

3. Click the **Google Chrome** icon to access the browser from your desktop or programs list.

4. Click on the link located in the bottom right-hand corner of Chrome to access the store.

5. Search for apps, themes, extensions, and/or games by using the search bar located in the upper left-hand corner of the webpage as shown in Figure 10.13.

Figure 10.13 Searching the Chrome Web Store

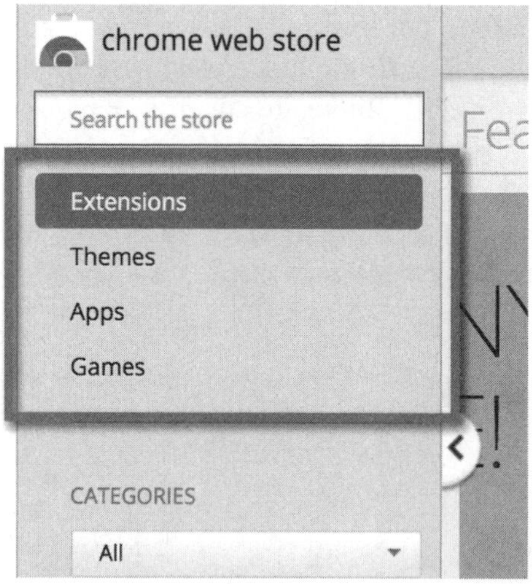

Chrome Apps and Extensions

So how are Apps and Extensions different?

Extensions	Apps
<ul><li>Can work on multiple websites</li><li>Is a utility</li><li>Modifies the way the browser works</li><li>Allows for automation</li></ul>	<ul><li>Usually have specific focus of content</li><li>Usually are part of *one* specific website</li><li>Can work offline</li></ul>

Examples	Examples
• Screencastify: Allows you to screen record and narrate any webpage you navigate to and create tutorials and demonstrate understanding of a web page. • EasyBib: Allows you to cite any website/article and build a bibliography of any and all webpages you navigate to. • OneTab: Allows you to take any and all tabs you have open in your current Chrome window and collapse down into one tab. You can then share this one tab/page as a link and recipients can view all the tabs you had open (this is very handy during direct instruction when navigating to several sites and you want a record of the sites you went to).	• Google Drive: Allows you to access all your Google files offline. • Task Timer: Allows you to create tasks, set goals for the amount of time for each task, and keep track of how much time you spend on each task. • VideoNot.es: Allows you to embed videos and take notes while you watch the video timestamping when the note was taken within the video.

View a curated list of some articles and resources that share some effective Chrome apps and extensions for middle school and beyond at Resource 10.15 on the companion website.

Google Photos

Many college and career standards want students to be college and career ready by the time they leave high school. Google Suite for Education provides experience with the tools they need to enter the workforce or college. Tools like Google Photos and My Google Maps are different and more specialized and are ideal to offer students experiences with enrichment. When students have time to discover places and photos, they will have a better understanding of the culture or features that make a location unique. A picture is worth a thousand words, and there are thousands of photos from different points of view concerning the same topic in these apps. For example, students who have taken photos of the White House can upload their own photos to their My Google Maps and describe their feelings and political motivations in a caption. When students get to contribute to the existing knowledge of the topic, it is our experience that the quality of work improves. Each time a photo is taken with a smartphone, a geotag is placed in the data file. When uploaded to Google Photos, you may add that tag to a map. For students, this would be a great start of the year project to upload their photos from summer break on the same map, and students could present where they have been and tell about the locations they visited.

To upload photos to a map follow these directions:

1. Open Google Drive.

2. Select **New.**

3. Select **Google My Maps** as shown in Figure 10.14.

4. Once opened, the My Google Map will have the menu bar shown in Figure 10.15.

5. Name the untitled map as shown with the arrow in Figure 10.15.

6. Add a marker, draw lines, add directions, and measure distance and areas with the toolbars shown in the box in Figure 10.15.

Figure 10.14   Open My Google Maps

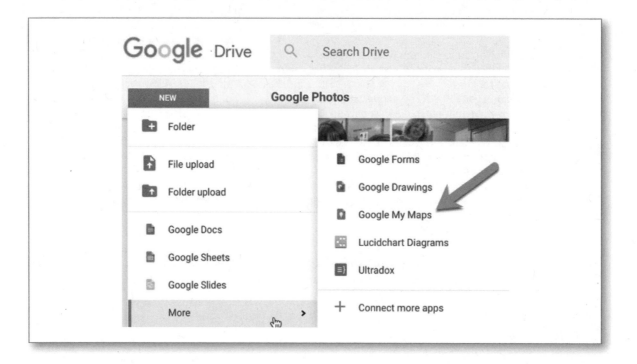

Figure 10.15   Toolbar for Creating Maps

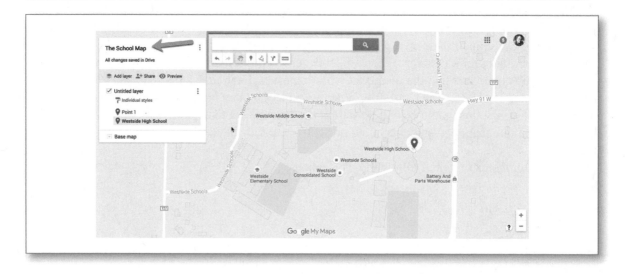

When the **add a marker** 📍 icon is clicked on a place on the map, a menu pops up as shown in Figure 10.15. This menu allows you to add uploaded photos and describe places on your map. Ask your students to be creative with this feature and create literature walks about their favorite book and show it graphically on the map. Use photos and videos from the places searchable from the web to illustrate the points of their presentation.

MAPS

Google Maps are not My Google Maps. My Google Maps are customizable. A plain old Google Map is just a very awesome mapping software that will allow you to find anything anywhere. Google Maps is a first-class map program that uses Google's search power to help users find anything in any place. Google Maps allows users to search for directions to and from places by car, walking, or public transportation. The search results for directions overlays routes onto the map and provides driving mileage and time of travel, including the current traffic conditions. Google Maps allows the user to view satellite images of locations and zoom in for detail. Users can also use the hybrid view to overlay roads and streets on satellite images. To search directions or locations on Google Maps, follow these steps:

1. Go to http://maps.google.com.

2. Enter a search term into the search bar as show by the arrow in Figure 10.16. Use the following search examples to get started using Google Maps.

   a. ZIP code

   b. City, state

   c. Physical address

   d. Landmarks example: *Grand Canyon*

   e. Places example: Cuban restaurants, Orlando, FL

3. Click the **Search icon** to reveal pins that are dropped onto the map, pinpointing the location on the map of your search (see Figure 10.16).

Figure 10.16 Dropped Pins and Information

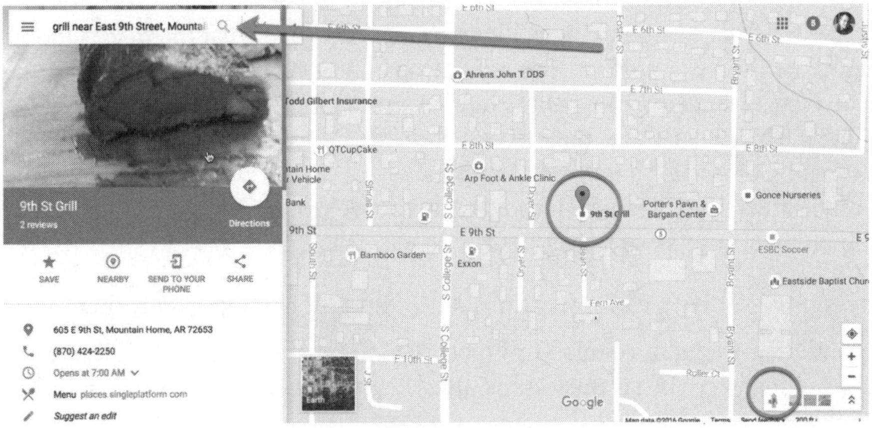

4. The dropped pin will indicate where the place is on the map. Use the **Directions** button to get turn by turn.

   a. Address

   b. Phone number

   c. Menu (if a restaurant)

   d. Picture of the location

To share the map, as in Figure 10.17

1. Click on the **Share** icon
2. Copy the link in the box
3. Paste the link in an email, instant message, Facebook, or Twitter post

Figure 10.17   Share Link to Map

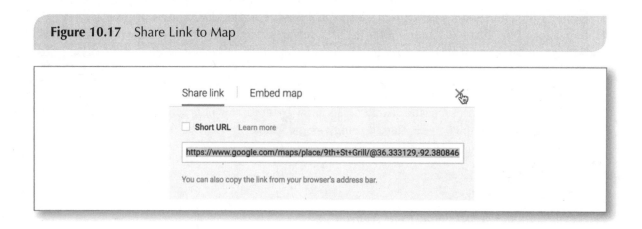

Street View and Pegman

Street View is a feature in Google Maps that lets the user see street-level imagery of a location in Google Maps. Google has a fleet of cars that have driven many of the roads in the world, and they have taken a 360-degree picture every few feet. The image captures buildings, passersby, and interesting landmarks. The purpose of this for the regular Google user is to be able to see what the location looks like from the street before they travel there. This gives them a way to know exactly what they are looking for when they arrive. In education, Street View could be used in a variety of contexts. Students can research places where Street View is enabled to see what the places look like as if they were standing there. For example, a search for Rome, Italy, places a pin next to the Colosseum. Activate Street View to see the Colosseum from the street. Sometimes Google has gone off the street with Street View. This means that they have taken their cameras inside buildings like the White House, the Roman Colosseum, and in a boat on the Amazon River. For a full list of Street View places, go to the Street View Gallery located at Resource 10.16. To use Pegman to activate Street View from any map, follow these steps:

1. Follow the steps to search for locations on Google Maps described earlier.
2. Click and drag **Pegman** (circled in Figure 10.16) onto the map where the user wants to see street-level imagery (if the street turns blue, Pegman has taken a photo from that location).
3. Use the arrows that are overlaid on the image to navigate the street.
   a. Using the arrows allows the student to virtually walk the streets of the location to explore the area.
4. Exit Street View by clicking on the in the upper right-hand corner of the map.

SCHOLAR

Google Scholar is an easy way to search for scholarly literature. Searching through Google Scholar will yield search results only from journals, scholarly books, articles, university libraries, and other trusted sources. Google ranks its search results in the same manner as publishers do. Google carefully measures the work's contribution to the field as well as the number of citations in other works. Google Scholar is a great place to start a research project. For example, senior research papers will require that the information be from trusted sources that are scholarly in nature. The students get a chance to read some of the abstracts and articles to gain a starting point of information. Often, students believe that information is true or trustworthy because it was published on the Internet. It will be valuable for students to know the difference between a plain Google search and a Google Scholar search as they become college and career ready. Reading evidence-based text and writing about its impact is an important skill. To access Google Scholar, follow these steps:

1. Go to http://scholar.google.com.
2. Type a search query into the search bar shown in Figure 10.18.
3. Review the results.
4. Narrow the results by selecting the parameters located in Figure 10.19.

The box labeled **A** indicates Articles/Legal documents: Click on one or the other to filter search results accordingly. In the box labeled **B**, click on a time interval. In box **C**, check to include or exclude patents or citations.

Figure 10.18   Search Photos by Location

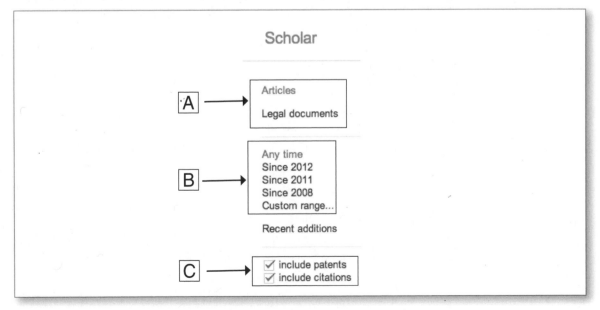

Figure 10.19   Scholar Search Parameters

COMMUNICATION

Everything is built on communication. It is the foundation of every relationship, and great educators know that proper communication with all stakeholders builds the best relationships. Teachers often see communication with students as their primary goal. Helping them understand concepts and knowledge is the core job of a teacher. But we know that being a teacher is much more about communicating with students. Coworkers, parents, and community members all play a role in the school system. Google can help you build a communication system that will save you time and organize your coworker, student, and parent relationships with ease. The G Suite is full of Even More communication tools that will foster the best relationships. "It's relationships, stupid!"

Google Voice

Google offers a free telephone number that is tied to your school or personal G Suite account. This feature is inadvertently turned off by the domain administrator in the admin console. It is a part of Gmail and Google Chat, and some school personnel see this as not good for student use. Westside High School allows the students and teachers to access the Google Voice number with their account. We want our students to be able to communicate with professionals in the workforce or another source that will help them in their scholastic journey. Teachers use it for parent communication. Follow the steps below to get Google Voice and examples of how to use it with your school community. Refer also to Figure 10.20.

1. Go to voice.google.com
   a. Log into your school G Suite account

2. Click Get a Voice number

3. Click **I want a new number**
   a. You want a new number because this is a way to communicate with parents that would not allow parents or students to view your personal phone number. When you create a new number, you get a 10-digit telephone number for free that only rings your Gmail account. Follow the rest of the steps to configure your new phone number.

4. Click Call me now for Google to call your current real phone number. This signals to Google that you are who you say you are. Malicious software programs could ask Google for countless phone numbers. This is a way they can prove that you are a human and not a robot. After you have verified your phone, go to Step 5.

5. Find a phone number:
   a. This step in the process allows the user to pick a phone number from a list that Google has secured. There are many numbers in this list and this will allow you to choose a number you want. For example, Michael's Google number is 901-466-MATH (6410). He lives in Northeast Arkansas, but at the time he got his number, there were no local area codes on the list of phone numbers Google controls. So, he picked a nearby area code of 901.
      i. Circle 1: Search by area code or zip code
         1. This will show a list of numbers with a particular area code or location.
      ii. Circle 2: Search by phrase or number
         1. This will show a list of available numbers that match a phrase. He got lucky and got the MATH phrase for his number. That is when he taught math at a nearby middle school.

iii. Circle 3: Click to search. You do not have to have both boxes filled with search terms. You may either choose by area code or phrase. Caution: If you narrow down your search by area code *and* phrase, you will most likely not find the number you are wanting. Each area code only has one of each seven digit number.

After you pick your number, it is yours associated with your G Suite account. The number is free and can call any United States domestic phone number for free. A teacher at Michael's school uses it for office hours. After a really difficult math lesson, the teacher will schedule office hours from 6 pm to 7:30 pm. During this time, students or parents may call the teacher on her school Google Voice number and ask questions. When the 7:30 pm time comes, the teacher will sign out of her G Suite account. This will force all other incoming calls to be sent directly to her Gmail account as a notification. As an administrator, Michael gives this phone number out to all his students and parents. It only rings when he wants it to and he can call from it anywhere he is connected to the Internet. It is great when Michael is away from his office phone to connect with parents and community members.

Figure 10.20   Google Voice

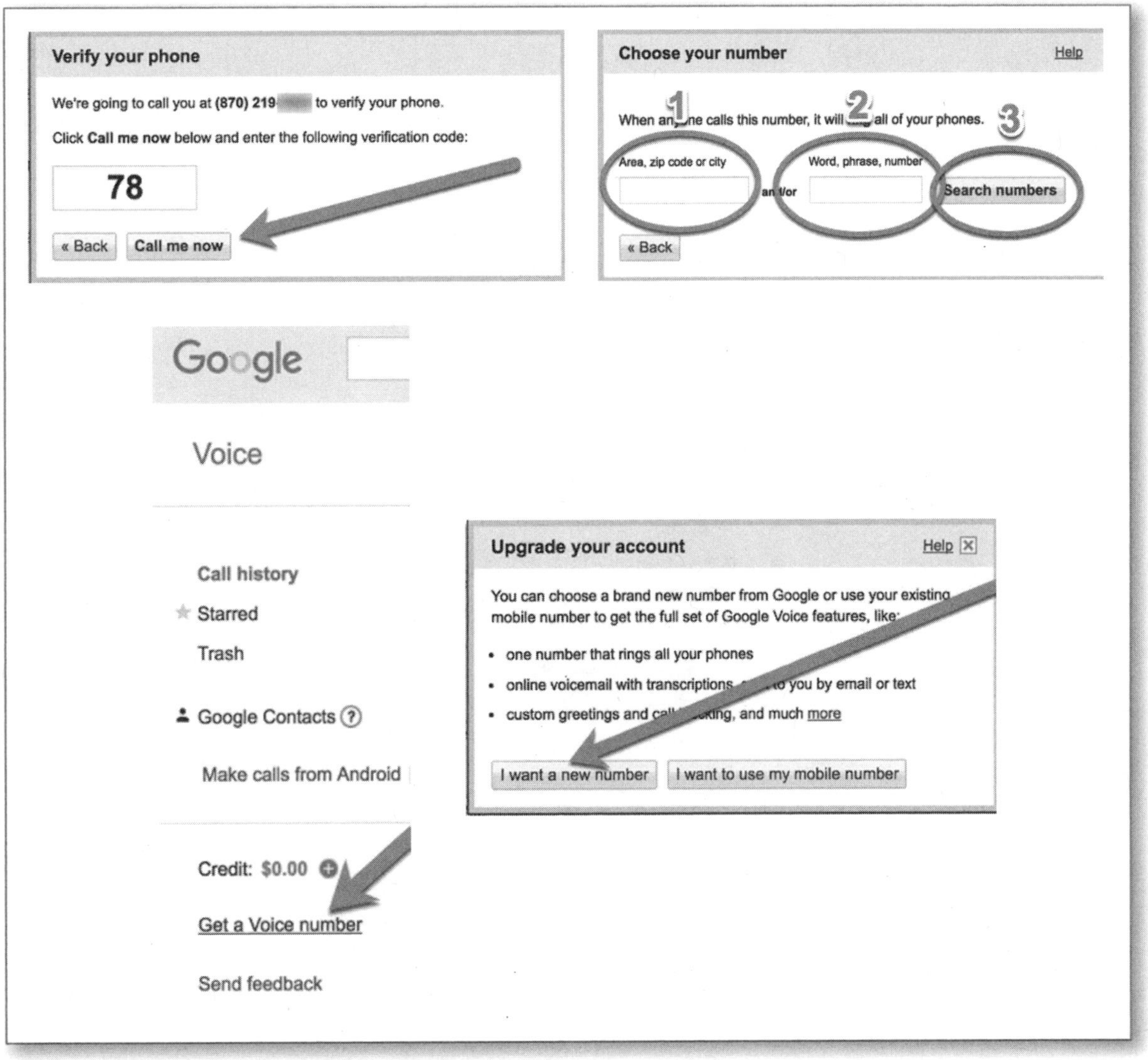

HANGOUTS

Google allows several communication tools. Some are easy to understand such as Gmail. Gmail has been around the longest and has some great features of communication. To take communication one step further from Google Voice and Gmail, Google introduced Hangouts. Hangouts are video chat, text chat, and collaboration tools built into the G Suite for Education. For example, on a recent snow day, Michael held a professional development class via Google Hangout video chat for his teachers. The task was simple and fun. When the weather started to look like snow or ice, he started talking to his teachers about a professional development activity they could do from home. Michael made it exciting and fun and put in a little competition. He emailed a premade link to the Hangout with instructions on how to win. First prize went to the teacher with the best pajamas, and second place went to the best bed hair. After the fun, Michael led a technology training on how to use Hangouts for communication with guest speakers. It went very well. Up to 15 participants can be live in the video chat at one time. If you want more than that you may broadcast your Hangout live to YouTube where an unlimited number of participants can access it; they just cannot participate in two-way dialogue. To access Hangouts do the following.

1. Go to hangouts.google.com or access the G Suite apps by clicking on the boxes as shown in Figure 10.21.

Figure 10.21 Access Google Hangouts

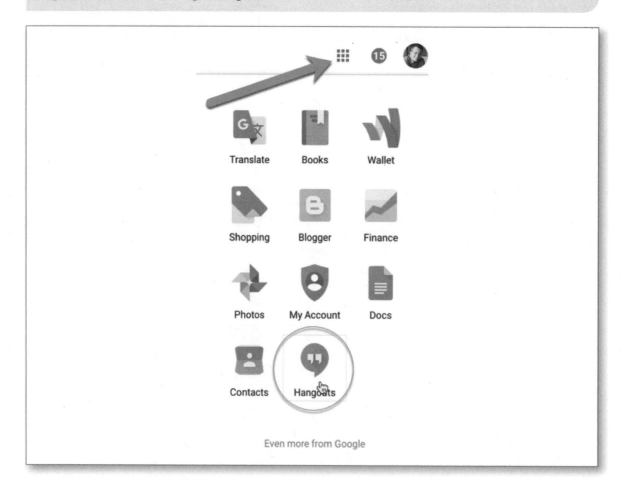

2. This will reveal the Hangouts landing page. From here you may start any type of G Suite communication with any of your contacts. You may also type an email address in the box where the arrow is pointing in Figure 10.22.

3. Select **Video Call**, **Text Chat (Message)**, or **Phone Call** to a phone number.

Figure 10.22   Create a New Conversation in Hangouts

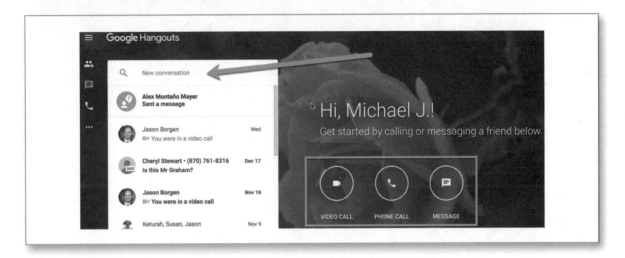

G Suite offers these communication tools to teachers and students for free. Teachers at Michael's school use the phone call feature to call parents and make a parent call log. Communication is the key to building all relationships in a school community. Use these features to connect to your stakeholders.

SUMMARY

Throughout this book, we have been learning how the G Suite for Education can be a great resource in implementing the various college and career standards. It is the goal of the standards to get every student college or career ready to face the challenges of life after high school. It is apparent that the Common Core State Standards and others like it want educators to infuse more technology into the learning environment. Standards like Anchor Standard 6 for Writing want students to "produce and publish writing using the Internet." G Suite for Education makes that a reality with the use of Google Docs. It seems like the team of Google employees that built G Suite for Education must have read the Common Core State Standards and then wrote software to improve the learning experiences of students.

Although the G Suite for Education package includes many apps that are perfect for school and learning, it does not contain all of the products Google offers. Search, A Google a Day, Google URL Shortener, QR code generator, Chromebooks, Chrome Web Store, Google Maps, and Google Scholar support the G Suite for Education package and give even more learning tools to students. Educators who are well versed in these tools can make an impact on the proper use of the Internet for learning. Students who have access to learn and work with tools like the ones found at Google will be well-prepped for success in college or a career. Look for lesson plans linked to specific Common Core State Standards in the next part of the book. The Lesson Plan Correlation Chart (found in the Resource section on the companion website.) will direct you to the appropriate lesson for your grade level. These lessons will refer to the use of G Suite for Education and the supporting tools learned about in this chapter.

We hope you have enjoyed this resource. But, remember, the learning is not over. Visit our website digitaledalliance.com to get even more lesson plans, content, and links to national and local conferences that we host.

RESOURCES

For more information about G Suite for Education, including

- lesson plans related to chapter content,
- domain setup for tech administrators' videos,
- overviews and Google training materials,
- the authors' favorite websites, and
- testimonials and interviews of schools currently using G Suite,

access Resources from this chapter on the companion website.

Lesson Plans

Grade Level	Lesson Plan Title	*All lesson plans and resources can be found on the companion website at: http://resources.corwin.com/googlemeetsms*	
Middle School	Historical Novel *My Brother Sam Is Dead* by Carol LaRow	http://goo.gl/SGkkn	Online Only
Upper Middle School	Datapalooza	http://goo.gl/hHZI2	#14

online resources http://resources.corwin.com/googlemeetsms

Index

CORWIN
A SAGE Publishing Company

Helping educators make the greatest impact

CORWIN HAS ONE MISSION: to enhance education through intentional professional learning.

We build long-term relationships with our authors, educators, clients, and associations who partner with us to develop and continuously improve the best evidence-based practices that establish and support lifelong learning.